For Kelvin, Tom and Lucy with
immeasurable gratitude and affection

ACKNOWLEDGEMENTS

I would firstly like to thank those at Metro Publications: Andrew for giving me the opportunity to write this book, Susi for her help and advice and Lesley for her patience with my endless questions. I am also indebted to Abigail Willis for her thoughtful editing and to Stephen Millar for his superb photography. My thanks and apologies to my long-suffering friends and family all of whom have shared my enthusiasm for the subject of this guide, whether they wanted to or not. I would especially like to thank Maxwell Hutchinson, who taught me more about architecture than any course or book ever could, and for his immense help with the last chapter of this book.

London Architecture

Marianne Butler

Photography by Stephen Millar

London Architecture

Written by Marianne Butler
Cover photographs by Stephen Millar
Photography by Stephen Millar
Walk photography by Metro
Edited by Abigail Willis
Maps by Lesley Gilmour
Design by Susi Koch & Lesley Gilmour

Published in 2004 by
Metro Publications
PO Box 6336
London
N1 6PY

Printed and bound in India by Thomson Press Ltd

British Library Cataloguing in Publication Data.
A catalogue record for this book is available from the British Library.

ISBN   1 902910 18 4

Contents

Cumberland Terrace

FOREWORD

London can justly claim to be one of the world's most architecturally fascinating cities. Admittedly, Rome has its great antiquities, New York its soaring 1930's skyscrapers, Haussmann's plan gives Paris its unique spacious grace, and Athens is of another era. But where else in the world does mould-breaking contemporary architecture lie within a stone's throw of over two thousand years of history?

Stand outside Richard Rogers 1980's Lloyd's building, which is still a most remarkable structure, turn through one hundred and eighty degrees and Norman Foster's Swiss Re Insurance 'gherkin' tower points skywards in an architectural gesture undreamed of before the third millennium. A sprightly five-minute walk will take you to the last remains of the two thousand year old Roman wall outside the Museum of London.

In a peculiarly British way these contrasting architectural styles cohabit peacefully. Britain, and London in particular, has its own idiosyncratic approach to architecture and architectural style. Admittedly, many of England's finest Gothic cathedrals are more French than British – no accident as most of them were built under Norman influence. From then on the British placed a pragmatic filter over the extreme swings of Continental architecture endeavour. The originality of Palladio's northern Italian villas was distilled into London's post-Fire churches by Wren, Gibb and Hawkesmoor. The exuberance of Italian Baroque wandered north to become the elegance of Georgian Bath. Regency terraced houses made a miniature Versailles look-alike available to all with party walls at 17'6" intervals.

In the second half of the nineteenth century however it was a different story. Britain led the way in the Industrial Revolution and with it coined a myriad of new architectural types, the railway stations, bridges and viaducts, mills and factories which sprang up throughout the country's industrial heartlands. Economic housing for the new urban working class and offices for the administration of Empire coincided with the greatest period of church building since the Middle Ages, in a style which, with a typical English nod and a wink is just that, Medieval.

In more recent times London has taken the very best of Continental Modernism from Germany, France and Scandinavia and cooked up a pragmatic British Modernism which is as peculiarly individual as the cut of an English gentleman's suit.

Post-modernism spread north across the English Channel and east across the Atlantic. London has its fair share of buildings which are woeful examples of 1980's post-modernism. Thankfully, following the economic collapse of the early 1990's after John Major's withdrawal from the European Exchange Rate Mechanism, the architectural scene was rescued and reinvigorated by the introduction of the National Lottery in 1994. Lottery millions gave London the Tate Modern, the Great Court at the British Museum and extensions to the Wallace Collection, the National Portrait Gallery and the Royal Opera House as well as creating… The Dome. London's Docklands, and particularly Canary Wharf, are an economic, if not an architectural, triumph. The barren wastelands of yesterday's docks have provided fertile soil for third millennium capitalism which regrettably seeks to express itself, in the main, in retro-Manhattan style skyscrapers. However, Foster's 'gherkin', quite literally, points the way to a different style and approach to London's high rise office buildings of the future.

London's current architecture owes a great deal to the impact of computer-aided design. Firstly, the form of buildings has been liberated from the dominance of the drawing board generated right angle. Norman Foster's GLA building and the Great Court at the British Museum would have been impossible without the flexible geometry of the microchip. Everywhere columns and beams have become deliciously slender with gravity-defying spans as the computer takes the drudgery and uncertainty out of the structural calculations. The third millennium affords the architect a whole new palate of materials to lighten and freshen the appearance of all buildings, large and small alike. And finally, the new computer-generated architecture is colourful. Plans can now be reproduced in accurate colours and conveyed through digital printing and photography – no watercolours or coloured pencils in sight.

Much of 19th-century architecture owes its genesis to cast iron and steel. Twentieth century architecture is dominated by the new freedoms and economies of reinforced concrete. So far, the 21st century is the architecture of transparency, of glass. Time alone will tell whether the world's aspirations for a low-carbon economy will cast doubt on the wisdom of lightweight enclosures and structures. Buildings are responsible for producing the largest proportion of carbon dioxide and also the vast proportion of embodied energy. Glass requires extensive heat for its production, is heavy and energy inefficient to transport and has less than admirable thermal characteristics. On the other hand new glass technology enables architects to dream new dreams and lighten the built environment with a delicate deftness of touch.

It is all too easy to see London's architecture simply in terms of the contemporary abundance of works by Norman Foster and Richard Rogers. Look back a decade or so and there are Terry Farrell's *grandes projets* with his English take on Post Modernism. Already, London's architecture can be seen as the work of a small number of forceful and opinionated architects. In the post World War Two period assured young men like Lesley Martin, Arnold Powell and John Moya and the entire London County Council Architects Department did their best to rebuild Britain with energy and enthusiasm. Victorian London would not be what is without the works of George Gilbert Scott; Regency London was created, in the main, by John Nash while Christopher Wren forged a new London out of the ashes of the Great Fire of 1666. Sad to say there is little left of pre-Fire London, the flames swept away the remains of the greatest Medieval city in Northern Europe taking with them the old Gothic St Paul's Cathedral, the largest structure of its kind in the world.

Marianne Butler's refreshing and tasteful guide to London's architecture shows us just how accessible all of this mêlée of styles and periods is. On any one of her walks the architectural enthusiast or someone approaching the subject for the first time will be able to experience this variety with little or no effort. Fortunately, London with its various 'villages' is a walking city. The square-mile that is the City of London can be absorbed in less than a day. The squares of Bloomsbury or Belgravia can be walked in an hour or so. John Nash's great urban plan from Regent's Park to Buckingham Palace is but an hour's walk with architectural variety at every twist and turn. Regardless of the location there is one simple rule about enjoying London's architecture, avoid the shop-fronts, the enticing interiors of cafés and bars – always excepting London's fantastic collection of Victorian public houses – and, quite simply, look up. All travellers habitually look down, maybe because the pavements have a habit of being somewhat hazardous. We become blind to the richness of the backdrop to our everyday lives, but cast your eyes upward and you will often be surprised by the architectural details that are just above the bland, contemporary shop fronts.

There is a lot to see in London's architectural landscape. It is not necessary to understand the subtle nuances of personality, style and function. With the help of this charming little book it is possible to take things, quite literally, at face value. Look and enjoy. On the other hand, read with care between the lines and wonderful stories tumble out of every door and window. London's buildings are as human and entertaining as Londoners themselves. And don't forget that there are 28,000 architectural guides available to everyone in London – the drivers of the city's black taxi-cabs. For the last twenty years, by a strange process of osmosis the London cabby has become as knowledgeable and opinionated about architecture as anybody in the capital. Hail a cab from outside, say, the Royal Exchange in the heart of the City and ask the driver to take you to Buckingham Palace. Once underway just ask them what they think about any building you care to mention. They will have an opinion and, in the main, it will be well informed.

London's architecture is for and about people. I am privileged to live in the very heart of what I consider to be the greatest architectural city in the world, and I can heartily recommend Marianne Butler's handy and accessible guide to everyone who wishes to explore London's unique architectural landscape.

Maxwell Hutchinson
Clerkenwell, London

Big Ben and Portcullis House

ABOUT THE AUTHOR

Marianne Butler has a Masters degree in ancient history from the University of London and works as a freelance researcher and writer. Most recently she has worked with the architect and broadcaster Maxwell Hutchinson on the book, published by Headline, of the much acclaimed 2003 Channel 4 series 'No 57 – The History of a House'. She divides her time between her old house and garden in the Scottish borders and the architectural delights of London.

Battersea Power Station

Introduction

I was born and brought up in a post-war New Town, which was socially essential but architecturally dull. Indeed I thought that Pete Seager had written his song 'Little Boxes' specifically about my particular corner of Hertfordshire… 'and the people live in boxes, little boxes all the same… there's a blue one and a red one and a pink one and a yellow one, and they are all made out of ticky-tacky and they all look just the same…'

As a child, the highlight of my year was the visit to London, ostensibly to see Father Christmas at the splendid Selfridges store. However, my imagination was truly captured by the architecture of the capital – taking in a film in Leicester Square meant sitting in the largest and plushest interior I had ever encountered. Welsh rarebit at a now defunct Lyons Corner House was a feast unsurpassed today, even by the delights of, say, The Ivy; and a simple stroll down any London street could reveal buildings of startling contrast in age, form and function. Today, of course, I find London and its architecture still as exciting as then and, fortunately, I am not alone in my enthusiasm

This guide is essentially a hop, skip and jump through the history of London and its buildings. Each chapter briefly describes a particular period and offers a selection of buildings that are reasonably representative of that era. Of course, the list is certainly not comprehensive given the space available and many popular buildings have been left out for one reason or another. Those that have been included are there essentially for their ease of access from central London and can be visited without too much fuss or expense. Indeed most are within the area covered by bus and tube one-day travelcards.

The aim of this guide is to forge or further an interest in London architecture for visitors, residents and those who come to the capital to work or play. I have tried to avoid jargon; it is one thing to know a spandrel from a spangle, but a beautiful building can be admired and understood without recourse to technical language.

Architecturally speaking we have much to look forward to in London – Daniel Libeskind's stunning 'Spiral' extension to the Victoria and Albert Museum will shortly be gracing the rather conservative Exhibition Road. Likewise, Renzo Piano's London

Bridge Tower, a soaring 1016 feet shard of glass, will transform an uninspiring corner of Southwark and provide 700 people with living and work space as well as giving a welcome facelift to the rather bleak railway station at its base. Exciting too is the long-awaited conversion of the iconic Battersea Power Station to a centre for the Arts – will it be as successful as the Tate Modern?

Invest in a bus or tube pass, wear some comfortable shoes and bring this guide – the best of London architecture will be waiting for you.

If you would like to make any comments about any of the buildings included in this guide please e-mail me at architectureguide@yahoo.co.uk.

Marianne Butler

How to use this book

The first part of this book gives an historical account of London's architecture. At the end of each chapter there are details of some of the best examples of the architectural style, and there are four area maps at the back of the book to help you locate the buildings. The second part of the book offers more practical information about exploring London's architecture with detailed walks and suggestions of where to eat, drink or shop while taking in some of the Capital's finest architecture. To appreciate London's skyline refer to the chapter 'Architecture with a View' with information about some of the best vantage points to see the city. At the back of the book is a diagram, 'London's Architecture at a Glance' which will help the reader to get a grasp of the different architectural periods and terms used within the book. This book should be of help to those that want to read about London's architecture and those that want to explore it.

In The Beginning

'And dream of London, small and white, and clean,
The clear Thames bordered by its gardens green'
William Morris

There is little evidence of pre-Roman habitation in the London area, just a few small settlements along the river Thames west of Whitehall. One explanation for this lack of habitation is that the river acted as natural barrier and border between tribes of Britons – the Atrebates, Regni and Cantiaci south of the Thames, approximately occupying the present counties of Berkshire, Sussex and Kent respectively. The north of the Thames, incorporating much of what is now Bedfordshire, Hertfordshire and Essex, was the home of the powerful Catuvellauni tribe.

For at least six centuries before the Roman occupation of Britain, the country had enjoyed substantial links with a trade network that stretched from the western Mediterranean, Spain, southern Gaul to northern Germany and the Baltic Islands. The Thames acted as a super highway transporting raw materials and goods from Britain's abundant natural resources copper from Wales, tin from Cornwall.

Archaeologists tell us that conditions in the area settled by the Romans were idyllic with the land almost entirely covered with a mix of open oak and hazel woodland. Smaller, clean and clear flowing rivers, such as the Fleet and the Walbrook, as well as streams poured into the Thames, then wider than it is today with small boggy islands at various points. The impetus for bridging the Thames, at a point not far from where London Bridge is today, may have been a military one but it also made for an attractive and convenient place to settle and trade.

Almost within living memory of the Roman conquest of 43 AD the southern half of Britain was a hive of activity: road building, setting up trading posts and establishing towns. Londinium, as Roman London was to become known, with its establishment as a major port, was central to this activity, at high tide the area could be reached by merchant ships that sailed up the Thames laden with goods from all parts of the Roman Empire.

Founded in about 50 AD on the north bank of the Thames, early Londinium must have resembled a frontier town of the Wild West filled with pioneering merchants and dealers. Settlement began in the area that is today the City of London. Flimsy, wooden dwellings, warehouses and a small fort were hurriedly constructed and the town rapidly expanded, becoming the largest town in Britain in just ten years.

However this fledgling town was destroyed in 60 AD by the Iceni tribe, from the area known today as East Anglia, led by their queen

Boudicca. Boudicca also razed Colchester and St Albans to the ground in her revolt against Roman rule. But by 70 CE Londinium was once again a boomtown with a programme of public works in place and within thirty years prestigious buildings such as the Amphitheatre, the Governor's Palace and Public Baths, all built from durable stone and tile, were gracing its streets. Domestic dwellings and shops however were still made from wood, closely packed together and generally situated on the busier, noisier streets.

The central, and perhaps most characteristic feature of any Roman town was the Forum, of which Londinium could boast the largest example in the northern Roman provinces, about 600 feet square in total. Situated approximately at modern Cornhill, such a building consisted of a large central open space surrounded by buildings that housed the town hall and legal centre. The open space was used by the populace as a venue for conducting religious and official business, as well as serving as a market place.

This was a period of great prosperity for the town and for architects and town planners this meant that new problems required new solutions. Continuous supplies of food and goods needed to be brought in from outside and it is about this time that the wooden landing stage that had passed as the town's port facility was superseded by a well-built quay with warehouses of commercial proportions.

Such was its importance, Londinium received a visit from Emperor Hadrian in 122 AD and by 200 AD a defensive wall surrounded the city. This wall, almost two miles in length, anywhere between 9 and 15 feet thick, was made from Kentish ragstone. The whole of Londinium was enclosed within – about 330 acres in total. Gateways that controlled entrance and exit into the area and allowed the passage of the major Roman roads were to the east Aldgate (leading to the road to Colchester), to the north Bishopsgate through which Ermine Street, the road to Lincoln and York, passed. Newgate was the entrance that allowed passage to and from the west along what is now the Strand while Ludgate also accessed a road west to Silchester. Cripplegate led only to the fort of the same name. Other gates, Moorgate, Aldermanbury and Tower were added during the medieval period.

During the 3rd century AD the population of Londinium began to shrink considerably, due in large to an economic downturn, however the citizens of the town were notably wealthier than ever before, with homes made from stone, or at least half-timbered, perhaps one or two

5

rooms with hypercaust heating and decorated with colourful mosaics and wall paintings.

The end of the 4th century saw the decline of the Roman Empire as a whole and by the mid 5th century Londinium was abandoned and its once grand public buildings and busy streets were left to fall into decay.

There is virtually nothing left to see of Roman London. Although archaeology can confirm the existence and position of buildings, what size they were and what materials they were made of, there is not much in the way of written evidence to tell us what the buildings actually looked like. To bridge this gap we have to consider what Roman architecture was like generally and apply this to London's remains in order to get some sort of picture of Londinium's principal buildings.

Many of the outward forms of Roman architecture are clearly taken from the Greek. In colonising Greece during the 2nd century BC the blossoming Roman Empire was able to exploit the skill of Greek builders who had perfected a standard post and lintel type of construction. Greek buildings were composed entirely of horizontal blocks supported by columns and walls – this was a style of architecture characterised by straight lines and a complete absence of arches or curves.

However such construction had its limitations. The span between columns was limited, as were the columns' weight bearing capacity, and therefore buildings could be no more than two storeys high. This was not enough for the Romans who wanted the architecture of their empire to make a strong statement of authority and this was very important to an acquisitive empire. The solution to the need for taller, more lavish buildings was found through the ingenious combination of the column and the rounded arch – a system that allows for a much higher load-bearing capacity.

The rounded arch is a distinctive feature of Roman architecture, as are the orders, or columns. The Romans had five different styles of columns, three of which were copies of Greek orders – Doric, plain with no fancy carving; Ionic, with fluted or scrolled capitals (that is the uppermost part of the column); and Corinthian with a capital decorated with carved acanthus leaves. All three Greek orders had fluted shafts. To this the Romans added the Tuscan order, like the Greek Doric but even plainer in appearance as the shaft was not fluted, and lastly Composite, similar to the Corinthian, but with more elaborate carving on the capital.

Capitals of the five classical orders and of the Modern Ionic Order

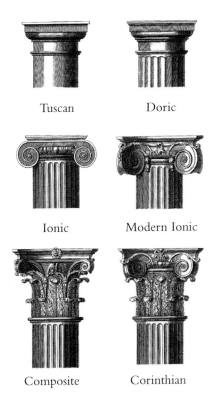

Tuscan

Doric

Ionic

Modern Ionic

Composite

Corinthian

The influence of Greco-Roman building cannot be overestimated, with many of their forms becoming part of the common language of western architecture. Indeed the very word 'architecture' is derived from the Latin and one of the most widely read and respected works on the subject is Vitruvius's De architectura libri decem (Ten Books of Architecture). Written sometime between 31 BC and 14 AD, Vitruvius' treatise highlighted the affinity between architecture and engineering and his work went on to influence a succession of architects over the ages, including Inigo Jones whose work in the 17th century is discussed in the following chapter.

What there is to see of Londinium

There are few Roman remains to be seen in London today, no unsurpisingly given that Londinium, being roughly the area o the present City of London, was subject to centuries of plunder neglect and destruction including the Great Fire of 1666. Howeve archaeologists are constantly turning up Roman finds examples o which can readily be seen in-situ in the undercroft of All Hallows b Tower Church on Byford Street (see p.19). In addition to these, thre Central London museums have extensive Roman displays which ca help us imagine what Londinium would have been like.

Guildhall

During the 1988 preparation work for an extension to the Guildhall in the heart of the City, short stretches of Roma wall were discovered. Much excitement ensued when it wa realised that what had been found was the site and remain of the amphitheatre – which would have been used for glad iatorial combat, animal fighting, public executions and reli gious ceremonies.

A line set into the paving in the square in front of the Guildhall denotes the location of the amphitheatre, whil archaeological finds relating to the site are in the basemen of the Guildhall Art Gallery – a short walk from the Museum of London.

Guildhall Art Gallery, Guildhall Yard, EC2P 2EJ; Telephon 020 7332 3700; Website www.guildhall-art-gallery.org.uk Nearest transport Bank LU (Central, Northern lines & DLR) Open Mon-Sat 10am-5pm, Sun 12noon-4pm; Admissio charge

British Museum

The Weston Gallery of Roman Britain houses an extensive display of artefacts from the Roman occupation, although not necessarily from Londinium. The museum also has a fascinating collection of Greek and Roman architectural remains which offer an excellent insight into the ways in which the various orders were used and the role of elements such as capitals, cornices and friezes.

The British Museum, Great Russell Street, WC1B 3DG; Telephone 0207 323 8299; Website www.thebritishmuseum.ac.uk; Nearest transport Holborn LU (Central and Piccadilly lines) and Russell Square (Piccadilly line); Open Sat-Wed 10am-5.30pm, Thurs-Fri 10am-8.30pm; Admission free (a charge may be made for temporary exhibitions)

Museum of London

A wonderful resource in the heart of the City of London. Archaeological finds and atmospheric room reconstructions show how Roman Londoners would have lived and worked while a section of old Roman city wall can also be glimpsed from the museum.

Museum of London, London Wall, EC2Y 5HN; Telephone 0870 444 3852; Website www.museumoflondon.org.uk; Nearest transport Barbican LU & Rail (Circle, Metropolitan and District lines) and St Paul's LU (Central line); Open Mon-Sat 10am-5.50pm, Sun 12noon-5.50pm; Admission free

Saxon, Norman, Gothic, Medieval & Tudor London

Westminster Abbey

The monk and historian The Venerable Bede (672-735) tells us that even after the end of Roman rule London was a 'mart of many nations'. For many years archaeologists and historians were baffled as to where the latest settlers in London, the Saxons and the Angles – Germanic tribes from Northern Europe who settled in Britain from the late 4th and 5th centuries onwards – actually lived. The first St Paul's, a wooden structure, was in place on the site of the present Cathedral by the early 7th century, but there is no evidence of other early settlement within the abandoned Roman city. It would appear that, initially at least, the Saxons avoided the site of Londinium and settled along the Thames valley at places such as Croydon, Mitcham, Rainham, Hanwell, and Twickenham.

However, during the building of the new extension to the Royal Opera House in Covent Garden in the 1980s, remains were found of the elusive Saxon town of 'Lundenwic'. They had settled a mile or so to the west of the ruined Roman city, underlying what is today the West End and the Aldwych, the name which may refer to the 'Ald wych' or 'old town'. It was not until the later Saxon period, from the expulsion of invading Danes by King Alfred in 886 until the Norman invasion of 1066, that the area within the old Roman walls was used again.

There is nothing left standing of Saxon pedigree, save a few traces at All Hallows Barking (see p.19), due mainly to their preference for building timber structures, which had no permanence above ground, or re-using Roman brick from the City area, thereby usually confusing matters. Because it is regarded as a time of cultural unenlightenment, the period of about 400 years between the departure of the Romans and the arrival of the Normans is often referred to as the 'Dark Age'. This is a little unfair given the beautifully crafted articles produced in this period, many fine examples of which can be seen in the British Museum.

However, one very important Saxon architectural legacy to posterity is the concept of the 'Hall' dwelling – one large room, open to the rafters, constructed of whole or split logs, with a fire for cooking and warmth at the centre. The size of the construction depended upon how many people had to be catered for. This simple structure was the basis of later 'Halls' for meetings and dining such as at Westminster, the City (Guildhall see p.31) and was central to community living in institutions such as the Inns of Law (see Section Two 'Walking London's Architecture' p.193) and the universities of Oxford and Cambridge.

The Norman invaders were prolific castle and church builders and the finest examples of both in London are to be found at the White Tower and St John's Chapel (see Tower of London p.21). The Tower was one of three castles built in the area, the others being Baynard's Castle, almost at the site of Blackfriars Station and Montfitchet Castle close by, the remains of which both perished in the Great Fire of 1666.

There are two notable characteristics of Norman architecture. The first is the use of enduring materials such as stone, or when that was not available they tended to 'make do' with Roman brick, as at St Albans Abbey. The second characteristic is the rounded arch, borrowed from Roman builders and the reason why Norman architecture is often called 'Romanesque'. The rounded arch was found to be strong in the extreme and experimentation with the pointed arch did not come until much later. The ground plan of a Norman church is always in the shape of a Latin cross. The altar is at the east end of the chancel – in the direction of Jerusalem and the main entrance is always at the west end.

Many Norman French words have been absorbed into our everyday language such as lodge, grange, vale and forest, and place names from this period still resound in London – Barbican, Savoy, Old Bailey, Charterhouse, Charing Cross.

The term 'Gothic' is a Renaissance term of abuse – describing a style the humanists found barbaric and anti-classical, but which embraced several changes in architectural thought and application. Between the 12th and 16th centuries these highly significant developments were achieved initially under the powerful Pope Innocent III, who was fortunate to be presiding over a unified church. However the Gothic style is generally held to have begun with the rebuilding of St Denis in France in the 1140s, under the auspices of Abbot Suger (1081-1151) – a man who knew what he wanted! He believed in the transcendental power of light and colour and this led him to demand large windows for stained glass. He was also fond of the idea that there should be lots of room for pilgrim perambulation on feast days.

What emerged from these requirements was the pointed arch and the rib vault, that is a groin vault with crossed arches exposed on the under surface, which was used from the late 11th century at Durham Cathedral and buildings in Italy and Picardy. However, combining these arches with large windows allowing light to flood in was a significant development. Immediately on entering a Gothic church one notices the impression of vast height. This is created partly by the real height of the building and partly by the optical illusion created by the columns, arches and ribs all pointing upwards. An exterior feature of Gothic church building is the presence of flying buttresses whose function was to counterbalance any outward thrust exerted on the seemingly impossibly thin and tall walls and thereby stop the whole building collapsing.

Much of London's Gothic building perished in the Great Fire of 1666 but good examples of the type can be seen in parts of Southwark Cathedral (see p.22) and the magnificent nave and fabulous flying buttresses at Westminster Abbey (see p.16). These are examples of Gothicism at its most evolved. For very early examples see the Temple Church and St Bartholomew the Great (see p.24 and p.23).

Medieval London had a rich and sophisticated government and simply by virtue of its wealth and size it was more independent than other cities. Some individuals became so rich they were able to lend vast sums to the crown if the king was in need of extra cash. One such wealthy individual was Richard Whittington, businessman, entrepreneur and philanthropist, who died 1423. He financed the first public toilets in the City, and was three times Lord Mayor of London. Whittington had financial dealings with three monarchs, Richard II, Henry IV and Henry V and was the same person portrayed in the apocryphal story of young 'Dick Whittington and his Cat', retold every year in pantomime!

Despite the proliferation of rich and powerful individuals, London was a place of extremes of wealth and poverty. The livery companies, some dating back from the early 12th century, not only looked after the interests of their members but also built enduring premises. The great churches and monasteries of this period are impressive, so too are the inns of courts and the houses of noblemen, but the back streets, dark and overhung, would have contained rough dwellings. The very poor would not have had ovens at home so hot food outlets would have been as familiar then as today. Whilst the main thoroughfares would have been kept relatively clean other lesser streets would have been smelly places littered with animal dung, industrial waste, such as discarded animal parts from leatherworkers, dirt and domestic garbage.

The average life expectancy for Londoners during this period was only early thirties, with an infant mortality rate of 30%. However, Bubonic plague, the 'Black Death' transfixed everyone, rich or poor. Attempts were made to zone activity in order to contain dirt and pollution, such as having specific areas for butchers on the edge of the City. Others took the view that health terrors were the product of immorality – a moral city was a healthy one – so prostitutes, beggars and lepers were subject to summary expulsion every now and then. Indeed the Palace of St James was built on the site of a former leper hospital for women, well away from the general populous. Rich citizens were able to invest in their spiritual wellbeing financing many monasteries in London, setting up alms houses and providing wards for unmarried mothers, as a way of protecting themselves from divine retribution.

The Renaissance was a rare period in that it was so self-conscious it gave itself a name – the word derives from the Italian 'rinascita' which means rebirth. Artists and humanists used the term to express the dramatic changes that occurred at the turn of the 15th century. London, along with the rest of Europe, was just emerging from a century of trauma – the 'Hundred Years War' and the Black Death had devastated the population and the accompanying economic recession affected many. Industry, farming and trade recovered gradually, and by the end of the 14th century a new confidence as well as a revival in international trade was being felt. Improvements in navigation brought wealth and the acquisition of new empires and the invention of moving type print brought standardisation in language and better communications.

In France and Spain a new style of architecture began to appear in court circles. The monarchy set the trend but little of this touched England. At this time Henry VIII was changing the face of London with the building of palaces in Whitehall, St James and Greenwich and the royal dockyards at Deptford and Woolwich, bringing much needed relief to the overcrowded City docks. The once dominant monasteries were now no longer the most impressive constructions in London. After the Dissolution of the Monasteries, which took place between 1535 and 1540, their land and buildings were sold to friends and supporters of the King, but not many of them could afford lavish new buildings, so adaptation was the order of the day.

It was Cardinal Wolsey who acknowledged Renaissance fashions by commissioning an Italian sculptor to produce roundels of the Roman Emperors for his fabulous new Hampton Court. However these decorations were attached to a new building that looked every inch a late medieval castle.

The Reformation had driven a wedge between England and Catholic Italy and so trade and political ties were established with the

Protestant Low Countries and as a nation England's ideas of the Renaissance were initially imported via Antwerp rather than Rome or Florence. Also the reigns of Mary and of Elizabeth saw little in the way of Royal building. Elizabeth chose to encourage her courtiers, the new men who rose up in wealth and influence under the Tudor monarchy, to build for her. The Queen preferred to be entertained in such 'prodigy houses' rather than at court, so she spent much of her reign going from one house to another, along with her colossal entourage. Such a house would be built with a range of state apartments – a great chamber, withdrawing chamber and bedroom fit for a monarch.

It was under Elizabeth's successor James, who came to the throne in 1603, that Renaissance architecture was embraced and the first building to be started in this new style was the Queen's House at Greenwich by Inigo Jones (see p.36).

But, what was so new about the Renaissance style? The architect now had to be mindful of the ideals of proportion, using Classical inspiration and mathematical precision to create unified, balanced structures. Inigo Jones (1573-1652) was the first architect in England to implement these ideals and had been fortunate enough to have travelled extensively in Italy, studying the Roman remains a full century before it became de rigueur for every fashionable young man of means to do so. He became Surveyor of the King's works in 1615 and in the following year received the commission from Queen Anne, wife of James, to design her a new pavilion at Greenwich.

His first work for the Royal household was as a masque designer working in collaboration with the dramatist Ben Jonson from about 1605, when they turned traditional court entertainment into a theatrical and intellectual display of excellence. Masques combined music, drama, dance and art and Jonson and Jones were the European masters of the genre – until they quarrelled and the partnership was ended in 1632. However, by this time, Jones was well ensconced as an architect producing England's first truly Renaissance buildings – the Banqueting House and the Queen's House, as well as the first Protestant Church and the first London Square (see p.40).

Jones had also worked on St Paul's Cathedral adding Classical elements to it. However, with the execution of Charles in 1649 and inauguration of the Commonwealth under Cromwell all such work was stopped and Jones's services were no longer required. Inigo Jones died in 1652, eight years before the Restoration that would witness a new contender for his crown of architect genius – Christopher Wren.

Examples of buildings from this period:

Westminster Abbey

Ever since William the Conqueror's coronation in the Abbey on Christmas Day 1066 all monarchs of England have been crowned here, with the exception of Edward V (usurped by Richard III) and Edward VIII (abdicated). Legend tells us that a monastery had been established on the site by the Saxons prior to the Norman Conquest, but this was subsequently sacked by the invading Danes. The monastery was restored by King Edgar (944-75) but soon fell into disrepair and we do not know what form its buildings would have taken.

It was the Saxon King Edward the Confessor who decided to build a magnificent church on the site, regardless of cost, and between 1045-50 he built what was in reality a classic Norman church – years before the Norman invasion of 1066. Edward had spent twenty five years in exile in Normandy and had not only admired its architecture but also understood the impact church building could have as a force within the kingdom. He had much admired the church of Jumieges Abbey, under construction between 1037-66, and this is what Westminster Abbey was based on – only Edward required his church to be larger than any church in Normandy. He also had his palace built alongside, thus establishing the site of the Palace of Westminster and subsequently Whitehall, thereby beginning the move by the monarchy away from the City, and the two becoming independent of each other.

Little is left of Edward's Norman church as subsequent monarchs have also endeavoured to leave their mark on the Abbey and what we have today is a spectacular monument to different architectural styles that need a book of their own to describe. However listed below is a very short list of some of the highlights:

Westminster Abbey

Pyx Chamber. This, and the undercroft, are the only remains of the original Norman church. This chamber, sometimes referred to as the Chapel of the Pyx, and the museum were formed from the undercroft of the monks' dormitory. The word 'pyx' means box and it was here that the monarch's money was held.

The Nave. Only 35 feet wide but the tallest in England at 102 feet. It was begun in 1246, making it the first example of High French Gothic architecture to be built in England. The tall, thin walls only stand upright with the aid of the massive external flying buttresses which are a work of art in themselves.

Chapter House. Begun in 1246, this octagonal room has a vaulted room of eight bays supported on a single pier. The huge windows with heraldic crests and the beautifully tiled floor date from 1259. From circa 1400–1547 the room was used for parliamentary meetings.

Chapel of Henry VII (also known as the Lady Chapel). Built between circa 1503-15 with superb pendant fan vaulting which makes this perhaps the most spectacular ceiling of its time.

There are also many works of art and monuments to see within the Abbey itself, including Poets' Corner which is almost a 'Who's Who' of English literature starting with Geoffrey Chaucer, who was the first poet to be buried here, in 1400.

Westminster Abbey, Dean's Yard, SW1; Telephone 020 7222 5897; Nearest transport Westminster LU (Jubilee, Central and District lines); Nave and Royal Chapels open Mon-Fri 9.30am-4.45pm (last admission 3.45pm), Sat 9am-2.45pm (last admission 1.45pm); Chapter House open Nov-Mar daily 10am-4pm (last admission 3.30pm), Apr-Oct daily 10am-5.30pm (last admission 5pm); Pyx Chamber and Abbey Museum open daily 10.30am-4pm; Admission charges vary (concessions available)

All Hallows Barking

This interesting church is not actually located in Barking but very close to the Tower of London in the City. It is so named because it was a daughter church of Barking Abbey, Essex (founded about 660 CE) and was first mentioned as such in documents dated 1086.

All Hallows can claim to be the only City church with standing fabric from the Anglo Saxon period and this is a section of the south-west wall and part of the north-west corner of the nave. Two sections of Roman tessellated pavement are also to be seen, one still in situ between the Saxon foundations of the tower and the other recently re-laid as part of the crypt flooring.

Most of the pre-17th century fabric of the church was destroyed in a fire in 1650 but the church was rebuilt between 1658-59, the only London church to have work carried out during the Commonwealth. The church again suffered extensive damage from enemy bombing during the 1939-45 conflict and drastic reconstruction was undertaken by Lord Mottistone of Seely and Paget architects who added a spire to the brick tower during the 1950s.

Do not miss the exquisite font cover dated 1682 and attributed to Grinling Gibbons – a feast of carved leaves, cherubs, fir cones and flowers.

Many historical figures are associated with this church – William Penn, founder of Pennsylvania was baptised here and John Quincy Adams, 6th President of the USA was married here in 1797, to name but two. This is the church of HM Customs and Excise.

All Hallows Barking, Great Tower Street, EC3R 5BJ; Telephone 020 7481 2928; Nearest transport Tower Hill LU (DLR, Circle and District lines); Open Mon-Fri 9am-6pm, Sat & Sun 10am-5pm

All Hallows Barking

Tower of London

The Tower of London, founded by William the Conqueror sometime after 1077, has been a royal palace, fortress, prison, place of execution, jewel house, mint, arsenal and royal zoo. Successive monarchs have added various buildings thereby bequeathing a complex of different architecture from various periods, such as the Cradle Tower (1348-1355), New Armouries (1663), Waterloo Barracks (1845), and the notorious Bloody Tower (previously known as the Garden Tower but re-named after its murderous associations).

The oldest, and most familiar, building within the walled 12 acre site is the White Tower. This huge, solid form was a bold statement by the conquering Normans to the local populace, but also provided a stout defence against any invading enemies and a place of refuge for the royal family in times of crisis. The Tower walls, 12 feet thick, are made from ragstone with Caen stone dressings specially shipped over from Normandy. The Caen stone dressings have mainly been replaced by Portland stone, but originally the stone was whitewashed and this is how the building got its name. The White Tower is a square building with turrets on each of the four corners, with the whole roofline being crenellated until the mid 16th century when ogee caps were added. Each of the three original floors (the fourth was added later) is divided into three distinct departments.

One of the architectural highlights of the Tower is St Johns Chapel on the second floor. This is perhaps one of the finest early Norman structures remaining anywhere. Massive, solid and unadorned with a tunnel-vaulted nave (unique in England) it exemplifies a wonderful use of space.

Tower of London, Tower Hill, EC3; Telephone 0870 756 606 (information line); Website www.hrp.org.uk; Nearest transport Tower Hill LU (Circle & District lines) & Tower Gateway DLR; Open Mon-Sat 9am-5pm, Sun 10am-5pm (1st March-31st Oct, Tues-Sat 9am-4pm, Sun & Mon 10am-4pm (1st Nov-28th Feb); Admission charge

Southwark Cathedral

Amidst the railway tracks, roads, blocks of flats and offices and in the shadow of the approach to London Bridge stands Southwark Cathedral. Built on the site of a much earlier church this former Augustinian Priory of St Mary Overie (meaning St Mary 'over the river') has its Norman and medieval plan still pretty much intact. This is despite serious fires in 1212 and 1390 which destroyed most of the fabric of the building. Subsequent rebuilding and renovation have nonetheless left the choir and retro-choir undisturbed and this is why the Cathedral can lay claim to being the 'oldest Gothic building in London'.

A very successful new building project was opened in 2001 providing the Cathedral with new ancillary accommodation, including a theological library, shop and refectory. The old and new parts of the building marry perfectly, which is due to the careful use of materials, being limestone and Norfolk flint under a Westmoreland slate roof. This extension, the work of architects Richard Griffiths and Ptolemy Dean, was nominated in the 2002 prestigious RIBA Stirling Prize for architectural excellence.

An interesting permanent exhibition called 'Long View of London' resides in the old refectory.

Southwark Cathedral, Montague Close, SE1 9DT; Telephone 020 7367 6700; Nearest transport London Bridge LU & Rail (Northern & Jubilee lines); Cathedral open daily 8am-6pm, exhibition open Mon-Sat 10am-6pm, Sun 11am-6pm; Admission charge for exhibition (concessions available)

Westminster Hall

The Hall was originally a Norman addition incorporated into the old Palace of Westminster built by Edward the Confessor as the principal residence of the monarch and remaining so until the reign of Henry VIII. Thereafter it was used mainly as a meeting place for Parliament, a use it has retained through to the present day. The Hall, described by many as the greatest royal hall in Europe, is, along with the

Jewel Tower (see below), the only surviving parts of the old Palace. Built by William II (also known as William Rufus) in 1099, some of the original masonry still survives but the Hall was heavily renovated during the reign of Richard II when the magnificent hammerbeam ceiling was added.

Also at the site is the Jewel Tower, built in the south-west corner of the original Palace grounds in 1365/66 to house the personal treasure of King Edward III. The Tower had been moated – an effective form of home security. The Tower now houses a small museum containing items relating to the old Palace of Westminster.

Westminster Hall & the Jewel Tower, Abingdon St, SW1 3JY; Telephone 020 7222 2219; Nearest transport Westminster LU (Jubille, Circle and District Lines); Open daily 10.00-18.00 (April-Sept), 10.00-17.00 (Oct), 10.00-16.00 (Nov-March); Admission charge

St Bartholomew the Great

This church was founded in 1123 as an Augustinian priory by Rahere a compassionate (he established the kernel of what is now a world famous hospital – St Bartholomew's) and enterprising monk. In 1133 he received royal permission to hold an annual fair which raised a considerable sum of money for his work – see Batholomew Walk p.194).

Very little of the 12th century church remains, however what we are left with is one of the most beautiful buildings in London. Originally a modest building of a choir, ambulatory and Lady Chapel, enlargement took place during the next one hundred years with the addition of transepts and a crossing and the lengthening of the nave giving the whole building the feel of a classic Norman church. (The splendid gateway of 1595 marks where the original nave finished).

The part of the priory serving as a hospital survived the Reformation but the monastery itself was closed, the church sold off to the parish and part of the nave demolished. The crypt was used as a wine and coal store; the Lady Chapel became private dwellings and a print works (Benjamin Franklin worked here during 1725); horses were stabled in the cloisters and a blacksmith operated in the north transept and a carpenter worked in the sacristy. The building was also used as a non–conformist meeting place and a school at various times throughout its history. It is a small miracle there was any fabric left to work with but the eminent architect Aston Webb spent from 1884-96 restoring the building to what we see today.

The church contains many notable features including an oriel window installed in 1517 overlooking the choir (probably to act as a watch tower to keep an eye on the gifts left at Rahere's tomb); the splendid, solid Romanesque pillars in the crossing; the earliest pointed arches in London (at the crossing) dating from 1145-60 and the only medieval font dated circa 1405 and in which the painter William Hogarth was baptised in 1697. The interior was used in the filming of 'Four Weddings and a Funeral' and 'Shakespeare in Love'.

St Bartholomew the Great, West Smithfield, EC1A 7JQ; Telephone 020 7606 5171; Nearest transport Farringdon or Barbican LU & Rail (Circle and Metropolitan lines); Open Mon-Fri 8.30am-5pm (closing at 4pm Nov-mid Feb); Sat 10.30am-1.30pm, Sun 8am-8pm

Temple Church

This church was built for the Knights Templar, an organisation formed at the end of the 11th century for the protection of Christian pilgrims journeying to and from the Holy Land. The churches they built throughout Europe were based on the circular design of the Church of the Holy Sepulchre in Jerusalem. This is one of the last surviving examples of such a church in England. Temple Church was consecrated in 1185 in the presence of King Henry II and was dedicated to St Mary. Associated with many historic events, such as the mediation between King John and the Barons in 1215, the Knights Templar nonetheless fell out of favour during the beginning of the 14th century. On confiscation of this church by the Crown it was leased to lawyers of the Middle and Inner Temples.

Temple Church

The circular nave of the Temple Church is a very fine example of the Transitional phase of architecture between the Norman and Gothic, indeed probably one of the first buildings to incorporate Gothic themes in England. The main piers in the nave are of Purbeck marble, its first use as a building material in London.

Many famous architects – Wren, George Gilbert Scott, Robert and Sidney Smirke, Decimus Burton to name but a few – have supervised restoration at the church at one time or another and their involvement is a testament to its architectural significance. A popular venue for concerts, the acoustics are superb, and it's very much a thriving, working church as well as an immensely interesting building to visit. Don't miss the life-size Purbeck marble effigies of knights dating from the 13th century.

For other buildings in the area of 'The Temple' see Fleet Street & Beyond Walk (p.204)

Temple Church, Temple Lane, EC4; Telephone 020 7353 3470; Nearest transport Blackfriars LU & Rail (Circle and District lines) Chancery Lane LU (Central line); Open to the public most days but times vary – please telephone to check

St John's Priory

Established in about 1140, the Knights Hospitallers' Priory of St John covered about six acres in Clerkenwell and was the English headquarters of the Order of St John, as it was known. The order was founded to give succour to pilgrims and Crusaders, but various changes in the Order occurred as late as 1877 when it became the St John's Ambulance Brigade.

After the dissolution of the monasteries during the reign of Henry VIII the Priory buildings were put to various uses – the residence of Queen Elizabeth I's Master of Revels; a pub; a coffee shop reputedly run by the father of the painter William Hogarth; and as the offices of 'The Gentlemen's Magazine'. However, St John's Ambulance Brigade now have their head office on the premises, thus bringing the story full circle.

What is left of architectural interest is a gem of a 12th century crypt over which a Georgian parish church was built. The original church was circular, similar to Temple Church. Also of note is the large and impressive St John's Gate, built in 1504, its grand size denoting the importance of the Priory. The museum contains many items of interest such as illustrated manuscripts and items relating to the history of the Order.

The Museum of the Order of St John, St John's Gate, St John's Lane, Clerkenwell, EC1M 4DA; Telephone 020 7324 4070; Nearest transport Farringdon LU & Rail (Circle and Metropolitan lines); Access to Priory by guided tours only, available 11am and 2.30pm Tues, Fri and Sat or by special arrangement (please telephone); Museum open Mon–Fri 10am-5pm, Sat 10am-4pm; Admission free (donations requested for tours)

Old St Pancras Church

Amid the turmoil of the current redevelopment at King's Cross patiently sits the Old St Pancras Church. Given its present surroundings, it is difficult to believe that this little church was, at one time, encircled by fields, and once served a country parish that stretched from what is now the Russell Square area all the way to Kenwood in Hampstead.

Pancratius was an orphaned boy living in the household of the Emperor of Rome who, on refusing to relinquish his Christian beliefs, was martyred in 304 CE; a basilica was later built in his honour on the Aurelian Way. During the time of the Roman occupation of London the River Fleet was navigable to just beyond where the church is sited today. Legend tells us that an encampment here raised the first place of worship in the name of St Pancras, the anglicised version of his name. What form this building took can only be guessed at as no trace of it remains. However a carved altar stone dating from the 6th or 7th century and an entry in the Doomsday Book of 1086 confirm the church's earlier existence. This makes it one of the oldest sites of continuous Christian worship in London.

By the end of the 18th century this little church was deemed too small and old for the fashionable inhabitants of the newly built houses in the Bedford Estate, in what is now the Euston Road area. Funds for a new church were sought and this little church fell out of favour. However, it is still very much a working church and well worth a visit.

The fairly substantial Norman church had been reworked during the 12th century and dramatically 'Normanised' during the 19th century, with mixed success. It is a pity that during this latter work the medieval tower was removed in order to extend the church west and add a south facing entrance porch and tower. The church was last renovated in 1979/80. The exterior was used in the film 'Four Weddings and a Funeral'.

The surrounding churchyard was disturbed somewhat during the establishment of King's Cross and St Pancras stations and one hopes the grounds are receiving sensitive and sympathetic treatment during current work. However there are many fine monuments in the churchyard including that of the eminent architect Sir John Soane and his family.

St Pancras Old Church, Pancras Road, NW1; Nearest transport King's Cross LU & Rail (Northern, Victoria, Circle, District and Metropolitan lines); For details of access and times of services telephone 020 7387 4193

St Helen's Bishopsgate

An interesting church that escaped damage in the Great Fire of 1666 and World War II only to sustain serious damage by IRA bombing in 1992 and 1993. The architect Quinlan Terry restored and reworked the interior between 1993-95 to provide a more flexible approach to the available space for worship. This little church, now almost hidden amid a thicket of tall, shiny office blocks, started life circa 1200-1215 as a Benedictine nunnery. However there was already a parish church on the site, possibly 11th or early 12th century, and the nun's new church was built alongside the existing building. This has given the church its odd appearance of having two 'main' entrances almost side by side, one for the nuns, and one for the parish. The naves are now one, but it is possible to trace their original configuration.

The church has a number of noteworthy features, not least of which is the Shakespeare window which dates from 1884 (he is believed to have lived nearby); a richly decorated pulpit dating from circa 1633 and a superb collection of pre-1666 monuments.

St Helen's Bishopsgate, Great St Helen's, EC3A 6AT; Telephone 020 7283 2231; Nearest transport Liverpool Street LU & Rail (Circle and Metropolitan lines); Open Mon–Fri 9am-5pm, entrance via St Helen's Church Office

Eltham Palace

Eltham Palace was built on a site that has been occupied by substantial houses since Saxon times. In 1275 it was owned by the Bishop of Durham who presented it to the first Prince of Wales, who became King Edward II. It was a favourite royal palace until Henry VIII's reign, when Greenwich was favoured. Eltham was sold off during the Commonwealth and was subject to an inglorious history until 1931 when the exceedingly wealthy Stephen Courtauld bought the lease and embarked on a six-year restoration programme of the old Hall. He also built an entirely new adjoining house. Within a mere eight years the lease was sold to the Army Education Corps and in 1995 the property was acquired by English Heritage.

St Helen's Bishopsgate

The Great Hall, with a superb hammerbeam ceiling, dates from 1475. It measures 100 feet by 36 feet, and is the only survival of the Palace's medieval splendour. The house built during the 1930s is Art Deco in style which whilst not pleasing the purists, does, provide a terrific contrast to the Hall and is fun to look at, if only to marvel at what the perhaps ill-advised rich chose to spend their money on! Of particular note is the entrance hall whose glass dome illuminates some extremely elegant period furniture and a circular carpet beneath. Both buildings are set in romantic moated gardens.

Eltham Palace, Court Yard, Eltham, SE9 5QE; Telephone 0208 294 2548; Nearest transport Eltham Rail; Open Wed, Thurs, Fri, Sun and Bank Holiday Mondays 10am–6pm (April–Sept) 10am–5pm (October) and 10am–4pm (Nov–Mar); Admission charge

Lambeth Palace

The palace and official London residence of the Archbishop of Canterbury, the most senior cleric of the Church of England, has occupied this site since 1207. This is the last remaining bishopric palace of any size along either bank of the Thames; the others all disappeared with the Reformation.

The simple but beautifully constructed undercroft of the Palace chapel dates from before 1240. The west doorway with its noted trefoiled opening are all that remain of the original building, the rest of which was damaged by Second World War enemy bombing and now restored. The water tower, also called Lollards' Tower, dates from 1435 and was used as a prison in the 17th century. The Gatehouse dates from about 1495 and is an excellent chance to see the red bricks used extensively in high quality Tudor building. The Great Hall of 1663, is also built of brick but with stone dressings and is a magnificent example of Gothic architecture with buttresses, pointed windows and a high-pitched roof with a splendid hammerbeam ceiling. Since the 19th century the Hall has been used as a library.

The principal offices and residence are the work of the architect Edward Blore (1787-1879) and all, according to the novelist Walter Scott, 'in the best Gothic taste'.

Lambeth Palace, Lambeth Palace Road, SE1; Nearest transport Lambeth North LU (Bakerloo line); Lambeth Palace is not open to the public but tours can be arranged by writing to the Booking Department at the above address. Lambeth Palace is part of the London Open House scheme (see Resources p.297).

Winchester House (remains of)

This was the London residence of the Bishops of Winchester from the 12th to the 17th century and would have been not too dissimilar to Lambeth Palace just along the Thames. The grounds of the House would have extended down to the river where the successive bishops came and went by barge. Nothing is left of the original 12th century building but what does remain dates from the early 14th century; just part of two walls of the Great Hall with a few doorways. However, perhaps of the greatest interest here is the remains of a rose window which was restored in 1972. Seeing it in its skeletal form one wonders if it could have looked any more beautiful with coloured glass.

Winchester House, Clink Street, SE1; Nearest transport London Bridge LU and Rail (Northern and Jubilee lines); Open access

Guildhall

There had been a guildhall (from the Anglo Saxon 'gild' meaning payment – a place where citizens paid their taxes) on this site for many years before this particular building was begun in 1411. Since enemy bombing in 1940, in which it was severely damaged and surrounding buildings destroyed, the Guildhall has stood exposed, but it was once part of a considerable medieval complex. Post-war restoration was carried out by Sir Giles Gilbert Scott who also added new office accommodation on the north wall. Further work during the 1960's added more offices and a new L-shaped library. The building of the new art gallery during the 1990s was delayed by the exciting discovery of remains of a Roman amphitheatre (see previous chapter). The art gallery, designed by Richard Gilbert Scott, was opened in 1999.

The Guildhall is the City's largest secular building and is still an important focus of official ceremonies and celebrations. Much of its 15th century perpendicular architecture is still in evidence – with its characteristic lightness of stonework and splendid windows with notably accomplished tracery.

Another interesting feature of the Guildhall is the 1788/89 porch by George Dance the Younger. This porch, made mainly from Portland stone, is arguably the earliest example of Indian influence in English architecture; a form which went on to be labelled 'Hindoo-Gothic'. At this time there was much debate amongst architects and intellectuals as to the origins of 'Gothic' and it is thought Dance was experimenting with these forms. Or, the inclusion of such eastern motifs and echoes may well just have been a nod of recognition towards the City's vital trading links with the Orient!

The Guildhall, Guildhall Yard, EC2P; Telephone 020 7606 3030; Nearest transport Bank LU (Central, Northern lines & DLR); The Guildhall is open to the public when not in use and entrance is free (telephone for details)

St Margaret, Westminster

If this church stood anywhere else in London it would probably receive far more attention. However, being in the shadow of the magnificent Westminster Abbey many visitors overlook this rather interesting church. Built between 1482-1523, but with a much earlier, perhaps late 11th century foundation, it is the only surviving pre-Reformation church in Westminster. Built in a Perpendicular style, that is the final flowering of the Gothic style, St Margaret 's interior was heavily restored during the 18th and 19th centuries, the last time by Giles Gilbert Scott in 1877. The church exterior is somewhat dominated by a tower built in 1734 – this was not a success and had to be partly rebuilt the following year but it is nonetheless a good example of Gothicism. St Margaret's has been the official parish church of Parliament since April 1614 and is where such notables as Samuel Pepys, John Milton and Winston Churchill were married.

This church has an interesting selection of stained glass windows ranging from the very early 16th century to a fabulous example of John Piper's work – an abstract titled 'Spring in London' and dated 1968. See Whitehall Walk (p.220)

St Margaret's Church Westminster, Parliament Square, SW1; Nearest transport Westminster LU (Jubilee, Central & District lines); Open Mon-Fri 9.30am-5.30pm, Sat 9am-2pm, Sun 1pm-5.30pm, Sunday service at 11am

St James's Palace

Although not open to the public (apart from the chapel, see below) there is plenty of St James's Palace to see from the street. The complex of buildings includes Clarence House, latterly the home of the late Queen Mother and now Prince Charles's London residence. The Palace was built by Henry VIII between 1531-40 at the same time Whitehall was under construction. St James's would appear to have been intended to house the monarch's heir rather than the king himself, so it is perhaps appropriate that a Prince of Wales is once more in residence. When Whitehall burned to the ground in 1698 St James's became the focus of the Royal court in London. This association however was relatively shortlived as George III thought St James's inappropriate for his new bride and moved the Court to Buckingham House (later Palace). A fire in 1809 destroyed much of the Palace. The State apartments as they appear today are the result of rebuilding and renovation by John Nash in the early 19th century.

The wall and gatehouse which face onto Cleveland Row are the oldest parts of the Palace, with the Tudor brickwork (red brick with blue brick diapering) dating from 1531-40 with later alterations. The gatehouse is typical of early Tudor design with its octagonal turrets; the ogee topped cupola and clock face, were added 1832.

The Chapel Royal is also part of the original range of buildings but was heavily renovated by Robert Smirke in 1836/37. The beautiful decorative ceiling dates from 1540 and is still very much intact. It was in this remarkable chapel that King Charles I took communion on the morning of his execution and Queen Victoria and Prince Albert were married here in November 1840.

Close by is St James's Park, which at one time was a swamp but which Henry VIII had drained in 1533 and stocked with deer for the royal hunt.

St James's Palace, Cleveland Row, Marlborough Gate, SW1; No public entry apart from service attendance in the Chapel Royal 8.30am and 11.30am Sundays (October to Good Friday only)

Staple Inn

This is a rare survivor of Elizabethan architecture in Central London and despite extensive restoration it is still a very impressive building. The front of this half-timbered building is in two halves – the slightly shorter half is probably just the older of the two, dating from 1586. Both parts have two overhanging storeys each and the shops on the ground floor, which are still just one room apiece, as they were originally planned. The Staple Inn gives us a tantalising glimpse of what London looked like prior to the Great Fire of 1666.

Staple Inn, Holborn, EC1; Nearest transport Chancery Lane LU (Central line); No public access – apart from shops on ground floor

Charlton House

Charlton House

The last remaining example in London of a truly Jacobean house. Built by Sir Adam Newton, tutor to the eldest son of James I, whom, had he not died as a teenager, would have become King Henry IX. Instead his younger brother became King Charles I – and the rest, as they say, is history! Constructed in the E-plan favoured at the time, Charlton House is a massive three-storey mansion with four symmetrical bay windows. It was built between 1607 and 1617 of red brick with stone dressing and each of the four towers that grace the corners is topped with an ogee roof. The interior contains a hall of double height, much fine panelling (mostly, alas, not original), interesting stone and marble fireplaces and a superb carved staircase. The House sits in very pleasant gardens and parkland.

It's well worth the effort to see this house not only for its own merits but to compare and contrast its bulkiness with Inigo Jones's work, especially the Queen's House (see p.36), began a mere four or so years later. Inigo Jones may well have been familiar with Charlton as he, like its owner and builder Sir Adam Newton, was in the employ of the Royal Household at the time.

Charlton House, Charlton Road, SE7 8RE; Telephone 0208 856 3951; Nearest transport Charlton Rail; Admission free. Charlton House is owned by the Borough of Greenwich and is used as a community centre. Concerts, meetings, classes and weddings frequently take place there so it's best to call ahead of a proposed visit to see which parts of the house are accessible and for opening times

The Queen's House, Greenwich

This riverside location was once the site of the Palace of Placentia, the birthplace of Henry VIII and his daughters Mary and Elizabeth. It was a favourite royal residence with an armoury and a tiltyard complete with romantic medieval towers and was conveniently close to the Royal Naval yards at Deptford and Woolwich.

The Queen's House

In 1616 work began on the Queen's House, which was commissioned for the wife of James I, Anne of Denmark who unfortunately died three years later and work stopped on the House. The house was covered in thatch and only completed between 1630-35 for Henrietta Maria, Charles I's queen.

The Queen's House was the first wholly classical building in England and is considered to be one of the most important buildings in British architectural history in that there simply had been nothing like it before. Inigo Jones built what was effectively a small (just 110 by 120 feet) two-storey square Italian villa in brick, with rusticated stone facings up to the first floor level on its north and south sides and plastered elsewhere; a pure white house contrasting with the heavy-looking piebald Tudor and Jacobean buildings of the time. The central loggia on the second floor overlooking Greenwich Park is pure Palladio, with a balustrade and Ionic columns with intricately carved capitals.

The interior contains many gems such as the royal apart-ments and the Great Hall, a forty-foot cube which Jones designed in accordance with Palladio's rules of proportion. The beautiful 'Tulip' staircase is worth a visit in its own right and is so-called because of the flower motifs on the finely crafted wrought-iron balustrade. It is notable also for being the first cantilevered spiral staircase in Britain. One of the most significant works of architecture in London, the whole building was restored between 1984-90. The renovation has proved a great success making the house a major Greenwich attraction, particularly as entrance is now free.

The Queen's House, National Maritime Museum, Greenwich, E10 9NF; Telephone 020 8858 4422; Nearest transport Cutty Sark Maritime Greenwich DLR and Maze Hill Rail; Open daily 10am-5pm; Admission free

The Banqueting House

On its completion the Banqueting House drew the comment from a contemporary observer that the building was 'too handsome for the rest of the palace'. Built between 1619-22 as part of the Whitehall Palace complex, really a collection of buildings of varying quality and style, Inigo Jones's Banqueting House was not only a more than satisfactory provision of a new reception hall and masquing house but also a momentous triumph in the history of English architecture.

The Banqueting House

Commenced after Jones's Queens House at Greenwich was started but completed many years sooner, the Banqueting House also incorporated elements of Palladio's Vicenzan architecture. The Banqueting House is approximately 110 feet in length and 55 feet in height, being therefore a double cube, its seven bays are divided by Ionic pillars with Corinthian pilasters above. Externally the two main elevations match. The three middle bays have attached columns whereas the outer bays have pilasters doubled at the outer edge of the building for emphasis. To add further interest to the façade different coloured masonry was used; Oxfordshire stone at the lower level with Northamptonshire stone above and Portland stone for all the main architectural detailing and the parapet, which runs the length of the building, both front and back. Portland stone was used during subsequent renovation, principally by Sir William Chambers during the late 18th century and by Sir John Soane in the early 19th.

An internal viewing of this building is very rewarding. The brick groin-vaulted undercroft, which originally sported a grotto and fountain, was the venue for Charles I and his friends' notorious drinking parties. The vast ceiling of the main room is an absolute corker. Divided into cornices and enriched with gilded carvings, it is more in keeping with classical Italian style than the rather fussy English fashion of the time. The whole building and its decoration, all coolly Classical, contrasts however with the ceiling panels, painted by Rubens, from which tumble colour and vigour. In place by 1635, the nine paintings proclaim the blessings of the reign of James I and glorify the Stuart dynasty. The paintings were commissioned by Charles I and one wonders whether he may have glanced upwards to take a last look at them as he was led through this room on his way to be executed outside in the cold on 30 January 1649.

The Banqueting House, Whitehall, SW1; Telephone 020 7839 8918; Nearest tube Westminster LU (Jubilee, Central and District lines) and Embankment LU (Circle, District, Bakerloo and Northern lines); Open Mon-Sat 10am-5pm (liable to close a short notice for Government functions); Admission charge

The Piazza and St Paul's Church, Covent Garden

It is hard to imagine when walking through the now bustling Piazza that this land was once used for growing provisions for Westminster Abbey. When Henry VIII closed the monasteries the whole area was given to Sir John Russell, the first Earl of Bedford and it was his ancestor, the 4th Earl who decided to develop the land. Between 1629–37 what developed was London's first real square, designed by the most fashionable architect of the day, Inigo Jones. Influenced by recent Parisian and Italian building, Jones produced a large square of individual houses behind a common, continuous façade in a Classical design. The development attracted wealthy residents who enjoyed the novelty of living in the grand terraced housing. The plan was dominated by Jones's church of St Paul to the south of the square. However, fashions change and within two decades the 5th Earl wanted a larger return on the invest-ment and had a fruit and vegetable market built at the centre of the square. The smarter residents promptly decamped to newer squares in town and less desirable occupants moved in. Jones's houses had all been demolished by 1890, due to expansion of the market.

What remains is the Georgian central market place, consid-ered the best preserved in England, built for the 6th Earl in 1828 and restored and renovated after 1974 when the market moved to larger premises in south London. The three terraces of market buildings now house small shops and restaurants and there is a daily craft market at the centre.

To get a flavour of what Jones's houses were like we can look at Bedford Chambers in the locality. Built 1877–79 by the eminent architect Henry Clutton and in a slightly larger scale, they do nonetheless resemble Jones's design especially in terms of proportion.

The Church of St Paul was built at the same time as the Piazza and was the first parish church to be built since before the reign of Queen Elizabeth. Jones's challenge was to build a church appropriate for the Protestant Church of England. His plans gave concern to his patron that the building would be likened to a barn to which Jones replied 'Then you shall have the handsomest barn in England'. The main body of the church feels wide for there are no side chapels or alter screen and the fittings are simple, with a notable carved wreath by Grinling Gibbons who is buried in the church-yard. Probably the most striking feature of the church is the portico with two square piers, one at each corner of the porch-front with two Tuscan columns between. However, even though this faces the rest of Covent Garden the main entrance to the church is through the rear of the building. The courtyard is a charming, quiet space in which to relax and contemplate.

St Paul's is known as the 'actors church', appropriately so given its location so close to Drury Lane. Many notable thespians have had their funerals and memorials held here and there is an interesting array of memorial plaques inside.

Covent Garden Piazza, Covent Garden, WC2; Nearest transport Covent Garden LU (Piccadilly Line)

St Paul's, Bedford St, WC2E 9ED; Telephone 020 7836 5221; Website www.actorschurch.org; Nearest transport Covent Garden LU (Piccadilly Line); Open Mon-Fri 8.30am-5.30pm, Sun 9am-1pm (closed Sat), Sunday service 11am

Fulham Palace

The eminent architectural historian Nicholas Pevsner called this 'one of the best medieval domestic sites in London'. Set in 13 acres of beautiful grounds by the Thames this was the country residence of the Bishop of London from 704 (acquired by the Saxon Bishop Waldhere) until 1973. Archaeological evidence shows that the site has been occupied since the Neolithic period.

Fulham Palace is an interesting mix of building styles – the earliest surviving part being the great hall which dates from about 1480 with 16th century additions. The hall under-went changes in decoration as well as function, from chapel to drawing room, as each incumbent Bishop endeavoured to make his mark on the Palace. The rest of the building is mostly Tudor (note the exquisite brickwork which makes an interesting comparison with the machine made bricks of the Victorian era also present) with Georgian and 19th century extensions.

Since 1973 the Palace has been leased to the Borough of Fulham and is now a successful museum with an interesting model of the building colour coded to help visitors identify the various architectural styles present.

Fulham Palace and Museum, Bishops Avenue, SW6 6EA; Telephone 020 7736 3233; Nearest transport Putney Bridge LU (District line); Museum open Wed-Sun 2pm-5pm (March-Oct), Thurs–Sun 1pm-4pm (Nov-Feb), Grounds open daily; excellent guided tours of the Palace available second and fourth Sundays in the month at 2pm; Admission charge

Wren & The Re-building of The City

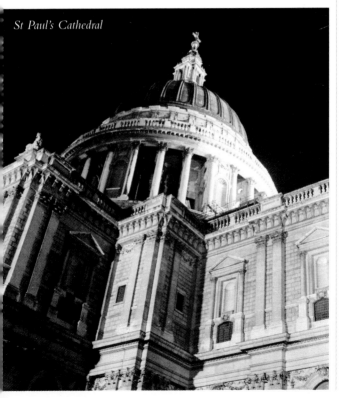

St Paul's Cathedral

At certain points in its history London has been a city of ruins and with its tindery mix of thatch and timber was accustomed to conflagration, whether by act of vandalism or by accident. The spark that ignited Thomas Farriner's bakery on 2nd of September 1666 in Pudding Lane started what history recalls as 'The Great Fire of London'. The fire raged for four days and nights and destroyed five-sixths of the City, 460 streets containing approximately 13,200 houses were lost, four of the seven City gates, 85 churches and 44 halls of livery companies were razed to the ground. The human misery caused by such catastrophe is incalculable but there were those who saw the sweeping away of the seething, stinking, plague-ridden streets with their mish-mash of buildings as an opportunity for urban renewal.

Even before the ashes of the fire had cooled plans for a more modern city were submitted to the Crown by, amongst others, Robert Hooke, John Evelyn and **Christopher Wren**. It is Wren's name that became synonymous with the re-building of the City, even though the vision he put forward was ignored.

Christopher Wren had spent the previous year, 1665, in Paris. Whether to avoid the plague that was ravaging London or to see for himself the extensive building work that was taking place under the glitteringly extravagant Louis XIV, this was the one and only time Wren ventured abroad. Imposing buildings, squares, theatres and aristocratic hotels (mansions) as well as the Chateau de Versailles and its gardens were being constructed in a style closely linked with the ideals of the Italian Renaissance. This was by virtue of the fact that architects of the calibre of Leonardo da Vinci and Cellini had been employed at the French court since the beginning of the century. Indeed during the summer of 1665 the great Italian architect Bernini was also in Paris having been summoned by Louis XIV to work on the Louvre. Bernini and Wren met only briefly but the encounter must have been an inspirational impact on the young man who was on the threshold of greatness himself.

Architecture in the 17th century was not yet a profession and Christopher Wren was not a trained architect but merely a gentleman-amateur. Educated at Westminster and Oxford, he was Professor of Astronomy and a scientist of outstanding reputation by the age of 29. His first venture into architecture arose when his aged uncle, who happened to be the Bishop of Ely, asked him to design the new chapel at Pembroke College, Cambridge which is considered to be a successful, if unimaginative, example of a classical building. His next buildings of note were both in Oxford, the Sheldonian Theatre and a new quad at Trinity College.

On his return from Paris in late 1665, Wren was appointed to restore St Paul's Cathedral, which shall henceforth be referred to as Old St Paul's to differentiate it from the post Great Fire building. Old St Paul's was one of the largest medieval cathedrals in England, 585ft long and 489ft high to the top of its spire. The main body of the cathedral was started in the 11th century and its spire renewed in 1315 after a fire. The spire was struck by lightening and rebuilt circa 1444 only to be struck again in 1561, when a decision was made not to re-build it. Without its hapless spire the building looked like a huge, squat ship, dwarfing all around it. We owe our knowledge of what Old St Paul's, and indeed the City as a whole, looked like from the drawings and engravings of Wenceslaus Hollar who worked in London in the 1650's.

Magnificent as it must have been, the old cathedral suffered neglect after the Reformation and much abuse during the Civil War when Cromwell's men, and their horses, were housed in the nave and various other parts of the building were let to traders. Stained glass windows, carved woodwork, effigies, statues and the Inigo Jones porch were wantonly destroyed and the dilapidated roof finally caved in. Wren's restoration plans were rendered unnecessary when the cathedral burnt to the ground along with most of the City.

The vision Wren and his contemporaries had for the City was for it to be re-built in a similar fashion to Paris or Rome with a regular street plan. However, the survival of London as an important commercial capital depended upon its immediate reconstruction and there was simply not the time, nor the will, to resolve the complicated land titles that each plot had accrued over the centuries. Therefore rebuilding could only be carried out on the lines of the existing streets. In October 1666 the King appointed Wren as one of three Crown Commissioners, to join with three nominees of the City to consider the methods of rebuilding and these were eventually encapsulated in a series of Acts of Parliament to safeguard against such a catastrophe ever happening again. These were:

i)   The structural standardisation of new-build houses in three specific types, all made from brick, with specified floor-heights and wall thickness'. This point in fact set a trend for house building throughout the whole country. The Commissioners had no say over the actual design of what was to be built even though the King demanded a 'much more beautiful city' to replace the old one.

ii)   The provision of a Thames-side quay and conversion of part of the River Fleet into a canal.

iii)   The authorisation for collection of a tax on coal imports into London to pay for a limited number of public works – this amount was subsequently found to be wholly inadequate and had to be trebled within a couple of years.

It took nearly three months to complete the demolition of the charred remains of the City and clear the rubble that lay everywhere. Labourers and skilled workers were brought in from all over the country to fulfil anticipated demand. Disputes between landowners and tenants had to be resolved and money had to be found to cover the cost of rebuilding. At this time there was no such thing as fire insurance – which came about as a result of the Great Fire - and little or no compensation, so only those City Companies, institutions, colleges and private individuals with enough capital invested elsewhere had the means to begin rebuilding immediately. Indeed many wealthy private individuals chose not to rebuild their London houses within the City but moved west instead.

Important buildings, such as the Royal Exchange, the Custom House (both of which perished in individual fires and were subsequently rebuilt), the College of Arms and many of the City Livery Companies' halls were under reconstruction within three or four years of the Great Fire, having been forced to carry on their business elsewhere in the meantime.

Perhaps as compensation for not being able to implement his overall plan for the City, Christopher Wren was charged with the task of personally overseeing the rebuilding of the City churches and St Paul's Cathedral. The whole project was to be financed from the aforementioned Coal Tax, which could only barely cover the actual construction and fabric of the churches; the interior fittings and decoration were to be the responsibility of the parish, although in most cases advice was sought from Wren. Of the pre-Great Fire churches 85 out of 107 had been destroyed and it was decided to only rebuild 51 of them. However many of the churchyards and burial grounds still exist and can be visited.

Wren was assisted by Robert Hooke and Edward Woodroffe - exactly how much input Wren had in each individual church is debatable, but he was in overall control. Many of the designs had to fit into awkward spaces and most of the churches are easy to pass by at ground level but they do display an astonishing variety of invention. This is particularly so with regard to the spires Wren added to each church which lent the City an elegance and an element of fantasy not seen before, and gave the country a blueprint for Protestant church building.

It was not until 1675 that Wren was able to start work on St Paul's Cathedral. His first design was rejected by the clergy who were hostile to its Classical lines. What they wanted was more or less a straight replacement of the Gothic Old St Paul's with its high nave and lower side aisles. What Wren envisaged was a high dome which would act as a focal point for the City as a whole. However Wren got his way by encouraging the clergy to agree to one design and then fundamentally altering it as the Cathedral was being built!

Wren's Monument

Examples of buildings from this period:

St Paul's Cathedral

The foundation stone for Wren's masterpiece, laid 21 June 1675, bears the inscription 'RESURGAM', Latin for 'I shall rise again', and was a relic from the Old St Paul's destroyed by the Great Fire of 1666. The new Cathedral, the fourth on the site, was completed in 1708, with the interior furnished by 1710. Christopher Wren personally oversaw the project from beginning to end – a unique feat, for nowhere else in the world has one Cathedral had just one architect and although his plans had to be approved by the Cathedral dean and chapter, what we see today is the pure product of Wren's genius. Whereas his City churches are essays in northern Protestant order, the design of St Paul's has its roots in the grand architecture of the Renaissance and the Baroque. The Cathedral bears comparison with, and indeed in some parts surpasses, Michaelangelo's St Peter's in Rome.

In order to provide a visually adequate substructure on which to place the dome Wren doubled the apparent height of the building by raising false screen walls on top of the aisle walls all round the cathedral. This also enabled him to conceal the flying buttresses that support the vault of the choir as well as giving the whole building a Classical feel. The porticoes that extend from the transepts and the much-photographed western towers were both influenced by buildings that were under recent construction in Rome, such as Rainaldi's Church of Gesu e Maria and Bernini's Santa Maria della Vittoria – so much inspiration from a city unvisited by Wren.

The familiar outline of St Paul's is due mostly to its great dome. It is almost hemispherical, and sits more sedately, more majestically than the elongated Roman type. However, this dome, that has dominated the London skyline for so long and is regarded by many to be the most beautiful in the world, is actually one of three structures. Such a large dome would have been fine viewed from the outside, but the observer inside the cathedral looking upwards would have had the feeling of staring into a vast cavernous hole and so, as with St Peter's in Rome, another smaller, saucer shaped dome was placed inside to solve the problem. Wren went further by placing a golden ball and cross, 23 feet high and weighing 7 tonnes, on top of the outer dome. In order to support its weight he introduced a third dome, or perhaps cone is a better description, made of brick and placed between the two others.

As wonderful as it is to gaze upon from the outside, a visit to the interior of St Paul's is a must. The crypt contains Wren's tomb; he was one of the first to be buried here when he died at the age of 91. Lord Nelson and the Duke of Wellington are also buried here as well as many others. There are numerous monuments and notable statues such as the one by Flaxman of Sir Joshua Reynolds. The crypt also holds the plans and models made by Wren of the Cathedral itself.

But no visit to St Paul's would be complete without a visit to the famous dome itself. A mere 259 steps takes one to the Whispering Gallery, so named because by a quirk in its construction a whisper against one wall can be heard on the opposite side. A further climb will take one to the Stone Gallery that encircles the outside of the dome and of course provides a fantastic view over London. However just 530 steps from ground level will take you to the highest point, the Golden Gallery – it is said Wren, in his mid-seventies, was hauled up here in a basket once a week to inspect the work in progress.

This iconic building celebrates its 300th birthday in 2008 and the Cathedral is in the throes of a £40 million-restoration campaign with an intensive programme of external cleaning and improved access for visitors with disabilities.

St Paul's Cathedral, Ludgate Hill, EC4; Telephone 020 7236 4128; Website www.stpauls.co.uk; Nearest transport St Paul's LU (Central line); Open Mon-Sat 8.30am-4pm (Cathedral occasionally closes at short notice for special services); Disabled access - please call 020 7246 8319 for specific information; Guide books and guided tours available from the Information Desk; Admission charge

Wren's City Churches

Before the Great Fire of 1666 the City of London had 107 parish churches, all highly individual, built in different periods and thus in various styles. Some would have enjoyed a wealthy patronage whilst others survived on a meagre budget supplied by poorer parishioners. The Great Fire destroyed 85 of the 107 and a decision was made that only 51 would be rebuilt. In addition St Andrew's Holborn, which whilst untouched by the fire and not strictly within the City was included as its crumbling fabric made it a special case. Wren was put in charge of the whole project, with Robert Hooke as one of his assistants, with the rather restrictive brief that the churches had to be rebuilt within their existing, frequently irregular and cramped plots. However notwithstanding plot limitations, Wren and Hooke designed and built an amazing variety of airy, well lit and functional buildings without a traditional Protestant church building reference to consult, they were influenced greatly by Dutch Protestant churches such as the Nieuwe Kerk in Haarlem.

Of these 51 churches only 24 complete buildings and six towers remain. These are listed below in alphabetical order rather than by merit or date.

Most of these churches are open to the public Monday to Friday, unless stated. Many have regular services of worship and lunchtime concerts – please telephone the individual church for details. All are of considerable interest but if you are only able to see one St Stephens Walbrook is highly recommended.

Christ Church, Newgate St

The first church on this site dated from the mid 13th century and was built by Franciscan friars (also known as Greyfriars). It was rebuilt in the early 14th century and was the second largest medieval church in the City, the largest being Old St Paul's. After the Dissolution of the Monasteries in 1536 the building was used as a store for wine rumoured to have been plundered from French ships. The chancel became a parish church and the King's printer set up shop in the nave. When Wren rebuilt the church after the Great Fire he made use of the medieval foundations and lower walls and the church therefore remained comparatively large. Enemy bombing during the Second World War destroyed the fabric of the main body of the church but the tower, regarded by some as the most beautiful in London, was mercifully spared. The spire, which has been likened to a square version of the one belonging to St Mary-le-Bow, was the subject of preservation work during the 1960s and a small garden has been formed where the church used to be.

Christ Church, Newgate Street, EC1; Nearest transport St Paul's LU (Central line); the tower can be viewed at any time

St Alban

As with so much of the City, the small area surrounding this tower has witnessed a great deal of history. It is believed that the first building on the site was the chapel of King Offa, dating back to the 8th century. An 11th century Saxon church certainly stood here and was enlarged over the centuries until it perished in 1666. Rather than design a completely new church, Wren appears to have been content to construct between 1682-8 a fairly faithful replica of what was lost to the Great Fire. The church was destroyed by enemy bombing in 1940, leaving Wren's beautiful Perpendicular Gothic tower standing forlorn and alone.

The tower was renovated during the 1960s and in 1984-85 it was converted into a private house and is now used as offices. Nothing remains of the churchyard used during the 18th and 19th centuries by the Barber-Surgeon's Company for burying the remains of executed criminals whose bodies had been used for dissection.

St Alban, Wood Street, EC2, Nearest transport St Paul's LU (Central line); the exterior of the tower can be viewed any time

St Andrew, Holborn

There has been a church on this site since at least 959 CE which although untouched by the Great Fire, had been pitifully neglected and Wren was charged with its rebuilding. The work started in 1684 and it took just two years to complete what was the largest of Wren's City churches. Wren kept the 15th century tower and refaced it in Portland stone. The interior is similar to St James's Piccadilly (completed 1682), also by Wren, with its barrel-vaulting, groin-vaults on Corinthian columns over the aisles and a two-storey Venetian window in the chancel. Again, enemy bombing during 1941 destroyed much of the building, the outer walls and tower surviving, but a faithful reconstruction was undertaken and the church was able to reopen in 1961.

Although the original furnishings have been lost, there is much of interest to look at inside the church. Three significant items, the organ, pulpit and font came from the Foundling Hospital. The organ is modern (1990) but sits within a case donated by the composer Handel in 1750.

On the outside wall of the west end of the church are 17th century statues of a young boy and girl from a nearby former parish school. St Andrew's now houses the Royal College of Organists.

St Andrew, Holborn Circus, EC4 3AB; Telephone 020 7353 3544; Nearest transport Chancery Lane LU (Central line) or Farringdon LU & Rail (District and Circle line); Open Mon-Fri 8am-5.30pm (Wed 8am-2pm, 6pm-9pm)

St Andrew by the Wardrobe

So named because of its proximity to the building where royal ceremonial robes and arms were stored from the mid 14th century. A church has occupied this spot since about 1170. This unadorned red brick rectangular church and plain tower was one of Wren's last City churches (1685-94) and so poor was the parish that funds derived from Coal Tax were also used to furnish the interior. 'Improvements' to Queen Victoria Street robbed St Andrew's of its churchyard and somewhat elevated the building so it is now very easy to pass by it without noticing it. Bomb damage in 1940 destroyed the original furnishings so what we see today is a collection from other Wren churches such as the font and font cover, made for St Matthew Friday Street which was demolished during the 19th century. There is a splendid stained glass window depicting the conversion of St Paul made for Bulstrode Park in Buckinghamshire in the early 18th century.

St Andrew by the Wardrobe, Queen Victoria Street, EC4A 3AB; Telephone 020 7248 7546; Nearest transport Blackfriars LU & Rail (Circle and District line); Open Mon-Fri 10am-4pm

St Anne and St Agnes

Wren designed this small church to a cross–in–square plan although it is believed Robert Hooke was heavily involved in its actual construction. A modest weatherboard pyramid with a square lantern tops the roof. The church sustained fire damage during World War II and the subsequent renovation did not include the original elaborate interior decoration, which suited the church's new role as a place of Lutheran worship. Services are now held in Amharic, English and Swahili.

St Anne & St Agnes, Gresham Street, EC2V 7BX; Telephone 020 7606 4986; Nearest transport St Paul's LU (Central line), Barbican LU and Rail (Circle and Metropolitan lines); Open Mon-Fri 9am-6pm, Sun 9am-8pm

St Benet

This delightful, small church of red and blue brick chequer-work is thought to be the design of Robert Hooke rather than Wren, though it is attributed to the latter. The exterior is heavily influenced by Dutch church building and inside there is some interesting 17th century furniture, such as a carved communion table. There has been a church on this site since at least the early 12th century and it is believed that the architect Inigo Jones was buried in the chancel on his death in 1652. However his memorial was destroyed in 1666. Much of the churchyard was lost in a road-widening scheme of 1870 and further 'improvements' left the church virtually marooned on its own small island! The nearby College of Arms uses St Benet for worship and since 1879 it has been the London Church of the Welsh Episcopalians and conducts services in Welsh.

St Benet, Paul's Wharf, Queen Victoria Street, EC4V 4ER; Telephone 020 7489 8754; Nearest transport Blackfriars LU & Rail (Circle and District lines); please telephone for opening times

St Bride

St Bride

Named for St Bridgit, the daughter of a 5th century Irish prince of Kildare, it is believed that a building of some sort has occupied this site since the Roman occupation of Britain. Many famous people are associated with this church. Wynkyn de Worde, apprentice to William Caxton who brought the first press to England in 1471, set up his printing works alongside the medieval church of St Bride's and thus inaugurated Fleet Street, 'the street of ink', as the centre for the printed word in England. Worde was buried in the churchyard in 1535.

Wren started work on replacing the medieval church in 1671 finishing seven years later. The magnificent spire was added in 1701-03. This is the tallest of all Wren's spires at 226 feet and is said to have inspired a local baker, William Rich, to create the first tiered wedding cake. The spire is telescoped in five stages, becoming slimmer as it reaches its peak, and is similar to an unexecuted design Wren made for the steeple of St Paul's Cathedral. The spire is notable not only for its height and beauty but also because it defiantly withstood enemy bombing during World War II severe enough to melt the bells within. However the extensive damage to the fabric of the church allowed the eminent archaeologist Professor Grimes to discover Roman and medieval remains that had lain hidden for hundreds of years. These remains are now on display in the Crypt along with a comprehensive and entertaining history of the church and the surrounding area.

Restoration work took place between 1955-57 and Wren's Classical barrel-vaulted ceiling, oval clerestory windows, and five-bay nave with paired Tuscan columns were faithfully rebuilt. However it was decided not to replicate the galleries that once ran along both sides of the nave. Of particular note is the trompe l'oeil painted by Glyn Jones that convinces the observer that there is a half-domed apse when there isn't!

St Bride's, Fleet Street, EC4Y 8AU; Telephone 020 7427 8754; Nearest transport St Paul's LU (Central line) Farringdon LU & Rail (Circle & Metropolitan lines); Open Mon-Fri 8am-5pm

St Clement Eastcheap

Wren built this, his plainest church, between 1683–87 to replace the 11th century church. The exterior is stuccoed brick with stone quoins and dressings. There is neither steeple nor cupola and the interior has been called too plain. However there are some interesting furnishings – namely the large pulpit and tester and a carved wooden font cover depicting a dove in a cage.

St Clement Eastcheap, Clement's Lane, EC4N 7AE; Telephone 020 7283 2711; Nearest transport Monument LU (District and Circle lines); Open Mon-Fri 7am-5pm

St Dunstan in the East

One of two churches in London named for a Saxon Archbishop of Canterbury. The original 13th century church was noted for its wealth and the prosperity of its parishioners; indeed the repairs that took place after the Great Fire were paid for by a private benefactor. Wren added the steeple in 1695-1701 in a Gothic style, no doubt to match the patched-up body of the church. Enemy bombing during World War II rendered the building a shell once again, and this is how it remains today, although a garden was planted in the ruins in the early 1970s.

St Dunstan in the East, St Dunstan's Hill, off Lower Thames Street, EC3; Nearest transport Monument LU (District and Circle lines); the tower and remaining walls can be viewed at any time

St Edmund the King and Martyr

There is very strong evidence that Wren's assistant Robert Hooke was responsible for much of the work on the body of this church. Another of Wren's assistants, Nicholas Hawksmoor, is thought to have designed the spire adorned with twelve decorative flaming urns and topped with a weathervane. These urns were inexplicably removed during late 19th century renovation by William Butterfield whose taste was for the Gothic rather than anything that even hinted at the Baroque. Funds are currently being sought to have these decorations, which were always the church's most notable feature, replaced.

There has been a place of worship on this site for almost a thousand years and it was named for the 9th century King of East Anglia, killed by Viking invaders. This same king also gave his name to the town of Bury St Edmunds in Suffolk.

St Edmund the King & Martyr, Lombard Street, EC3V 9AN; Telephone 020 7626 9701, Nearest transport Bank LU (Central, Northern lines & DLR); Open Mon-Fri 10am-4pm

St Edmund the King and Martyr

St James Garlickhithe

Perhaps one of the unluckiest buildings in London – the original Norman church was destroyed in the Great Fire, Wren's church was subject to 'Victorianisation' during the 19th century, it was bombed during World War II and then a tall crane, working on a nearby building, fell on it 1991. Happily it survived and what the visitor sees today is very much what Wren executed in 1674. Of particular note is the spire, thought to be mostly the work of Wren's assistant Nicholas Hawksmoor, and the interior woodwork.

St James Garlickhithe, Garlick Hill, EC4V 2AL; Telephone 020 7236 1719; Nearest transport Mansion House LU (Circle and District lines); Open Mon-Fri 10am-4pm

St Lawrence Jewry

Named for a 3rd century Roman who refused to denounce Christianity this church has been the Corporation of London's official place of worship since the Guildhall chapel was demolished in the early 19th century. Unusually for a City church it stands detached from any other building and the whole church is stone-faced, fitting for a building stand-ing at the head of King Street. King Street was one of only two new roads built in the City immediately after the Great Fire, the other being Queen Street, these roads were built to ease the route between the Thames and the Guildhall.

The interior of St Lawrence is an essay in white walls, gold leaf and magnificent chandeliers and when built 1670-87 was one of the most expensive of Wren's churches. Badly gutted by enemy bombing on 29th December 1940, the church was fully restored in 1957.

St Lawrence Jewry, Gresham Street, EC2V 5AA; Telephone 020 7600 9478; Nearest transport Bank LU (Central, Northern lines & DLR); Open Mon-Fri 7.30am-2pm

St Magnus the Martyr

Built 1671-76 with its 185 feet steeple added in 1703, this church was named for St Magnus the Viking Earl of Orkney who lived 1080-1116. The church stood at the approach to the Old London Bridge and a constant stream of people passed its door. Indeed so busy was the route that in 1762 the approach was widened and Wren's church was reduced by two bays at its west end, somewhat isolating the solid, square tower in the process.

The visitor will not fail to notice that, in comparison with other Wren churches, the interior is fairly sumptuous. The furnishings for Wren's City churches were the responsibility of the parish and St Magnus is fortunate in having many of its original fittings which unusually are very much in continental Baroque style. Some additions were made during the 1920's when the church was embellished further for Anglo-Catholic worship.

Some fine paintings are contained within the church – Moses and Aaron on the reredos, and a Virgin and Child in the style of Van Dyck. There is an interesting model of the Old London Bridge and on the west exterior wall is a clock dating from 1709, which was a famous London land-mark for some two hundred years until it was obscured by nearby 20th century buildings.

St Magnus the Martyr, Lower Thames Street, EC3R 6DN; Telephone 020 7626 4481; Nearest transport Monument LU (District and Circle lines); Open Tues-Fri 10am-4pm, Sun 10am-2pm

St Margaret Lothbury

The original church on this site dated from the 12th century with 15th century additions. Wren's church was built between 1683-92 with the plain square tower completed in 1700. The tower and its distinctive fine lead spire are thought to be the work of Robert Hooke.

Entrance to the building is via the stone-clad south side, through the tower, much in the style of London medieval churches. Indeed Wren may well have kept the old foundations and building pattern here. Much of the exquisite furnishing comes from now demolished London churches such as the superb carved font which was originally at St Olave Jewry.

St Margaret Lothbury, Lothbury, EC2V 8EX; Telephone 020 7606 8330; Nearest transport Bank LU (Central, Northern lines & DLR); Open Mon-Fri 8am-5pm

St Margaret Pattens

The unusual name of this church has two possible explanations – either it is named for a wealthy parishioner canon of St Paul's, Ranalf Patin or the name refers to the pattens, wooden shoe covers, which may well have been made in the vicinity.

The original 12th century church on this site apparently collapsed and was rebuilt in the 16th century. Wren's church was built between 1684-89 with the lead-covered spire, added 1698-1702, thought to be by Nicholas Hawksmoor. The exterior of the church is built mainly of Portland stone and the interior consists of a plain rectangular nave.

Many of the interior furnishings survive including now rare examples of twin canopied churchwardens' pews, an hourglass in an iron stand used for timing sermons and a punishment bench with a carved Devil's head.

St Margaret Pattens, Eastcheap, EC3M 1HS; Telephone 020 7623 6630; Nearest transport Monument LU (District and Circle lines), Open Mon-Fri 8am-4pm

St Martin within Ludgate

St Martin within Ludgate

Situated close to the west end of St Paul's Cathedral on a site near the old Lud Gate, Wren's church of 1677-86 incorporates part of the Roman city wall. The church is built on a centralised plan, a cross inside a square - the cross being defined by columns supporting the barrel vaulting. From the tower rises a lead spire, which is thought to be influenced by Dutch design.

The church of St Martin was fortunate to suffer little from 'the improvements', renovations and World War II bomb damage and is therefore a relatively good example of Wren's design. However, Robert Hooke's diary tells of at least thirty-one visits to the site at both the design and construction stages so what we could be looking at is perhaps more correctly a fine example of work by Hooke rather than one by Wren.

St Martin within Ludgate, Ludgate Hill, EC4M 7DE; Telephone 020 7248 6054; Nearest transport LU St Paul's (Central line); Open Mon-Fri 11am-3pm

St Mary Abchurch

This church was built by Wren between 1681-86 on the site of a medieval church. Is constructed of dark red brick with stone quoins. A tower on its north-west corner carries a slender lead-covered spire. The rather plain exterior is of Dutch influence and gives no hint of the sweetest of Wren's interiors.

The small interior has no aisles and is made to look spacious by the placement of a shallow dome on eight arches. This dome was splendidly painted in 1708 by William Snow and colourfully depicts a heavenly choir with sun rays and clouds. Also of major interest is the very large carved reredos known to be by Grinling Gibbons, the only such example of his work on this ambitious scale in the City.

Enemy bombing during World War II caused extensive damage to the church; the dome had to be restored which took seven years to complete and the precious reredos was found to have been blown into two thousand pieces. Miraculously this was put back together again in a programme that took five years to complete.

St Mary Abchurch, Abchurch Lane, off King William Street, EC4N 7BA, Telephone 020 7626 0306, Nearest transport Bank LU (Central, Northern lines & DLR); Open Mon-Thurs 10.30am-2.30pm, Fri 10.30-12noon

St Mary Aldermary

'Aldermary' denotes that this church of St Mary is the oldest in the City. At first sight one can hardly believe that this is a Wren church given that it is one of the finest examples of 17th century Gothic revival in the country. The main body of the church was built with money from a private benefactor under the supervision of Wren and this may go some way to explain the deviation in design from other contemporary City churches. Stone refacing during the late 19th century exaggerates this difference. A visit inside the church reveals a unique example of a Wren fan-vaulted ceiling with some late 19th century carved Gothic furnishings and panelling.

St Mary Aldermary, Bow Lane, off Queen Victoria Street, EC4N 4SJ; Telephone 020 7248 4906; Nearest transport Mansion House LU (Circle and District lines); Open Mon-Fri 11am-3pm

St Mary le Bow

If a child is born within the sound of Bow Bells, so the legend tells us, he or she can declare themselves to be a Cockney. Cynics may now comment that it would be hard to hear the bells above the roar of the passing traffic. However the 11th century medieval church previously on this site had to contend with the cacophony from a very busy market, place of pillory and execution, as well as a sometime jousting ground, outside in Cheapside.

On commencement of work on the site after the Great Fire Wren not only found he could reuse the medieval crypt but was also delighted to find part of a gravelled roadway on which to build the church tower. The steeple cost almost as much as the rest of the building and is at 224 feet, second only to St Bride's in height and was the first to be built on a post Great Fire church (1678-80). Internally the Basilica of Maxentius in Rome apparently inspired the square nave with its three wide arches on piers.

Enemy bombing in 1941 caused extensive damage to the steeple and bells, but as a testament to Wren's superb team of craftsmen, the tower remained upright. However the interior had to be radically repaired and all the furnishings were renewed during 1956-64.

St Mary le Bow, Cheapside, EC2; Telephone 020 7248 5139; Nearest transport Bank LU (Central, Northern lines & DLR) or St Paul's LU (Central line); Open Mon-Thurs 6.30am-6pm, Fri 6.30-4pm (see also in 'Eat and Drink Architecture' p.258)

St Mary at Hill

Wren was able to reuse three walls and most of the tower of the medieval church on this site first mentioned in the 12th century. However 19th century renovations, during which 3,000 bodies were exhumed from the churchyard and re-interred at Norwood Cemetery, and a serious fire in 1988 requiring extensive repairs has left the church a mixture of periods. Nevertheless Wren's Greek cross plan is still very much in evidence.

For many years this church has been associated with the fish trade which was carried out at nearby Billingsgate and the surrounding streets, and the fishmongers still hold their Harvest Festival service at St Mary's.

St Mary at Hill, Lovat Lane, between Eastcheap and Lower Thames Street, EC3R 8EE; Telephone 020 7626 4184; Nearest transport Monument LU (District and Circle lines); Open Mon-Fri 11am-4pm

St Michael Cornhill

St Michael Cornhill

As with St Mary at Hill, St Michael's contains a mix of periods. It would appear that the body of the church was rebuilt after the Great Fire at the behest of the parish rather than Wren and his Commissioners. Perhaps Wren felt that repair rather than rebuild was the order of the day. However the original medieval tower was demolished and rebuilt between 1715-22 by Wren's office in a Gothic style to a design by Nicholas Hawksmoor. George Gilbert Scott carried out renovations between 1857-60 in the High Victorian Style removing most of the original furnishings but adding a superb Gothic porch on the north side.

St Michael Cornhill, Cornhill, EC3V 9DS; Telephone 020 7248 382; Nearest transport Bank LU (Central, Northern lines & DLR); Open Mon-Fri 8.30am-5pm

St Michael Paternoster Royal

There has been a church on this site since at least 1100. The building that perished in the Great Fire had been built in 1409 by the infamous Lord Mayor of London, Sir Richard (Dick) Whittington, who lived close by. Wren built its replacement between 1685-94 as a plain rectangular church with a tower, which has arched windows and a pierced parapet. To this was added a steeple (1713-17) considered to be one of the most beautiful in the City.

This is one of the last churches to be repaired (1966-68) following severe damage sustained by bombing in World War II. However, much of the furnishings from the 17th century survived such as the carved reredos. There is also a charming stained glass window depicting Dick Whittington.

The term 'paternoster' refers to the rosary makers who worked in the locality and the 'royal' in the church's name is thought to be a corruption of 'La Reole', after the area of France that a nearby wine-importer had business dealings with.

St Michael Paternoster Royal, College Hill, Upper Thames Street, EC4R 2RL; Telephone 020 7248 5202; Nearest transport Mansion House LU (Circle and District lines); Open Mon-Fri 9am-5pm

St Nicholas Cole Abbey

Not very far away from St Paul's Cathedral and the Millennium Bridge, this church has a splendid spire surmounted by a gilded ship. 'Cole Abbey' is thought to be a corruption of the term 'cold harbour', ie a temporary shelter for travellers.

This is among Wren's plainest churches, a simple rectangle with an uncovered ceiling. St Nicholas received extensive damage in 1941 and its position amid busy roads has given it a somewhat isolated air. From 1982 the church was used by the Free Church of Scotland who have recently moved to alternative premises – ideas are currently been forwarded as to its next use.

St Nicholas Cole Abbey, Queen Victoria Street, EC4V 4BJ; Nearest transport Blackfriars LU & Rail (Circle and District lines); Currently not open to the public

St Peter upon Cornhill

Wren, assisted by Robert Hooke, built this church between 1677-84 and its crowded site, occupied by churches since at least Saxon times, gives us a glimpse of what London was like before 19th and 20th century road widening schemes left some churches marooned.

One of this church's boasts is that Felix Mendelssohn played the newly installed organ here in 1840. He obviously enjoyed the experience as he returned for an encore two years later!

St Peter upon Cornhill, Cornhill, EC3V 9DS; Telephone 020 7283 2231; Nearest transport Bank LU (Central, Northern lines & DLR); viewing by arrrangement, telephone for details and opening times

St Stephen Walbrook

St Stephen Walbrook

Located behind the Mansion House in close proximity to its neighbours it would be easy to dismiss this church with its dull exterior at street level, despite its magnificent spire. However, this is one of the most remarkable church interiors in London, if not the whole country. It is known for certain that Wren was closely involved in the design and construction of St Stephen - he was even paid a 20 guinea bonus because the finished project delighted the parishioners so! Wren probably used the building of this church as an experimental model for St Paul's Cathedral and he certainly involved the same group of craftsmen.

This is one of the largest of the City churches of this period and what greets the visitor is a light and airy interior. Sixteen carefully spaced Corinthian columns, all of equal height, give the nave an exquisite sense of division. The beautiful dome sits on eight arches supported by eight of the columns. Very little alteration took place during the 18th and 19th centuries but extensive renovation work needed to be carried out during the 1980s when the whole building was in almost in danger of collapse. This work, costing approximately £1.3 million, was done with great care and sensitivity however a controversial reordering around a new altar, an 8 foot circle of Travertine marble by Henry Moore, has its critics. Light-coloured wooden curved benches replaced the old box pews and as a whole the new arrangement emphasises Wrens centralising tendency. Nevertheless, the lovely, carved wooden reredos does give the impression of having been left stranded.

The eminent 16th century composer John Dunstable and the architect and playwright John Vanburgh (1664-1726) are buried here. It is from this church that the then rector, Chad Varah, founded The Samaritans.

St Stephen Walbrook, Walbrook, EC4N 8BN; Telephone 020 7283 4444; Nearest transport Mansion House LU (Circle & District lines); Open Mon-Thurs 10am-4pm, Fri 10am-3pm

St Vedast alias Foster

Vedast was a Frankish saint who also has a church dedicated to him in Lincolnshire.

A church was known to have been on this site in 1170 which was rebuilt in 1519 only to be destroyed by the Great Fire. A new church was initiated by the parish after 1669, using the medieval foundations and which was completed by the Rebuilding Commissioners by 1672. Wren added the steeple in 1709-12 and it is considered to be his most Baroque.

The church received extensive damage from enemy bombardment in the Second World War and the 17th century furnishings in St Vadast mainly come from other Wren churches.

St Vedast alias Foster, Foster Lane, Cheapside, EC2V 6HH; Telephone 020 7606 3998; Nearest transport St Paul's LU (Central line); Open Mon-Fri 8am-6pm

From Restoration to Georgian

"Oh bear me to paths of fair Pell Mell!
Safe are thy pavements, grateful is thy smell."
John Gay

Chiswick House

When the monarchy was restored to Britain in 1660, Charles II and his entourage brought back from their enforced exile continental ideas and tastes that were to change the face of much of London. One of the first projects the King undertook on his return was the remodelling of St James's Park and opening it to the public. The Park's main feature was a straight canal, tree lined in the French style. Pall Mall was laid out alongside the Park, this too has a continental flavour as its name refers to pell mell (pallo a maglio in Italian) a game played with a mallet and ball and popular with the Court.

The wealthy in society built their houses in the newly fashionable West End of London – St James's, Soho, Westminster, Piccadilly and Mayfair. Following Inigo Jones's example in Covent Garden of 1629 the London square became a desirable place to live as well as a golden opportunity for speculative building. Terraces of tall houses resembled one large mansion enabling those with aspirations to be vague as to how much of it they actually lived in! Squares laid out in this period were St James's (1661), Leicester (1670), Golden (1677) and Bloomsbury, which is thought to have been the first, planned in early 1661 by the Earl of Southampton.

Three sides of Bloomsbury Square contained ranges of terraced houses, built within tight specifications, whilst the fourth side was taken up with the Earl's own large abode, Southampton House. Here, as with other schemes, the aristocratic model of development went on alongside smaller-scale speculative building. Most of the Square has been subsequently rebuilt, however numbers 9-14 retain some fabric and certainly the proportions of the original houses.

Some of the building schemes executed in the 1660s, particularly those in Soho, were shoddily constructed and needed replacement when their 60-year lease expired. Subsequent redevelopment, during 1730/40s, was dominated by the fashion for the Palladian Revival style.

The renewed interest in the work of Inigo Jones (see Chapter 1.2 p.15, 36-41) was a reaction to the Baroque architecture perfected by Wren and Vanbrugh (see Greenwich Walk p.250). The architect Colen Campbell mooted a national architectural style over the 'affected and licentious' Baroque, which was considered to carry too many associations of foreign tyranny and absolutism, and a return to the 'Antique Simplicity' found in the Queen's House, Greenwich and the Banqueting House, Whitehall.

However, the return to the works of Jones and Palladio required a reinterpretation. Instead of being a vehicle for Stuart pretensions, Palladianism was viewed as a way of adapting the buildings of Roman antiquity to suit the governing classes – as the Roman patrician travelled from his country estate to the Senate, so the English gentleman travelled from his country estate to Parliament. The work of Burlington and Kent especially embraced Palladio's architectural philosophy (see p.86-88).

By 1760 Neoclassicism, had become fashionable, by-passing Palladianism to return to the pure forms of Greek and Roman architecture, as practised by Robert Wood, James Stuart and Robert Adam (see p.89).

London was by far the largest City in Europe by 1700, with a population of 600,000, but most of its citizens did not enjoy the privilege of good living conditions; the writings of Smollett and the paintings of Hogarth show a world of squalor and want. Many of those flooding into London were refugees, particularly Huguenots from France after the persecution of 1685, who settled in the East End, working mainly in the textile trade. The Government became alarmed at this influx of non-conformists with unknown political allegiances and so, in 1711, the Building of Fifty New Churches Act was passed to reassert the primacy of the Established Church to be paid for from a tax on the purchase of coal. The brief was to build the churches in stone with towers or steeples, no doubt influenced by Wren's City churches. Only twelve of the churches were built, the most notable being – St John's Smith Square (Archer, see p.259) St Mary-le-Strand (Gibbs, see p.85) and St Mary Woolnoth, (Hawksmoor, see p.80).

The 18th century growth in state and commerce generally led to buildings for specific official purposes, for example the Admiralty (see Whitehall Walk p.220) and Sir William Chambers' creation, the first purpose-built office complex in Europe at Somerset House (see p.215). Barracks, hospitals, theatres, opera houses, and coffee houses, banks and bridges were built. London became the first 'consumer society' in the world as shops sprang up all over the capital. It had been usual to convert ordinary houses but purpose-built shops with large windows were now becoming commonplace – number 34 Haymarket has probably the oldest shop front in London and numbers 165-167 Bond Street date from the 1770s.

Gentlemen's clubs were an 18th century invention, and were often named after their original owner. Two such can still be found in St James's Street, Westminster and are, more or less, in their original form. Boodles was built in 1775/76 in the Adam style but not by Adam himself. Brooke's, dating from 1776/78 is by the architect Henry Holland.

Another 18th century phenomenon was the emergence of the architect as an arbiter of taste and design, the forerunner of the modern architect. An architect could so designate himself by virtue of his academic training in the subject. His whole approach to design and construction based on theoretical knowledge rather than observation and practical experience, the tools by which a master mason or master carpenter learned his trade. That is not to say a medieval mason would have been ignorant of geometry – how else would he have been able to build the Gothic churches with their impossibly tall walls. Cooperation between master masons and other master craftsmen would have been paramount to the production of fine buildings.

The rise of the architect began back in the 17th century when the taste of the patron, in London, the royal household and particularly the Stuart dynasty, co-incided with that of Inigo Jones. Jones was well-travelled and well-versed in the work and writings of Andrea Palladio, the master of Italian Renaissance architecture. Palladio interpreted all that was elegant about Roman building and applied this vision to 16th century villa and palazzo building with notable success. Jones used Palladio's theories in his own work at the Queen's House, Banqueting House etc (see Chapter 1.2, p.36-37). He was able to do so, in part, because Palladio set his ideas to paper in his architectural treatise *I quatro libri dell'architettura*, (The Four Books of Architecture), published in 1570. Architecture was henceforth the marriage of the practical to the theoretical.

Inigo Jones paved the way for others, such as Wren, Vanbrugh and Nash who, like him, were holders of posts within the Royal Works. However, although positions within the Works were prestigious and, to a large extent, lucrative, the knowledge gained therein was not felt to have been passed on thoroughly enough. It therefore became usual from the early part of the 18th century for practising architects to take on articled clerks, who learned their profession 'on the job' and at the drawing board, attending lectures and, if funds were sufficient, travelling in Europe, principally to Northern Italy, Rome and Greece.

The Royal Academy of Arts, founded in 1768, incorporated architecture into its remit and appointed a Professor of Architecture. In 1791 a group of leading London architects set up 'The Architects' Club' with a mission to define the profession and qualifications of an architect. A few years later, in 1809, The London Architectural Society formed to provide lectures and a library. In 1810 the first tentative steps were taken to institute a Royal Academy of Architecture, but its first official meeting was not held until 1835.

Below are listed, as far as possible, in date order, the 18th century's leading architects and some of their work still to be seen in London. Many were 'amateur' architects in that they did not rely on their architecture practice to earn a living, and were wealthy gentlemen in their own right. Most had travelled abroad, some extensively on the 'Grand Tour', and this is where many found the inspiration and incentive to try their hands at architecture.

Royal Hospital Chelsea

Sir Christopher Wren (1632-1723)

See the previous chapter for St Paul's Cathedral and the City churches. A description of Wren's work in Greenwich can be found in 'Walking London's Architecture' (see p.250) and information about the Monument is contained in 'Architecture with a view' (see p.285). Other buildings by Wren are:

St James's Piccadilly

The area surrounding the church was granted to Henry Jermyn, Earl of St Albans in 1662 for residential development. In 1672 Wren was commissioned to design and build the new parish church, which was eventually consecrated by the Bishop of London on 13 July 1684. Built of red brick with Portland stone dressings St James's is a supremely elegant building; its interior is wide and spacious with galleries on three sides supported by square pillars. Handsome Corinthian columns carry the barrel vault of the nave.

The font and reredos are by Grinling Gibbons and are stunning examples of his work and make a visit to this charming church even more worthwhile. Sculpted in white marble the font depicts scenes from Genesis, whilst the reredos of carved limewood is of garlands of flowers and a pelican with her young. The Churchyard holds a lively craft market on most days.

St James's Church, 197 Piccadilly, W1J 9LL; Telephone 020 7734 4511; Nearest transport Piccadilly Circus LU (Piccadilly and Bakerloo lines); Open most days but please call beforehand to check

Royal Hospital Chelsea

Built at the behest and expense of Charles II as a home for war-wounded and elderly soldiers the Royal Hospital was inspired by the magnificent Hôtel des Invalides in Paris. Although nothing like as grand as the Paris model it is considered by its residents to be a 'homely' space in which to live. Built between 1682-91, 476 old soldiers had moved in by 1689.

Built in two coloured brick with some stone dressings, the Hospital was Wren's largest domestic commission. The buildings are arranged around three open courtyards, the longest of which fronts the road and houses both the Hall and Chapel. The Hall, contains some superb paintings, including two by the 18th century portraitist Allan Ramsay, as well as tattered banners of some long-ago military campaigns and the Chapel.

The central courtyard, the Figure Court, is enclosed by buildings on its northern, eastern and western sides, but the southern side is open with a view to the grounds and the river. The statue of Charles II dressed as a Roman Emperor, from which the Court takes its name, is the work of Grinling Gibbons. It has recently been re-gilded and is now very bright indeed.

Visitors are welcome here and permitted to visit the Hall, Chapel and courtyards. The Long Wards are not open to the public as they are still very much in use by ex-soldiers, known as Chelsea Pensioners, whose scarlet uniforms cut quite a dash in this part of town.

The Royal Hospital, Royal Hospital Road, SW3; Telephone 020 7881 5209; Nearest transport Sloane Square LU (Circle and District lines); Open daily 10am-12noon, Mon-Sat 2pm-4pm (except between Oct–March and Bank Holidays); Visitors are welcome at Sunday morning services – Holy Communion at 8.30am Matins at 11am; Conducted tours are available (with a Chelsea Pensioner guide); Please telephone for information and bookings

Royal Hospital Chelsea

Nicholas Hawksmoor (1661-1736)

Born in Nottingham he was, by the age of 18 employed in London as Sir Christopher Wren's 'domestic clerk'. He assisted Wren in making drawings for St Paul's Cathedral and many of the City churches. He also assisted Vanbrugh on his two most fabulous buildings, Castle Howard in Yorkshire and Blenheim Palace in Oxfordshire. In 1711 Hawksmoor was appointed one of two surveyors to oversee the Fifty New Churches Act, and at last recognised as a major architectural force in his own right. Part of the genius of Hawksmoor was his mastery of architectural forms from Classic through Gothic and Renaissance to Italian Baroque, but in a style that remained utterly personal, and almost impossible to categorise.

See 'Walking London's Architecture' for details of Hawksmoor's work in Greenwich (p.250).

St George-in-the-East

Built between 1714-29, with its tall west tower and octagonal lantern set slightly back into the body of the church. Four shorter towers, each containing a spiral staircase to the gallery, have lanterns that resemble pepper pots. This noble church was burned out during World War II and it remained a sad, roofless site until 1963 when the ingenious idea of building a smaller church within the old, breathed new life into the Hawksmoor shell.

St George in the East, Cannon Street Road, E1; Telephone 020 7481 1345 ; Nearest transport Shadwell LU (DLR & Metropolitan line); please telephone for opening times

St Anne, Limehouse

Started in 1714 as one of the first of the 'Fifty Churches' of
the 1711 Act, it was not completed until 1724 and then
remained unused for six years through lack of funds with
which to pay the clergy. The huge portico at the west
entrance and the tower are characteristically complex. The
tower is said to be Hawksmoor's version of a 15th century
lantern tower and is complete with a clock (said to be the
second highest placed clock in the country after the Big Ben
clock face on the Houses of Parliament). The tower and
clock were a landmark for generations of sailors, on their
way to or returning from every corner of the world, alas the
ships pass no more.

The interior is impressive with four huge, full height
columns dividing the nave and there is a superb stained glass
window at the east end by Charles Clutterbuck depicting
the Crucifixion of Christ installed during a very faithful
reconstruction of the interior by Phillip Hardwick, following a serious fire in 1850. St Anne's received further renovation and cleaning between 1983-93 by Julian Harrap.

St Anne's Limehouse, Commercial Road, E14; Telephone 020
7987 1502; Nearest transport Westferry (DLR); Open
Mon-Fri 2pm-4pm, Sat and Sun 2.30am-5.30pm; Services
on Sundays 10.30am & 6pm

St Mary Woolnoth

Aptly described as situated 'on the prow' of Lombard Street
and Bank, this church's curious name dates back to a Saxon
noble called Woolnoth, or possibly Wulfnoth, who founded
a temple on the site. Hawksmoor's church is the only one
built in the City under the 'Fifty Churches' Act of 1711.
Given a very cramped site, he created a unique exterior,
especially when one considers his other churches were built
on 'greenfield' sites. The interior feels larger than expected
and its design is based on the Egyptian Hall, as described by
the Roman writer Vitruvius.

The church has been threatened with demolition many times, especially during the 19th century when City sites were at premium and 18th century church architecture was a low priority. St Mary Woolnoth is unique in having an underground station below it, during the construction of which The City and Southern London Railway cleared the church vaults, transferring the bodies buried there to a cemetery in Ilford, and sunk lift shafts directly beneath the church.

St Mary Woolnoth, Lombard Street, EC3; Telephone 020 7626 9701; Nearest transport Bank LU (Central, Northern lines & DLR); Open Mon–Fri 9am to 4.30pm

Christ Church, Spitalfields

Another glorious example of Hawksmoor's genius and considered by many to be his best church, yet it has suffered a chequered history and was the subject of near-demolition during the 1960s. It was started in 1714, and consecrated in 1729 but became neglected over the ensuing years and had to be closed in 1957 as it was felt to be a dangerous structure. Conservationists fought and won a hard battle and money was raised for the restoration of Christ Church by selling-off St John's, Smith Square as a concert hall (see 'Eat and Drink Architecture' p.258).

This church is now used extensively during the Spitalfields Festival and for other concerts during the year. It is a truly fantastic architectural tour de force; to look at the giant columns and plaster decorated ceiling is worth the journey alone!

Christ Church, Commercial Street, E1; Telephone 020 7247 7202; Nearest transport Aldgate East LU (District and Hammersmith & City lines) or Liverpool Street LU & Rail (Central, Circle and Hammersmith & City lines); Please telephone for opening times

St George's Bloomsbury

It is easy to walk and drive past St George's rather grimy exterior without knowing that it is considered to be one of London's most authentically Classical churches. Hawksmoor has taken Pliny's description of the Mausoleum at Halicarnassus (one of the seven wonders of the ancient world) and applied it to the stepped steeple of this Christian church. The creamy interior is a perfect foil for the rich wooden fittings. Also note the altarpiece niche, an amazing work of marquetry and quite unique for a London church.

St George's, Bloomsbury Way, WC1; Telephone 020 7405 3044; Website www.stgeorgesbloomsbury.org.uk; Nearest transport Holborn LU (Central or Piccadilly lines) or Tottenham Court Road LU (Central or Northern line); Please telephone for opening times

West Towers, Westminster Abbey

This project was Hawksmoor's last and he died before it was completed. These towers show his extraordinary ability for imitation and innovation and are one of only two examples of his Gothic work in London, the other being the tower of St Michael, Cornhill. So well do they sit with the rest of the west end of the Abbey, it is hard to persuade the casual onlooker that the towers only date from the 18th century!

West Towers, Westminster Abbey, The Sanctuary, SW1; Nearest transport Westminster LU (Jubilee, District & Circle lines); Can be viewed any time

Sir John Vanbrugh (1664–1726)

Of Vanbrugh one contemporary said 'Van's genius, without thought or lecture, is hugely turn'd to architecture'. However, Vanbrugh's life was an extraordinary one even if we do not take into consideration his architectural achievements: he was also in his time a wine merchant, soldier, prisoner (in the Bastille of Paris) as well as a successful playwright (The Relapse, The Provok'd Wife respectively are just two of his plays still performed today).

It is not known when Vanbrugh decided to try his hand at architecture but by 1669 he was designing Castle Howard in North Yorkshire for the Earl of Carlisle. By 1702 he was Wren's principal colleague on the Board of His Majesty's Works and the following year was appointed to the Board of Directors of Greenwich Hospital and to the building project which would occupy much of his time and talent. Until, that is, he was given the opportunity to create his most memorable building – Blenheim Palace in Oxfordshire, a gift to the Duke of Marlborough as a mark of royal gratitude for his military achievements against the French. A master of the Baroque, his work was flamboyant, theatrical and exuberant. His massive and muscular style worked best when applied to the large-scale projects he undertook and Vanbrugh was fortunate to practice in an age when men of considerable means desired magnificent houses for themselves. Towards the end of his life Vanbrugh did, however champion architects of the Palladian movement, such as Burlington. For Vanbrugh's other work in Greenwich see 'Walking London's Architecture' (p.250).

Vanbrugh Castle

In 1718 Vanbrugh bought twelve acres of land at Maze Hill in order to build homes for himself and his family, while he was working on projects at Greenwich nearby. His own is the only building remaining and is now divided into private apartments and thus not open to the public.

Finished in 1726, this turreted, palatial building, resembling a Scottish castle or fortress still stuns and amuses the unsuspecting! It is thought to be Britain's first sham castle – a sort of Gothic pile without a trace of Gothic detailing!

Vanbrugh Castle, Westcombe Park Road, SE3; Nearest transport Maze Hill Rail; No public Access

Thomas Archer (1668-1743)

Born to a wealthy Warwickshire family and educated at Oxford, he travelled in Europe for four years. During his time in Italy he studied the
work of Bernini, and the influence is evident in Archer's designs which
are almost pure continental Baroque.

St Pauls's Deptford

Pevsner described St Paul's as 'One of the most moving 18th
century churches in London: large, sombre and virile'. Built
1713-30 as part of the 1711 'Fifty Churches Act', it is
certainly one of the foremost Baroque churches in London,
if not the country. The visitor is greeted at the west end by
a large semi-circular portico, surmounted by a tall English
steeple. The interior has notable features such as a curving
Venetian window at the apse on the east end, great solid
Corinthian columns and the original pulpit with graceful
iron stairs.

St Paul's, Diamond Way, Deptford, SE8 3DS; Telephone 020
8692 0989; Nearest transport Deptford Bridge (DLR);
Services daily, please telephone for opening times

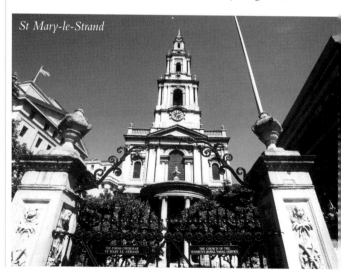

St Mary-le-Strand

James Gibbs (1682-1754)

Born into a modest Scottish Catholic family, Gibbs was unable to fund the 'Grand Tour' and as a young man stayed with relatives in Holland before enrolling at the Scots College in Rome with a view to taking Holy Orders. However, fortunately for us, the young Gibbs decided that his real calling was architecture and he became a pupil of the great Carlo Fontana. Consequently Gibbs had a thorough, professional training in Italian architecture, unlike his contemporaries who were merely observers. On his return to England in 1709, the only obstacle to a glittering career was his religion. Ironically, one of his first major commissions was to design the church of St Mary-le-Strand as one of the 'Fifty New Churches' under the Act intended to promote Protestant worship! Not adverse to self-publicity, he published two editions of his drawings and in 1732 published his *Rules for Drawing the Several Parts of Architecture*.

Gibbs' church of St Martin-in-the-Fields is described in 'Walking London's Architecture' in the Whitehall Walk (see p.220) while the Bartholomew Walk contains information on his work at St Bartholomew's Hospital (see p.194).

St Mary-le-Strand

Marooned in the middle of a busy London thoroughfare and a short walk from the delights of the Covent Garden area this small church is worth dodging the traffic to visit. The advantage of it being stranded on an island is that it can be viewed from all sides. Dating from 1714–17, this building, probably more than all his others, reflects Gibbs' training under Fontana, even though Gibbs had to make modifications to please his masters. The original design for the tower was too 'Roman' for Whigish taste and so something a little more Palladian was produced instead. The semi-circular entrance porch is exquisite as is the interior with its richly coloured stained glass windows, particularly the work in the apse by Sidney Toy (1947).

St Mary-le-Strand, Strand, WC2; Nearest transport Temple LU (District & Circle lines); Church open Mon–Fri 10.30am-3.30pm, Sun 10am-1pm with a service at 11am

William Kent (1685-1748)

Although from a very humble family, as a prodigiously talented painte
Kent enjoyed the patronage of wealthy gentlemen who financed hi
study visits to Italy over a period of ten years. In the winter of 171!
whilst in Rome he met the Earl of Burlington who became not only
his most important patron but also a lifelong collaborator and friend
On his return to England in 1719 Kent received commissions from the
great and wealthy. He was called upon to restore Ruben's painted
ceiling at the Banqueting House and in 1739 became Portrait Painte
to the King, although this post was never fulfilled.

Kent had taken an interest in architecture during his stay in Italy and
had studied the works not only of Palladio but also buildings in Rome
such as those by Guilio, Romano and Raphael. The influence of these
latter two artist/architects can be seen in Kent's preference for rusticated
wall-surfaces over the smooth exteriors assocoiated with Palladian
architecture.

Among Kent's most prestigious works outside the capital are the garden
buildings at Stowe in Buckinghamshire and Holkham Hall in Norfolk
on which he collaborated with Lord Burlington. His most enduring
London projects, The Horse Guards and The Treasury Buildings are
both described in the Whitehall Walk (see p.220). Another superb
example of Kent's London work is 44 Berkeley Square, a house built fo
a cousin of Burlington's and dating from 1744-45 (no public access to
the interior).

Lord Burlington (Richard Boyle, 3rd Earl of Burlington 1694-1753)

He inherited extensive properties in the country and London at the age of ten and this wealth enabled him to travel and patronise the talented. He championed the music of the young Handel, the paintings of Kent and supported the Italian sculptor Guelfi. He employed the talent of Colen Campbell in his quest to restore the principals of Palladian architecture to the position it enjoyed at the time of Inigo Jones, before the cultural wilderness that was the Commonwealth intervened. Campbell and Burlington collaborated on the remodelling of the latter's family home in Piccadilly, which was subject to further, more extensive, alterations during the 19th century.

However by the early 1720's Burlington was acting as his own architect, assisted by Henry Flitcroft, who was later to design the church of St Giles-in-the-Field (at St Giles High Street, WC2). Their earliest work is the Dormitory at Westminster School (gutted during World War II and much altered since with no public access).

Chiswick House

Described by Sir Kenneth Clark in his book Civilisation as a 'masterpiece of domestic architecture', Chiswick House was inspired by Palladio's famous Villa Rotonda – but it is no slavish copy. Built between 1727-29 the house was designed by Burlington to be the setting for his extensive art collection. This was housed on the first floor along with a bedchamber and dressing room for Lady Burlington. The lower floor housed Burlington's library and his private apartments. The domestic offices, kitchen etc, remained in the existing Jacobean house close by. The plan of Chiswick House is a square with an interior of octagonal halls and a slightly flattened dome, also octagonal with four small windows. The elegant exterior double staircase leads to the portico which, even with six solid Corinthium columns, appears to float. On either side of the portico are statues of Jones and Palladio by the leading 18th century sculptor Rysbrack.

The aforementioned Jacobean house was demolished in the 1780's in order to add wings to Burlington's villa, but these were taken down shortly afterwards. Chiswick House stayed mostly within the ownership of Burlington's family but by the early 1950's it needed extensive repairs.

Connoisseurs of architecture will have fun spotting Burlington's influences in the house and references to the works of classical interpreters Palladio and Scamozzi. For the rest of us it is just a joy to behold – a sparkling gem of a building set within an exquisite public park.

The gateway is of note in that it was originally designed by Inigo Jones for a house in Chelsea and erected at Chiswick in 1738.

Chiswick House, Burlington Lane, W4; Telephone 020 8995 0508; Nearest transport Chiswick (District line); Open Wed, Fri & Sun 10am-5pm, Sat & Bank Hols 10am-2pm (1st April-31st Oct); Admission charge

Chiswick House

Robert Adam (1728-92)

Born the second son of William Adam, a successful Scottish architect and entrepreneur, Robert Adam enjoyed a background of relative privilege. He moved in intellectual circles, had access to his father's excellent library and was sufficiently wealthy to be able to live like a gentleman and travel in Europe, Italy in particular. However, Adam was not a gentleman of leisure and, like his father, was thoroughly versed in the craft of building. One important result of this was his concern that every detail of a scheme, right down to the doorknobs, should be designed by him. However, this involvement in the business side of building was seen as taking part in trade and this set Adam apart from many other architects who, like Burlington, for example, were of landed gentry stock.

On his return from his extensive travels in early 1758 he decided to settle in London and was soon joined by his two brothers James and William junior. In 1761 he was given one of two new posts of Architect of the King's Works (the post until then had been 'Surveyor of the King's Works'). The other post went to Sir William Chambers who was Adam's rival rather than his colleague. Nevertheless over the next thirty years Robert Adam went on to expand the repertoire of English domestic architecture from strict Palladianism to include a much wider range of classical sources.

Adam proved his scholarship by producing three volumes entitled *Works in Architecture of Robert and James Adam*, and for almost thirty years he was one of the most sought after and busiest architects in the country. Yet there are very few purely, from the foundations to the chimney tops, Adam buildings. That said, he was a master of renovation and interior design, as three of his most important houses Syon, Osterley and Kenwood, all described below, illustrate.

Syon House

Originally the site of a 15th century abbey and of a noble house since 1547, Syon House has belonged to the Percy family, Earls and Dukes of Northumberland, since 1594 and was extensively reconstructed by the tenth Earl in the 17th century. However, the title died out with his son and was not recreated until 1750 when Sir Hugh Smithson became Earl of Northumberland. It was for him that Robert Adam refashioned the old house by creating a first floor or piano nobile level and a complete set of parade rooms, through which the guests and hosts would promenade at the frequent fashionable parties. These new rooms were created within the old structure. The outside of the house looks nothing like a conventional 18th century classical house.

Entrance to the house is through the Hall to the Ante-room, the Great Dining Room and the State Drawing Room to the Gallery. This principal route takes the visitor through a sequence of splendid chambers, each different from the last yet all related by similar uses of classical motifs. Adam uses colour in a dramatic fashion. The prevailing colours of the Hall are ivory and black (in the marble floor) but the next room, the Ante-room is an essay in sumptuous gold. All the decorations are built in, with no pictures on the walls, instead there are two plaster panels with trophies of Roman arms and another classical scene in plaster relief over the fireplace. What Adam has done here is to draw on a wide range of sources, mixing ancient Greek and Roman motifs in a frankly idiosyncratic manner and then arranged them in a richly unified scheme.

Syon House is set within 200 acres of Thames side parkland, within which is a 40 acre garden designed by Capability Brown.

Syon House, Syon Park, Brentford, TW8 8JF; Telephone 020 8560 0882; Nearest transport Gunnersbury LU (District line); House open Wed, Thurs, Sun & Bank Hols 11am-5pm (March-Oct); Grounds open daily 10.30am-5pm or dusk if earler; Admission charge

Osterley Park

Osterley Park

Osterley Park was originally built as the country seat for Thomas Gresham in 1575. The house was bought in 1761 by wealthy banker Robert Childs, who enjoyed living in the height of fashion and, like many of his contemporaries, employed Robert Adam to transform his home. As with Syon, the old-fashioned exterior of the house belies its interior with red brick wings around a courtyard, with towers at each corner topped with ogee caps. Adam added a magnificent screen of Ionic columns to form a double portico at the centre of the front elevation, the house being entered by a short flight of stairs. Inside, the decorative scheme of the Etruscan Dressing Room is particularly sumptuous, Adam drawing on ancient Herculaneum and the classicizing work of his contemporary Josiah Wedgwood for inspiration.

The house and grounds have been owned by the National Trust since 1949 and the house, considered to be the most perfectly preserved of all Adam's work, is set in extensive farm and parkland. The romantic pleasure ground has a magnificent lake complete with anglers, water fowl and a flashing kingfisher. The stable block has interesting Elizabethan brickwork and an early 18th century cupola and clock. All this is a mere 45 minute tube ride from the centre of London.

Osterley Park, Jersey Road, Isleworth, Houndslow, Middlesex, TW7 4RB; Telephone 020 8232 5050; Website www.osterleypark.org.uk; Nearest transport Osterley (Piccadilly line); The park is open daily 9am-7.30pm (or dusk if earlier); Please see website for house opening times and admission prices

Kenwood

Kenwood stands on the crest of the ridge between Hampstead and Highgate and looks towards central London. On the site of a much older house, Kenwood was rebuilt in about 1700 and between 1764-79 was remodelled by Robert Adam for its owner William Murray, 1st Earl of Mansfield. To the existing brick house Adam added the porch, library and ante chamber, embellished and decorated the remainder of the interior and encased the whole exterior in white stucco. The wings of the house are a post-Adam addition.

On the north façade of the house Adam added the huge portico, with four fluted Ionic columns and Grecian scrolled capitals supporting the massive pediment. As you pass through the portico look up to see the rather striking decoration beneath the pediment.

The Library, sometimes referred to as 'The Great Room', is regarded as one of the finest 18th century British interiors. The room is an unusual shape, a double cube with semi-circular apses and a coved ceiling inspired by ancient Roman baths.

Kenwood houses a renowned art collection, which includes works by Jan Vermeer, Frans Hals and Rembrandt as well as portraits by Gainsborough, Reynolds and Romney.

This elegant house sits in extensive grounds, landscaped by Humphry Repton circa 1793, which beautifully incorporates some fine 20th century sculpture by, among others, Reg Butler, Barbara Hepworth and Henry Moore.

The Iveagh Bequest, Kenwood, Hampstead Lane, NW3 7JR; Telephone 020 8348 1286; Nearest transport Golders Green LU (Northern and Hampstead Heath line); Open daily 10am-5pm (1st April-31st Oct), 10am-4pm (1st Nov-31st March); Admission free

Apsley House

Built 1771-78 by Robert Adam for Lord Apsley, but extensively remodelled by James Wyatt and his family from 1807 onwards. Further renovations have largely ignored its Adam origins, although a few of the rooms still conform to his ideals – if you look really hard!

Originally the house address was 'No1 London' because it was the first building past the tollgate into the capital for travellers eastward. Apsley House was once the home of Arthur Wellesley, 1st Duke of Wellington, soldier and politician, and today houses the Wellington Museum and a glittering array of artworks acquired courtesy of the Iron Duke's military successes, among them paintings by Velasquez and Correggio.

Apsley House, 149 Piccadilly, W1; Telephone 020 7499 5676; Nearest transport Hyde Park Corner LU (Piccadilly line); Open Tues-Sun & Bank Holiday Mon 11am-5pm; Admission charge

Adelphi

This building's name is derived from the Greek 'adelphoi' meaning 'brothers' and so-called in honour of the enterprise undertaken by Robert, John and William Adam on a three-acre site on the north bank of the Thames just off the Strand. Between 1768 and 1774 terraces of houses were built here using a series of arches and subterranean streets to counteract the awkward site which sloped from the Strand to the river. Only a few of the original houses remain – numbers 6-10 Adam Street WC2. The buildings are now offices and can only be viewed from the outside. Nearby are the buildings of the Royal Society of Arts, also by Adams and completed in 1774. Built from stone with a temple front of fluted Ionic columns they are worth having a look at.

Royal Society of Arts, 8 John Adam Street, WC2; Telephone 020 7930 5115; Nearest transport Charing Cross LU & Rail (Bakerloo & Northern lines); Open to the public first Sunday of the month from 10am-1pm; Admission free

Note: See also the south and east side of Fitzroy Square, designed by Robert Adam as one of his last large works but heavily renovated since. Also Frederick's Place, a small enclave of 18th century domestic architecture in the heart of the City. Began in 1775 these houses were built as small, individual units rather than a uniform terrace and many have since been 'Victorianised', although it's interesting trying to spot what remains of Adam's original vision.

John Nash (1725-1835)

Nash was the leading architect of the English Regency period pursuing a neo-classical vision with the patronage of the Prince Regent. He began his working life as a designer of country houses with the landscape gardener Humphry Repton, and by the early 19th century had become a prosperous member of the Whig party and in an ideal position to put his architectural ideas into practice in the capital. The forging of a form of classical architecture with stucco walls, huge porticos and various orders of columns and entablatures defined the Regency style. Among Nash's key works are the Regents Park Terraces, All Souls Church (1822-24) as well as the layout of Regent Street and Trafalgar Square. For more information about Nash refer to the John Nash Walks (see p.230).

Sir John Soane (1753-1837)

'The ruling passion of my life (is) to be distinguished as an architect', so said Sir John Soane, the son of a Reading bricklayer who went on to enjoy great success in his chosen career. Soane was indeed a distinguished architect and was awarded many prestigious surveyorships (Whitehall, Bank of England) and was Professor of Architecture at the Royal Academy for many years.

Soane was a pupil of George Dance junior whose most distinguished building is All Hallows, London Wall EC2. Dance was made City Surveyor on the retirement of his father, George Dance senior (who was responsible for St Boltoph, Aldgate, EC3 and the Mansion House, Mansion House Place EC4, the official residence of the Lord Mayor). It has been suggested that Dance junior and Soane introduced what the latter liked to call 'the poetry of architecture' into the rather austere classical tradition, by which he meant the role that natural light could play in a building. Soane's buildings are characterised by an innovative approach to lighting and fenestration with devices such as top lighting and coloured glass used to particular effect.

Bank of England

Soane was appointed to the Surveyorship in 1788 at the commencement of this major building project. The Bank, quite naturally, needed to be wrapped in a secure, window-less wall and thus most of the interior needed to be top-lit which is where Soane's genius lay. Alas, most of what he built has since been rebuilt in the name of progress. However, the very finest of his work at the Bank, the domed Stock Office built in 1792, is, thankfully, preserved and now accommodates the Bank of England Museum.

Bank of England Museum, Bartholomew Lane, EC2R 8AH; Telephone 020 7601 5545; Nearest transport Bank LU (Central, Northern lines & DLR); Open Mon–Fri 10am-5pm; Admission free

Dulwich Picture Gallery

Designed and built between 1811-14 this was Britain's first public art gallery and a natural vehicle for Soane's clever use of top lighting. Using brick with stone dressings, Soane managed to produce a wonderful building with a very limited budget. Thanks to a major restoration programme the galleries once again look magnificent and an exciting new bronze and glass 'Visitor Wing' by Rick Mather houses an excellent café.

The gallery contains some outstanding works of art by Poussin, Rembrandt, Murillo, Gainsborough and Watteau, amongst others.

Dulwich Picture Gallery, College Road, SE21 7AD; Telephone 020 8693 5254; Website www.dulwichpicturegallery.org; Nearest transport West Dulwich Rail; Open Tue-Fri 10am-5pm and Sat, Sun & Bank Hols 11am-5pm; Admission charge

Sir John Soane's Museum

Soane moved to this house in 1812 and in 1833 obtained an Act of Parliament that enabled him to leave it to the nation intact, as a museum for the study of 'Architecture and Allied Arts'. It is packed with the items he collected throughout his long life – architectural drawings, models, casts, pieces of sculpture, stunning items from antiquity, a collection of some of the best paintings by Hogarth – including all eight stages of The Rakes Progress, as well as some very good sculpture by, amongst others, Flaxman and Banks.

Make an appointment in advance and you will be able to peruse some of the 30,000 architectural drawings Soane collected, including some by Wren and Robert Adam.

Soane's Museum is actually three houses knocked into one and the exterior is more eclectic than its Georgian Mannerist Neo-classical neighbours. Soane added a three storey stone loggia to the façade, topped with statuary. The interior contains a series of architectural delights: the oval staircase which sweeps gracefully up to the yellow drawing room, the clever use of mirrors to create light and space in the main ground floor room, the neo-Gothic 'Monks Parlour' and the basement rooms whose arrangement is reminiscent of a Roman catacomb which has been crammed with interesting objects. On the first Tuesday evening of the month, the museum is open between 6pm-9pm, with parts of the house lit by candlelight – not to be missed!

Sir John Soane's Museum, 13 Lincoln's Inn Fields, WC2A 3BP; Telephone 020 7405 2107; Nearest transport Holborn LU (Central and Piccadilly lines); Open Tues-Sat 10am-5pm; Admission free

Sir John Soane's Museum

Sir Robert Smirke (1781-1867)

At the age of sixteen Smirke began working in the office of Sir John Soane, but left within months to work with George Dance junior. Smirke enjoyed an immensely successful career, being awarded some very plum commissions. A dedicated Greek Revivalist, it has been suggested that his work consisted of the same couple of Grecian formulae used over and over and that his reputation for reliability and as a good business manager outweighed his architectural flair.

British Museum

Arriving at the corner of Great Russell Street, particularly from Gower Street, its hard to imagine that such a narrow street could possibly accommodate a museum, let alone this monumental neo-classical building. It was built by Smirke 1823-47 as a massive extension to Montague House, the original, rather modest museum building, and was designed to a courtyard plan. Wings and floors were added piecemeal, when funds allowed. The first phase was built on the east side specifically to house George III's library acquired by the Museum in 1823. The King's Library, as the wing is known, has recently been renovated and re-opened to the public as the Enlightenment Gallery, but minus the books (which are housed in the new British Library – see p.180).

The façade, one of the most memorable and imposing in London was the last part of Smirke's project to be built in 1847, when Montague House itself was demolished to make way for the great Ionic colonnade and portico.

The architect's brother, Sidney Smirke, designed and built the domed Reading Room, finished in 1857, which filled Robert's courtyard. For a description of the 21st century alterations to this see 'Eat & Drink Architecture' (p.258).

British Museum, Great Russell Street, WC1B 3DG; Telephone 020 7636 1555; Website www.thebritishmuseum.ac.uk; Nearest transport Holborn LU (Central and Piccadilly lines) or Russell Square LU (Piccadilly line); Galleries open Sat-Wed 10am-5.30pm, Thurs & Fri 10am-8.30pm; Round Reading

Room open daily 10am-5.30pm & first Thurs in the month until 8.30pm; Great Court open Sun-Wed 9am-6pm & Thurs-Sat 9am-10pm; Admission free

See also The Custom House, Lower Thames Street, EC3. In 1825 Smirke rebuilt the centre block of the 1813/17 building by David Laing, after a partial collapse of the structure. Smirke also added a bold new colonnade to the riverside façade of King's College, Somerset House's nearest neigbour. Built 1829-31 the College was to be the Anglican equivalent of the 'Godless' University College in Gower Street!

Other 18th Century buildings of note to visit:

Dennis Severs' House

Not a museum but a living image of how life once may have been within the walls of this house. The house was the brainchild of its late owner, Dennis Severs, an American artist who 'created' a fictional Huguenot family, the Jervis's, placed them in this real 18th century house and then let them fill the space with what might have been.

Set in the heart of Spitalfields, Dennis Severs' House is also close to Hawksmoor's Christ Church (see p.81)

Dennis Severs' House, 18 Folgate Street, E1 6BX; Telephone 020 7247 4013; Nearest transport Liverpool Street LU & Rail (Circle, Metropolitan and Central lines); Telephone for recorded information on opening times and admission charges

Dr Johnson's House

The lexicographer, writer and conversationalist Samuel Johnson (1709–84) lived in this atmospheric house whilst he wrote his Dictionary of the English Language. The house, built in 1700, contains furniture and fittings dating from Dr Johnson's time here. This house is a real gem, an oasis of calm surrounded by a sea of offices.

Dr Johnson's House, 17 Gough Square, EC4A 3DE; Telephone 020 7353 3745; Nearest transport Chancery Lane LU (Central line) and Blackfriars LU & Rail (Central and District lines); Open Mon-Sat 11am-5.30pm (March -Sept), Mon-Sat 11am-5pm (Oct-April); Admission charge

Dr Johnson's House

John Wesley's House

Whilst thought to have been designed by George Dance the Younger, as part of a large complex, this attribution is uncertain. Only one house and the adjoining chapel were built in 1778/79 and this is where John Wesley (1703-91), evangelist and founder of Methodism, spent his last eleven winters – he spent his summers touring the country and preaching.

The four-storey stuccoed building with Coade stone dressings is a good example of a Georgian town house. Since 1898 the house has been a museum and a focus of many visits to London, particular by American Methodists. The interior has been, as far as possible, restored to look as it did when Wesley and his many helpers were in residence.

Perhaps the most touching feature of the house is the small room leading off Wesley's bedroom. This small room, simply furnished with a chair, kneeler and small bureau, which holds a candle and bible, is known to Methodists as the 'power house', for it is here that Wesley spent the first hours of each day in prayer.

The Chapel is a small, but good example of Georgian design, with a porch that was added later, in 1897. Wesley is buried in the chapel graveyard and there is a splendid bronze statue of him by J Adams Acton dated 1891.

John Wesley's House and Chapel, 47 City Road, EC1Y 1AU; Telephone 020 7253 2262; Nearest transport Old Street Rail & LU (Northern line) and Moorgate Rail & LU (Circle, Metropolitan, Hammersmith and City lines); Open Mon-Sat 10am–4pm, Sunday & Bank Holidays 12pm–2pm; Admission charge, concessions available, free on Sundays

Keats House

This was the home of the eminent poet John Keats (1795–1821) who was twenty three years old when he moved into the eastern half of this house (it used to be a pair of semi's). At this date Hampstead was not really part of London but a fairly secluded village surrounded by fields. Keats wrote some of his finest poetry whilst living here, including 'Ode to a Nightingale' whilst he was sitting under a plum tree in the garden. Sadly he died at the tender age of twenty-five, having written some of the most memorable poetry in the English language, whilst on a trip to Italy.

The house is decorated and furnished as it would have been when Keats was in residence.

Keats House, Keats Grove, NW3 2RR; Telephone 020 7435 2062; Nearest transport Belsize Park and Hampstead LU (Northern line) and Hampstead Heath Rail; Open Tues-Sun 12noon-4pm (5pm during summer months); Admission charge

Geffrye Museum

This excellent museum takes the form of a series of rooms each one displaying the interior of a period home, from Elizabethan times up to the present. The museum is housed in a row of beautifully built 18th century almshouses and also features a lovely garden with period garden 'rooms'.

Geffrye Museum, Kingsland Road, E2 8EA; Telephone 020 7739 9893; Website www.geffrye-museum.org.uk; Nearest transport Liverpool Street LU & Rail (Central, Circle and Metropolitan lines) or Old Street LU & Rail (Northern line); Open Tues-Sat 10am-5pm, Sun & Bank Holidays 12noon-5pm; Admission free

Geffrye Museum

Victorian London

For much of the 19th London resembled a giant construction site. Industry, imperialism, philanthropy and the coming of the railways brought massed building projects to the capital and each new institution needed to find an appropriate architectural language. The cottage hospital required a different form of expression to the railway station, music hall or the department store, and on occasion the forms they chose could be controversial. When the Houses of Parliament burned down in the 1830's it was decided by the Government that its replacement must be of a Gothic or Elizabethan design. Had the accident happened twenty or thirty years earlier we may well be the proud custodians of a Classical building. At that time Classical was associated with learning and authority, Gothic with religion, palazzo for pomp and Egyptian with the exotic. However a surge of nationalism throughout Europe in the 1820s and 1830s saw some British artists, craftsmen and architects looking back to the medieval Gothic, a style which was seen as 'English' and thus appropriate for the Houses of Parliment.

Most of the major railway termini were built between 1836-76, and within that forty years much of London was carved up as the railway companies vied with each other to acquire land. Over 7,000 people were rendered homeless when The Great Eastern Railway inched its tracks towards Liverpool Street Station. Trains provided relatively cheap travel to the new suburbs for City clerks and other white collar workers, but these were not generally the people who were rendered homeless by this 'progress'.

The first terminal to be completed to the north of London was Euston station, which took its name from 'Euston Grove', the picturesque nursery garden it was built on. Open and ready for business in 1837 the line initially only went as far as Boxmoor, just outside Hemel Hempstead. However, the following year the line was extended to Birmingham, the 112-mile journey taking just over five hours. In celebration of this feat the railway company commissioned the eminent architect Philip Hardwick (1792-1870) to design a grand entrance to the station. This he did in spectacular fashion with a huge, severe Greek Doric entrance portico 72 feet tall. Four stone pillars supported the arch, which at the time was the tallest structure in London.

Hardwick also built two hotels on the site and in 1849 his magnificent booking office was unveiled. The Great Hall, as it was aptly called, was 125 feet long, 62 feet wide and the same in height, with a deeply coffered ceiling. It had a marble floor and, at one end, a double flight of curved steps leading to the offices and boardroom of the railway company. Drawings of the Hall show a place so large and splendid that one could be forgiven for thinking it was a large church or cathedral.

In the early 1960's the Hall, Arch and other buildings nearby were felled, again in the name of 'progress', and to howls of protest, and the travelling public were given one of those bland 'you could be anywhere' stations in its stead. Mystery and urban myth surround the whereabouts of the remains of the Euston Arch to this day.

King's Cross station opened in 1852 and St Pancras station in 1862 (see p.121). They, along with Euston station, spilled commuters in their thousands on to New Road (now called Euston Road) to find their own way to office and workshop until the coming of underground trains and a bus network. It is estimated that by 1850 just over 200,000 workers went to the City every day on foot, most from major railway stations.

'Underground' line trains linking major London stations began operation with the opening of the Paddington to Farringdon branch of the Metropolitan Railway in 1863. By 1884 the route encompassed the centre of London and thus the Circle line was born. Deeper excavations were needed for lines such as The City and South London Railway which ran between Stockwell and King William Street in the City from 1890, and which forms part of today's Northern line.

Many villages and small towns around London were swelled by mass housing built for commuters, people who once would have 'lived above the shop', or at least in very unsatisfactory conditions nearby. This is especially so south of the river Thames, where places such as Clapham, Peckham, and Southfields grew rapidly. The population of Streatham, for example, in 1811 was 2,729 – by 1900 it was 70,000, due in the main to the opening of Streatham Hill station in 1856. The plain 'two-up, two-down' house with a garden proliferated in the new suburbs and are still very much in demand today. During the 19th century industrialisation and mass production touched almost every aspect of life and this is true of building too. Brick, in particular, became widely and easily available as well as cheaper. Red brick was more usual before about 1870 and after that date the yellowish-brown locally produced, stock brick made from London clay, which indeed is known as London Stock brick, became more popular.

London's population shift was particularly dramatic in the City and Westminster, 123,000 and 241,000 people respectively in 1841 declining to 27,000 and 183,000 by 1901. Those who stayed in the centre of London were generally those at either end of the economic scale. The wealthy still built mansions in town, but in far fewer numbers than the century before. The price of building land soared during the 19th century and the mansion block, with large, spacious flats complete with designated servants quarters became practical and fashionable.

The poor existed among the rookeries and slums of Seven Dials, St Giles and the edges of the Fleet Valley, in close proximity to a festering open sewer. Slum clearance became a priority when new roads needed to cut through such areas – St Giles was pulled apart 1841-47 when a thoroughfare from Oxford Circus to High Holborn became necessary.

Peabody Flats

The slum problem and continuing outbreaks of cholera led to the publication of the Report on the Sanitary Conditions of the Labouring Classes in 1842, which resulted in various philanthropic organisations taking on the practicalities highlighted by the document. Again, blocks of flats were seen as the solution and from the mid 1840's model dwelling were constructed with various degrees of success. In 1862 American philanthropist George Peabody gave £500,000 of his fortune to a Trust for the provision of 'cheap…healthful dwellings for the poor' and between 1864 and 1890, 5,000 such dwellings had been provided, designed by the architect H A Darbishire. The flats were usually in blocks of five or six floors; fairly close-set and made of striped brick. As a mark of their enduring quality, there are still currently approximately 12,000 Peabody properties on 70 estates of varying size in inner London.

Philanthropy extended to hospital provision and the improvement of existing facilities. Just one example of many at this time occurred in the 1890s when the wealthy furniture manufacturer John Blundell Maple made a vast donation to University College, Gower Street in order that a new hospital be built at, what was then, the only university outside Oxford and Cambridge to award medical degrees. Between 1896-1906 Alfred Waterhouse designed a spectacularly innovative cruci-form-shaped building in red brick and terracotta Gothic style, which was in contrast to the Classical form of the rest of the College's buildings. The hospital's offices and operating theatres were placed at the centre with wards suitably isolated in the wings of the cross pattern. The building is now used by the University's Medical School with no public admission. However it is usually part of the Open House scheme – see 'Resources' at the end of this book (p.297).

Asylums for the long-term care of people who were mentally and physically disabled or needed psychiatric care were also created, usually on sites outside of London such as Banstead in Surrey and St Albans in Hertfordshire. Orphanages were built such as the London Orphan Asylum in Clapton (1823-25), a huge Greek Doric building. Local authorities were obliged to at least attempt to provide public libraries funded by ratepayers following the Free Libraries Act of 1850. When a new municipal building was erected it was usually built in red brick. Public baths were provided to serve a dual purpose, firstly as recreational swimming pools and secondly as baths for those with little or no washing facilities at home.

Prison planning and construction was of special interest during the 19th century. Pentonville Prison, built 1840-42 by Sir Joshua Jebb, took Jeremy Bentham's Panopticon plan of 1791, which exposed the confined to 24-hour observation, and while also drawing on models of American provincial prisons and ideas of solitude and silence. The crank, a hard-labour machine, which produced nothing but 'exhaustion of the body and boredom of the mind', was invented at Pentonville. Mercifully the 'crank' is no longer in use, even if the prison is.

The Education Act of 1870 ushered in the compulsory provision of schooling for children and necessitated the building of hundreds of schools all over the capital. Church schools favoured designs in the Gothic vein; Board schools preferred red brick and gables.

London in the 19th century was the booming, industrialised, self-confident hub of an Empire. In 1851 this confidence manifested itself in the Great Exhibition held in Hyde Park, inspired and championed by the young monarch's husband, Prince Albert. The purpose of the exhibition was to put on a global display of manufactured goods and works of art in order to 'encourage competition and encouragement'. Britain was a rapidly industrialising country using raw materials from all over the world and the Exhibition functioned like a giant shop window.

The event, which was a total success with six million visitors viewing the wares of 17,000 exhibitors, was held in what became known as the 'Crystal Palace'. The structure made from glass and cast-iron and six times the size of St Paul's Cathedral was designed not by an architect but by a gardener, Joseph Paxton. He had previously designed and constructed the Palm House at Chatsworth in Yorkshire, but the Hyde Park project was on a much bigger scale – taking nine months to construct, not by conventional builders but by members of the Royal Engineers! The entire 'Crystal Palace' was dismantled and reconstructed in a park in Sydenham, south-east London but perished in a fire in 1936; only its name lingers on.

Those who witnessed the array of goods on display at the Great Exhibition wanted to be able to purchase such items for themselves. Department stores came into being such as Harvey Nichols in Knightsbridge, a purpose built shop of 1889-94. However it was more usual for a small shopkeeper to simply expand into neighbouring premises.

London in the 19th century saw massive change – the consequence of that change has been debated ever since, and the jury is still out. However, one enduring legacy of the century is some very interesting architecture. Unfortunately, one negative side to the Victorian's enthusiasm for progress and construction is that there tended to be casualties, buildings that were simply in the way. Even Wren's churches weren't safe – St Benet Fink in Threadneedle Street in the City was demolished to make way for the Royal Exchange in 1842. Many other architectural gems, such as the splendid St Stephen Walbrook, were saved by public outcry – but only by the skin of their teeth.

Examples of buildings from this period:

Palace of Westminster and Houses of Parliament

The need for a new Palace of Westminster arose from the fire of October 1834, which destroyed the totally inadequate set of buildings that housed Parliament. It was decided to build a new Houses of Parliament on the same site and what we have as a result is one of the most immediately identifiable buildings in the world.

The Palace had been the site of the principal residence of the kings of England from the 11th century until 1512 when it was destroyed by fire and the remaining buildings were used as the administrative centre for the crown. Parliament met in St Stephen's Chapel, sitting in the choir, one group facing the other, and this gave the seating configuration to the chamber of the House of Commons as we see it today.

The only buildings surviving from the 1834 fire are Westminster Hall, the crypt of St Stephen's Chapel, the cloisters and the Jewel Tower. The architect Charles Barry, who won the commission in 1835 following an open competition, cleverly incorporated all of these remains into the design of the new Palace of Westminster.

The government had specified to all those submitting designs that the new building must be in a Gothic or

Elizabethan style; only a handful of the hopeful contestants chose the latter. Debate was taking place at the time over the merits of 'Gothic' architecture, seen as English and Christian, versus 'Classic', which was seen, by some, as foreign and pagan. Charles Barry had previously celebrated the 'Classic' in his distinctly Italianate Travellers Club in Pall Mall, so he was a rather odd choice for the commission in that respect. However, Barry employed the talent of A W Pugin, a keen 'Gothicist', who at the time of his appointment at the Palace of Westminster had published his 'manifesto' wordily entitled *Contrast or a Parallel between the Noble Edifices of the Middle Ages and the Corresponding Buildings of the Present Day, showing the Present Decay of Taste*. The partnership appears to have developed well. As a middle-aged, respectable, workaholic architect, Charles Barry had to deal with the grinding tedium of endless battles with numerous committees that were involved in such a huge project. His private practice was to suffer financially as his time and energy were spent working on Westminster Palace. Indeed, he died in May 1860, at the age of sixty-five, just weeks before the building was completed.

Pugin, on the other hand, was an intelligent and exacting young man of twenty-three when he started work with Barry. Employed initially to draw the many complex plans for the building, he was an immensely gifted draughtsman. Later he was officially employed to work on the Palace interior as 'superintendent of woodcarving', but with a brief to design everything from the stained glass in the windows to the coat hooks. Pugin too died before the project of Westminster Palace was completed, aged forty, insane, and a patient at the Bethlam hospital in south London.

Two towers dominate Barry and Pugin's building. Firstly there is the Clock Tower which was completed in 1852; it is 316 feet high, 40 feet square and the top can be reached by climbing 393 steps. The clock is the largest in Britain and has worked perfectly since 1859. The great bell, known as Big Ben, strikes the quarter hour and each hour and was cast at the Whitechapel Bell Foundry in east London.

The most massive tower is the Victoria Tower at 323 feet tall and it is perhaps this, combined with the long stretch of rhythmic façade, which gives the building its familiar shape. The Gothic detailing of the exterior is so overt the building could easily be taken for a very large English cathedral! The Tower is used for storage and currently holds papers relating to the 1.5 million or so Acts of Parliament passed since 1497.

The interior contains almost 1,000 rooms, including the House of Commons, Commons Lobby, Central Lobby, Lords Lobby, House of Lords, Prince's Chamber, Royal Gallery. There are also 11 courtyards, 8 bars and 6 restaurants (none of which are open to the public). Prince Albert chaired the committee that took responsibility for the interior decorations, helping to choose suitable subjects for the many frescoes as well as the positioning of statues and other details.

Whilst it is possible to visit the interior of the Palace, the best view of all is probably from a boat on the Thames or, if that is not possible, observe the fine detailing of the south façade by standing in Victoria Tower Gardens.

Houses of Parliament, Palace of Westminster, SW1; Website www.parliament.uk/parliament/guide/palace.htm; Nearest transport Westminster LU (District and Jubilee lines); Palace open to the public at certain times, entrance by ticket – please apply to your local MP or your embassy (apply at least eight weeks ahead), alternatively visitors can queue outside the St Stephen's entrance for admission that day but admission is not guaranteed, guided tours are also available; Admission free, see website for more details

Houses of Parliament

Banco Commerciale Italiana, Gresham Street

Originally built for the Queen's Assurance Company in 1850 by Sancton Wood, a pupil of Smirke, it is now occupied by an Italian bank, somewhat appropriately given the Italianate nature of its architecture. The open arcade on the ground floor has slim Tuscan columns, a fairly recent innovation in the City at the time, but one that was to become popular, and the upper floors have close-set windows, which occupy most of the stone-faced façade. This is a fairly early example of the Italianate style being expressed in office accommodation; until this date the style had been considered acceptable for gentlemen's clubs and little else (for example – Charles Barry's Travellers Club, Pall Mall, 1832).

The top storey, with its very small windows, is a fairly recent addition replacing a pitched roof with large chimneystacks. This was 19th century office building of the grandest order on a prominent corner site and is a welcome survivor; so many of its contemporaries have been bulldozed.

Banco Commerciale Italiana, 44 Gresham Street, EC2; Nearest transport Bank LU (Central, Northern lines & DLR); No public access inside the building

113

All Saints Church, Margaret Street

This church was the pioneer building of the High Victorian phase of the Gothic Revival and is perhaps one of the finest examples of architect William Butterfield's work. Just a short step from the consumer chaos that is Oxford Circus, All Saints is the expression of the Ecclesiological Society's movement to restore Catholic privileges (before the 19th century the celebration of the Eucharist every Sunday within the Anglican tradition was not practised).

Completed in 1859, Butterfield was able to incorporate the Society's requirements for a church, a choir school and a clergy house on a plot that is a mere 100 feet square. He did this by placing the church at the rear with the school and house at the front, level with the street, and arranged around a small courtyard. The spire is 227 feet high and was influenced by the great spire of St Mary's, Lubeck; with the nave 63 feet in length and 73 feet in height. Controversially, but with great success, Butterworth chose to build in pink brick (at the time more expensive than stone) in a bold chequered pattern, the first major building on such a scale to be built from brick rather than stone.

Walking from the outside into the spectacular interior is an experience not to be missed as one is greeted with a riot of colour and patterning in granite, alabaster, marble and tiles. The Lady Chapel designed and decorated by the artist Ninian Comper in 1911, and richly decorated in a late Gothic style, is of particular note.

All Saints, Margaret Street, W1; Telephone 020 7636 1788; Nearest transport Oxford Circus LU (Victoria line, Central line and Bakerloo line); Open daily 7am-7pm

Albert Memorial

When Queen Victoria's consort died in December 1861 at the age of 42 it was mooted by the Lord Mayor of London and others that a national memorial should be erected in Prince Albert's honour. Various plans by some of the country's most eminent architects of the day were submitted and the Queen chose Sir George Gilbert Scott's design, to be funded partly by national subscription and a massive £50,000 donation from the Government.

Scott's work stands tall at 175 feet and at its centre is a larger than life bronze statue of the seated Prince holding a copy of the catalogue from the 1851 Great Exhibition; the over-seeing of this event was thought to have been his proudest achievement. There are a further 175 life-size statues arranged at different levels and these groups of marble figures represent the four continents of the world; agriculture; manufacturing; commerce; engineering; architects; poets and musicians; painters; sculptors; astronomy; geology; geometry; rhetoric; music; astrology; medicine; physiology; faith; hope; charity; temperance; justice; fortitude and prudence. In addition there is a host of bronze angels. All these figures, which are the work of leading British sculptors of the day, are housed under an iron-framed canopy raised on a flight of stone steps.

The whole project was completed in 1872 and was hailed as 'a fitting memorial to our blameless prince' as well as being dismissed as 'vulgar'! Sir George Gilbert Scott considered it to be his finest piece of work and certainly the whole memorial is a testimony to High Victorian Gothic architectural taste and values.

During World War I the original gilding from the memorial was removed lest enemy Zeppelins were attracted by its shine and was only restored during an £11 million, four-year restoration programme completed in 1998.

Albert Memorial, Kensington Gardens, SW7 (opposite the Albert Hall); Telephone 020 7495 0916 to book a guided tour; Nearest transport Knightsbridge LU (Piccadilly line)

Holborn Viaduct

Being stuck in London's traffic is nothing new and even before mass car ownership the capital's roads were often at a standstill. The Holborn Viaduct was built in 1863-69 as part of a congestion relief measure and to form a link between the West End and the City. It was designed by William Haywood, the City Surveyor and spans Farringdon Street, which runs part of the course of the Fleet river, now trickling down to the Thames in pipes under the road.

The most noticeable element of the Viaduct is the cast iron bridge, being 1400 feet in length and 80 feet wide resting on granite hexagonal piers. The marvellous open ironwork is painted red and gold and looks much better than it sounds! The parapet has four bronze statues representing 'Science' and 'Fine Art' on the north side and 'Commerce' and 'Agriculture' on the south.

The Viaduct is best viewed from Farringdon Street but there are staircases at either end of the bridge to access the upper level.

Holborn Viaduct, EC1; Nearest transport Farringdon Rail & LU (Circle, Metropolitan, Hammersmith & City lines); Access is open and free

Royal Albert Hall

Prince Albert had suggested that profits from the very successful Great Exhibition of 1851 should be used to build museums, schools and, in particular, a central hall containing a library and exhibition rooms. Following the Prince's death in 1861 and the building of the Albert Memorial, it was hoped to use some of the money raised for that project to build such a hall, but funds proved inadequate. However in 1863 the idea was conceived to finance the building by selling 999-year leases on seats in the hall and over 1,300 were sold at one hundred pounds each. This allowed the purchasers free entrance to every concert – an arrangement still in existence today but modified to allow owners access to just eighty concerts a year.

With a capacity of 8,000 people, this huge elliptical hall (not round, as most casual observers believe), was designed by Captain Francis Fowke. His design was based on the work of Gottfried Semper, a close friend of Prince Albert and architect of the renowned Dresden Opera House. The foundation stone was laid in 1867 by Queen Victoria, who unexpectedly announced that the building was to be called 'The Royal Albert Hall'; until then it was known as the 'Hall of Arts and Sciences'. The Prince of Wales officially opened the Hall four years later; his mother felt the occasion 'too emotional' to attend.

The brick domed building is decorated in marble and terracotta, the latter being in profusion in the area, such as the neighbouring blocks of flats and Alfred Waterhouse's Natural History Museum built nearby in 1873-81. Four double height entrance porches and a balcony encircle the building as does the magnificent frieze entitled 'The Triumph of Art and Letters'.

The interior of the main hall has three tiers of boxes, stalls and a huge gallery, but the acoustics were dreadful and a problem for many years. The eminent conductor Sir Thomas Beecham said that the Hall could be used for a hundred things – but music was not one of them! In the late 1960's a solution was found for the notorious echo by suspending huge fibreglass diffusers from the ceiling, which look like giant fungi but do the job!

The Hall hosts many varied events but none more famous than the annual festival of music 'The Proms', which run from June to September.

Royal Albert Hall, Kensington Gore, SW7; For concert and ticket enquiries please telephone 020 7589 3203; Nearest transport Knightsbridge LU (Piccadilly line)

Linley Sambourne House

This house gives us a marvellous opportunity to see the interior of a late Victorian house which has been preserved rather than 'recreated'. It was the home of Edward Linley Sambourne (1844-1910), chief political cartoonist at Punch magazine and is full of his work and his collection of photographs. He lived here from 1874 until his death in 1910.fimagination

The house was built 1858-60 of brick with good quality stucco enriching the exterior and is part of the grid of streets in the popular Holland Park area of London (Phillimore Gardens and Essex Villas complete this small complex). The interior is a picture of cluttered Victorian domesticity with heavy drapes, some original William Morris wallpaper still in situ and a downstairs lavatory the quality of whose workmanship needs to be seen to be believed!

Linley Sambourne House, 18 Stafford Terrace, W8 7BH; Telephone 020 7602 3316 (info and bookings); Nearest transport High Street Kensington LU (Circle and District lines); Open Saturdays & Sundays by guided tour only; Admission charge

Leighton House

From the outside, this unassuming house with its red brick façade gives nothing away about its quite extraordinary interior. Architect George Aichison (1825-1910) designed the body of the house in 1866, but the interior is a pure reflection of its owner's highly aesthetic taste. Lord Frederick Leighton was a highly successful and respected artist, the first professional painter to be knighted, one-time President of the Royal Academy and who counted Queen Victoria as one of his customers!

Lord Leighton had travelled extensively abroad since early childhood and his house was a marvellous backdrop to his extensive collection of paintings and memorabilia. At the centre of the house, both physically and spiritually is the Arab Room, believed to be based on the chamber of the

12th century Islamic Palace of La Zisa at Palermo. The walls and floors are decorated with Leighton's unique collection of Moorish tiles with additions by William de Morgan. In the middle of this room is a pool and fountain. A 'Silk Room' was added in 1895 to house part of Leighton's collection of paintings and to this was added a zenana, originally a place where women could watch proceedings but remain unseen, which overlooks the Arab Hall and adds to the sensuous air of exoticism. It is in the Arab Hall where Lord Leighton held his famous soirées at which he entertained the great and the good. However in order not to encourage the outstaying of any welcome, Leighton only had two bedrooms in this large house!

Visitors to the house can also see Lord Leighton's studio and paintings by his contemporaries such as John Millais, Edward Burne-Jones, and of course some of his own pictures.

Leighton House, 12 Holland Park Road, W14; Telephone 020 7602 3316; Nearest transport High Street Kensington LU (Circle and District lines); Open Wed-Mon 11am-5.30pm (closed most bank holidays; Admission charge

St Pancras Chambers, formally the Midland Grand Hotel

St Pancras Station and The Midland Grand Hotel

A frequent response to the question 'What is your favourite building in London?' is often 'St Pancras Station'. The station is undoubtedly a wonderful feat of engineering, however what most people think of as St Pancras Station is in fact the Midland Hotel, a completely separate building.

At the beginning of 1866 Sir George Gilbert Scott's design for a hotel to mark the extension of the Midland railway to a London terminus was chosen by the Directors, even though Scott's design was larger and more expensive than other plans submitted.

There is hardly any relationship between Scott's hotel and the Terminus, designed by W H Barlow. Barlow's plan for the south end of the train shed was adapted to include a second gable and glazed screen thus protecting the hotel from the noise and pollution of the station. Barlow's roof over the platforms is 689 feet long with an unprecedented clear roof span of 245 feet 6 inches across the station. The twenty-five ribs of channel and plate iron lattice ribs rise some 100 feet to meet in a very slightly pointed apex. The ironwork at the station was made by the Butterfly Company and was originally painted sky-blue. The terminus is listed Grade I.

Grade I listing has also been granted to Scott's hotel which was opened in 1876 to great acclaim: '...obliterating its rivals; making Euston appear the old fashioned muddle it was and King's Cross a very ordinary piece of austere engineer's building'. It is interesting to note that the contemporary view of Scott's Gothic design made the 30 odd year old Classic Euston Station 'old fashioned' – such was the rapid and violent change of taste in the 19th century.

The frontage of the hotel, 565 feet in length with a 270 feet tall clock tower and a wider 250 feet tall west tower, is a mass of balconies, windows, gables, dormers, ironwork, columns and carving. The interior is richly decorated throughout with finely carved details on capitals, turrets, stringcourses and friezes, much of which is made from honey-coloured Ancaster stone. Columns are of polished limestone, pink from Devonshire and green from Connemara, and much of the detailing of the principal window surrounds is in Red Mansfield sandstone. The wooden panelling is also finely carved. The flooring is either of geometric ceramic tiles made by Minton and Company or specially commissioned Wilton Axminster carpet.

The hotel had 250 bedrooms, a sumptuous curved dining room and a Grand Staircase, which is one of the finest examples of High Victorian decoration. Also provided was a Ladies' Smoking Room, the first in London, which must have been quite shocking when it opened! The hotel was the most opulent in London at the time of its opening and at fourteen shillings a night (which included breakfast, dinner and a personal attendant!) it was considered to be quite expensive.

However, the demand for en-suite facilities and the rising costs of employing an army of staff to run the business smoothly meant that by 1935 the hotel had to close. From that date until the 1960's the building was renamed 'St Pancras Chambers' and used as offices, amid bids for its demolition (it was at this time the building received Grade I listing status).

During the 1980's the building failed its fire certificate requirements and has been empty ever since. However during the early 1990's British Rail and English Heritage funded the £10 million structural renovations and exterior cleaning of the building so badly needed. Internally, beneath layers of 'slapped-on' office paint is the original fabulous decoration, just waiting for time and money to be lavished on them once again. We are all waiting and watching with interest.

St Pancras Station and St Pancras Chambers, Euston Road, NW1; Telephone 0207 304 3921 (for tours information only); Nearest transport King's Cross & St Pancras Rail & LU (Victoria, Northern, Circle, Metropolitan lines); Public access to the building is possible 10am-5pm on most weekdays – this is limited to the ground floor rooms only, guided tours of a larger proportion of the building are available Saturdays and Sundays 11am-1.30pm (please call to confirm first); Please telephone for admission costs and details of wheelchair access

London Oratory Church of the Immaculate Heart of Mary

Pevsner called this church 'the most thoroughgoing 19th century import of the Italianate style' and indeed one could be forgiven for the feeling of having been transported to Rome when visiting the Oratory.

Completed in 1884, the church was a celebration of the English Catholic revival of the latter-half of the 19th century and was the first Catholic church of substance built in London since the reformation. It was designed by the young Herbert Gribble, himself a Catholic convert, who was a mere 29 years old when he was given this huge commission. However it was not until 1896 that the west front and dome, which give the church its familiar face of today, were added.

The interior has a broad nave some 50 feet in width giving an impression of spaciousness. Instead of aisles Gribble built side chapels. The whole building is light and richly decorated with some striking altarpieces and statues.

In the nave there are huge marble statues of the Apostles carved by Giuseppe Mazzuoli between 1679-1695 for Siena Cathedral. Also of particular note is Rex Whistler's altarpiece of the English Martyrs in the Chapel of St Wilfred. Completed in 1938, this triptych shows St Thomas More and St John Fisher (both of whom had been canonised in 1935) on the side panels with a depiction of executions at Tyburn at the centre. A fine First World War memorial by L Berra is grouped with an Italian marble pieta.

It is rumoured that during the Cold War era the London Oratory was used by the KGB as a dead letter box – one can only congratulate them on their excellent choice of building!

London Oratory, Thurloe Place, Brompton Road, SW7; Telephone 020 7808 0900; Nearest transport South Kensington LU (Central, District and Piccadilly lines); Open Mon-Sat 6.30am-8pm; Admission free

Edwardian London &
The Rise Of Modernism

Senate House

The Edwardian period was short, Edward VII was monarch for a mere nine years, from 1901-10, and yet the very term 'Edwardian' conjures a powerful image of ladies in large hats, boating parties, amusing automobiles and ponies in paddocks. False though this image may have been for the majority, the economic climate around 1900 meant that architects such as the eminent Edwin Lutyens were commissioned by clients whose new-found wealth from retail, coal and textiles afforded them picturesque houses and a small stake in the land. What they really wanted, but couldn't quite afford, was a country house and pedigreed estate, so their desires were satisfied with oversized stairwells and room layouts which gave odd vistas but still felt informal. The exteriors tended to be vaguely Tudor with hipped gables and tall chimneys.

Referred to as the 'Domestic Revival' movement, Lutyens translated some of this emotion to his London buildings and the office blocks he designed were treated to his genius for composition and balance (see Ex-Country Life Offices p.134). However, Lutyens soon became unfashionable, being seen as a self-flaunting Victorian who failed, or refused, to 'move with the times'.

The Edwardian period may well have been a short one but in reality it saw the introduction of a plethora of styles and movements; Post-impressionism, Fauvism, Expressionism, Cubism. These new conceptual themes and philosophies in building were more popular on the Continent at the beginning of the century and it would take time and the catastrophe of a war to bring such radical ideas to Britain to any serious degree. Even then they usually remained as ideas rather than anything material.

Art nouveau, which had been expressed as far back as the mid 19th century in decorative forms such as the ornamentation on the capitals of Blackfriars Railway Bridge and Holborn Viaduct, was still popular. So too was the Arts and Crafts Movement although there are now few examples of its architecture in London (see entries for Euston Fire Station and Cheyne Walk houses p.131 and p.133).

Familiar Gothic Revival forms were still used for church building while large scale public buildings were more often than not of a 'Wrenaissance' form, that is a sort of grandiose baroque in the mode of Wren and Vanbrugh. The French form of classical baroque, as taught by the influential Ecole des Beaux Arts in Paris was also deemed a suitable form for large scale buildings such as banks. The distinctive Venetian form of baroque was used for the ground breaking Methodist Central Hall which at once marked its independence from forms of Anglican church building (see p.138).

Advances in technology at the dawning of the 20th century affected architecture. The advent of electric lighting, first installed in the City at the now demolished Lloyds Bank in Lombard Street in 1887, meant that by the turn of the century the provision of natural light within buildings became less of an issue. The first passenger lifts were introduced in 1890 and this together with the introduction of concrete and steel framed buildings ten years later, meant that larger, taller buildings were possible.

This was good news for the City in particular where numbers pouring in each day increased dramatically in the first quarter of the century; 364,000 people in 1911 compared to 437,000 in 1921. The City prospered year on year, it was after all the financial capital of the Empire and even when industry and manufacturing no longer boomed as they had done in the previous century, the City was still 'doing nicely'. Even the dark days of the 1914-18 war were fully recovered from by the early 1920s. However, the Great Depression of the early 1930's shook the very foundation of the City.

Westminster was very much aware of its place as the capital of the Empire. Street widening schemes took place as much for aesthetic reasons as for the accommodation of the motor car. Gentlemen's clubs were built and thrived. Shopping occupied happy hours for those who could afford it, and it appeared that more and more could do so. When Nash built his Via Triumphalis, he made provision in Regent Street for small shops who gave customers a personal service or who sent staff out to their houses, and where haute couture was usual. By the beginning of the century these arrangements were seen to be wholly inadequate by shopkeepers who complained about the lack of space for the stock to satisfy this new army of shoppers.

Mr Gordon Selfridge opened his department store in Oxford Street on 15 March 1909, bringing to London his brand of Chicago consumerism and in Knightsbridge Harrods was expanding at a pace that required new premises to be built and in 1905 the first part of its terracotta emporium was opened (see Shopping and Architecture p270).

Hotels and restaurants also saw business booming. The Ritz Hotel, built on Piccadilly was of a pioneering design (see Eat and Drink

Selfridges

Architecture p.258) whilst, at the other end of the scale, the now defunct Lyons tea-rooms were also doing well and in 1909 the first Lyons Corner House was opened in purpose built premises in Coventry Street. The novelty of 'brand' architecture, good, value for money fare and waitresses nicknamed 'nippies', because of their speed of service, served a truly classless clientele. Indignation ensued recently among acquaintances of mine of a certain age when the Lyons chain was favourably compared to the McDonalds Restaurant chain; it was rather like having one's favourite aunt compared with a harlot.

Cinema and theatre audiences grew steadily. This was the era of Frank Matcham who built the magnificent Coliseum in 1902-04 (see p.134) the Hackney Empire in 1901, both the subject of recent major renovations, and the London Palladium, in 1910.

Certainly much of the impetus for the Edwardian love of outings to shops or cinemas was the ease of transport within the capital. In 1900 the opening of the Central line took passengers from Bond Street to the Bank of England in what seemed like no time at all.

However, this cosy vision, false or not, of Edwardian life as expressed in its architecture was to come to an end with what was then called the Great War, the European conflict of 1914-18. The mood of those involved in the world of the arts throughout Europe had been changing, perhaps from the end of the 19th century and certainly from the beginning of the 20th. This change was characterised by a consistent rejection of tradition and a self-conscious effort to explore other possibilities of living. The fact that such philosophies were being considered by a wide swathe of the arts, painting, literature and music as well as architecture, in a Europe-wide forum, is significant. Seen by some as the response to the carnage of World War I and the subsequent rise of social equality, it may simply have been the response to photography. To have access to images which previously could only have been seen by the very few privileged enough to travel must have had an impact on many levels.

The term 'Modernism' has been given to this shift in thinking and was particularly important in the field of architecture and is most properly identified with the Modern Movement. This was the 20th century European movement which sought an architecture appropriate to modern society and which used all the technical advances at its disposal, such as the reinforced concrete frame. The Modern Movement also sought to sever ties with the past, particularly with the 19th century.

The first wave of the Modern Movement in architecture was by 1917 already being defined by a small group of Dutch artists, designers and architects, named after their influential magazine, De Stijl. This movement was dedicated to clean, uncomplicated abstract purism and a fondness for straight lines. The early Modern Movement can also be closely identified with the setting up of the Bauhaus school in Germany in 1919. This groundbreaking unit thrived until repressed by the Nazis in 1933. The first Bauhaus director was Walter Gropius (1883-1969) who taught the ideal of the committed craftsman knowing his place in the arts. However it was the ideal of functionality in architecture that was the main Bauhaus message whereby practical considerations and not aesthetics determined the form of a building. At its heart was the desire to improve the material conditions of modern society through good, honest design.

Any idea of a supposed resonance with the Arts and Crafts and William Morris can be scotched by the fact that the Modern Movement did not look back to a golden age of medieval craftsmen for its inspiration but instead explored all the possibilities available through modern technology. The breaking- down of social and cultural barri-ers were also of concern to Modernist architects.

However, those who commissioned building works in London, and Britain as a whole, had been traditionally suspicious of anything foreign, including architecture, unless it has a Roman or Greek pedi-gree! Nonetheless émigré architects such as Erno Goldfinger succeeded in bringing the Modern Movement to London during the 1930s (see Willow Road p.152).

Britain never did develop its own Bauhaus equivalent, adapting instead an Arts and Crafts aesthetic. Mock Tudor, 'Tudorbethan' and Jacobean-style was the order of the day, particularly in domestic build-ing from the 1920s onwards. Buildings were, typically, half-timbered with a mix of bricks and pebble dash and featured wooden framed windows with iron casements and a generous dose of stained glass, with, perhaps an elaborate chimneystack or a slate hung roof.

Despite the economic depression of the 1930s house building continued apace. Speculative builders lined the roads heading out of town with ribbon developments and filled the suburbs with houses, usually in semi-detached pairs and these more often than not were owner-occupied rather than rented. In 1919 there were approximately eight million homes in Britain but by 1939 there were twelve million. Many of these houses were built in the London area.

Generally smaller than the houses of the previous generation these 1930s houses are often mocked and derided. The perceived bastardisation of designs such as the aforementioned Arts and Crafts resulted in the 'Moderne' (sometimes referred to as 'sun trap'), the less-decorated style of the 1930s semi with large bay windows and generous use of chrome. However, given the level of privacy these houses afforded combined with the luxury of indoor plumbing, they must have seemed like a glimpse of heaven itself to their owners.

Art deco was universally admired throughout Europe from the time of World War I, reaching its peak in the 1920s and 1930s. The style was even admired in London and art deco here found its expression in cinema design, office building and high end bars and restaurants. Some of its finest examples are to be found in the old newspaper offices in Fleet Street (see Walking London's Architecture p.204).

There is even more of a hint of art deco in the work of the architect Charles Holden, whose work in London is much admired, even though his name may not be instantly recognisable. He was commissioned by Frank Pick, the head of London Transport during its glory years of the 1920s and 30s, to design more than fifty London Underground stations. Holden was also the architect of the London Transport Headquarters (see p.141) as well as other major projects (Arnos Grove Station, Senate House and Zimbabwe House, see p.146, 150 and 137). His work had a distinct clear and uncluttered geometry giving London the optimistic architecture that it so deserved, having survived the bitter economic Depression of the 1930s.

Then came World War II and from the 7th September 1940 the enemy Blitzkrieg relentlessly pounded London killing 15,000 people and destroying thousands of buildings. When the war ended and the damage was surveyed what, everyone asked, would lift London's spirits now?

Examples of buildings from this period:

Euston Fire Station, Euston Road

W E Riley & LCC Architects Department   1901-02

A lovely example of an Arts and Crafts influenced building in the style adopted by London County Council. There are two similar such buildings in Hampstead but this one must surely be one of the most overlooked gems in this area. Situated to the east of the Euston Station complex, the top floor of the building was designed as the residence for the Chief Fire Officer of the station.

This remarkable fire station is built from red brick and Portland stone. Note the tall, plain chimneypieces and the exquisite lettering over the doors facing the Euston Road.

Euston Fire Station, Euston Road, NW1; No public access to the interior

Euston Fire Station

Westminster Cathedral

John Francis Bentley   1903

Westminster Cathedral or, more correctly, the Metropolitan Cathedral of the Most Precious Blood, is the principal Roman Catholic church in England. Cardinal Vaughan had been the instigator of the building of a cathedral here and wanted something built as quickly as possible but a shortage of funds was always going to hamper any project that was too ambitious. Nonetheless, John Francis Bentley, a Roman Catholic convert, was appointed architect and his inclination was to design something Gothic in nature. This was thwarted by Cardinal Vaughan who felt an early Christian basilica would compete less with nearby Westminster Abbey.

Bentley was dispatched abroad to do his own 'grand tour' of Italy, travelling to Rome and other principal cities but it was a visit to St Vitale in Ravenna that 'really told me all I wanted'. On his return work started almost immediately and by the time Bentley died in 1902, he had witnessed the completion of his cathedral, apart from the tower. Ironically, the first service in the cathedral in 1903 was the funeral of Cardinal Vaughan.

The cathedral nave is made up of three great domed bays each 60 feet in width, with chapels set to either side. At the east end a fourth domed bay serves as the Sanctuary and has the Lady Chapel and Chapel of the Blessed Sacrament off. The cathedral's exterior form is dominated by a spectacular campanile 284 feet high and the whole building is strikingly faced in red brick with bands of Portland stone.

Much of the interior is derived from Italian sources, such as the pulpit which is in an appropriately early Christian style by Leonori dating from 1899. A great deal of the decoration is unfinished simply through the lack of funds, but the whole is perhaps the more endearing for this.

Eric Gill's unforgettable reliefs of the Fourteen Stations of the Cross which decorate the piers of the nave are worth a visit alone. Look out for the inscription at the foot of the Sanctuary steps marking the Mass celebrated here by Pope John Paul II during his visit to London in 1982. This was the first Mass to be celebrated in England by a reigning pope.

Set amongst the frankly bleak offices and shops of Victoria this is one of the more surprising and memorable buildings in London.

Westminster Cathedral, Ashley Place, Victoria Street, SW1; Telephone 020 7798 9055; Website www.westminstercathedral.org.uk; Nearest transport St James's Park LU (District & Circle lines) or Victoria Rail & LU (Victoria, District & Circle lines); Open Mon-Fri 7am-7pm and Sat & Sun 8am-7pm (Cathedral closes at 5.30pm on public holidays); Telephone for details of wheelchair access

38 and 39 Cheyne Walk

C R Ashbee   1904

These properties are important examples of the work of the influential Charles Robert Ashbee (1863-1942), Arts and Crafts architect and designer par excellence. Although he was heavily influenced by William Morris and John Ruskin as well as the principles of Socialism, Ashbee's house building was confined to the upper end of the artisan class. These houses are the only two remaining from a group of eight, one having been demolished as late as 1968 to make way for some frankly boring flats.

The detailing on these houses, the ironwork railings for example, was the product of Ashbee's influential School and Guild of Handicraft, a cooperative group of craftsmen.

38 and 39 Cheyne Walk, SW3; Nearest transport Sloane Square LU (Circle and District lines); Private dwellings – no public access

Ex Country Life Offices

Sir Edwin Lutyens   1904

Lutyens built these offices as a new head office for his friend and client Edward Hudson who had founded the magazine 'Country Life' in 1897. This was his first commission in London but was followed by many more.

Wren's work at Hampton Court Palace is clearly echoed here in the flat front, sash windows and carved stone decoration. The quirky window placed within the entrance pediment is a nice touch. The chimneystacks have looked a little insignificant since windows were added to the attic level in the mid 1950s.

Country Life Offices, 2-10 Tavistock Street, WC2; Nearest transport Covent Garden LU (Piccadilly line); Private offices – no public access

Coliseum Theatre

Frank Matcham   1904

The home of the English National Opera since 1968, when the company was known as the Sadler's Wells Opera Company.

Designed by Frank Matcham for the impresario Oswald Stoll as a variety house the talents of Ellen Terry, Sarah Bernhardt and Diaghilev's Ballet Company have graced its proscenium stage – a revolving stage at that, the first in England. At its opening this theatre had the largest audience capacity (2,358) in London and was pure Edwardian – some at the time said elephantine – baroque. The exterior has a terracotta façade with a domed short column on top, supporting a huge globe that once revolved until Westminster City Council made it stop, for reasons that would baffle us ordinary mortals.

The interior had always been a little awkward and the facilities for staff and patrons had become outdated by the time a four-year programme of improvements was begun in 2000. A certain amount of restoration to Matcham's original design, which had been re-built over the years, was also included.

The £30 million project was completed almost on time and has been praised by critics and audiences alike. The glass barrel roof to the St Martin's Lane façade has been reinstated and the improvements to the public facilities, including better front of house and foyer arrangements are a joy. All patrons now enter from St Martin's Lane, but before this arrangement those in the 'gods' had to negotiate the daunting flight of stairs from the door in the adjacent alleyway.

New bars and catering facilities help smooth things along and superb views are afforded from the glass-barrelled roof looking towards Trafalgar Square.

Interestingly, another of Frank Matcham's London gems, the Hackney Empire, has also benefited from a massive and recently completed programme of improvements.

The London Coliseum, St Martin's Lane, WC2N; Telephone 020 7836 0111; Nearest transport Charing Cross Rail & LU (Northern and Bakerloo lines); Open Box Office in foyer Mon-Sat 10am-curtain-up (about 7.30pm); Tours of the building available - please telephone the Box Office 020 78632 8300 and for information on wheelchair access

Central Criminal Court (Old Bailey)

E W Mountford   1907

Designed by E W Mountford (1855-1908) and completed in 1907, the building's most dominant feature is its dome, which was inspired by the one at the Royal Naval Hospital Greenwich and which also echoes the huge dome of nearby St Paul's Cathedral. Considered to be the finest example of Neo-English baroque inspired by Wren, Vanbrugh and French classicism it was built on a solid base of Cornish granite with Portland stone facing on the upper part of the building, the material favoured by this movement. The original building contained four courts and ninety holding cells but this has been extended to nineteen court rooms over the years. The richly decorated marble Grand Hall and Lower Hall have lunettes painted by Gerald Moira with scenes from the Old Testament and English history. The building's most famous feature is the 12 foot high statue of Justice cast in bronze and covered with gold leaf which stands on top of the dome. In her right hand she bears the sword of retribution and in her left hand she holds the scales of justice. Interestingly this Justice is not blindfolded but all-seeing.

Built on the site of the notorious Newgate Prison and place of public execution since at least the second half of the twelfth century the Court has tried many famous cases – including William Penn, Daniel Defoe, Oscar Wilde, William 'Lord Haw Haw' Joyce, Dr Crippen, and the Kray brothers.

Central Criminal Court, Old Bailey, EC4M; Telephone 020 7248 3277; Nearest transport St Paul's LU (Central line); Open Mon-Fri 10am-1pm & 2pm-5pm; Admission free; Please telephone for details of wheelchair access

Zimbabwe House

Charles Holden   1907-08

These offices were originally built for the British Medical Association and sold to the Southern Rhodesian High Commission in 1930.

Pevsner described this building, an early work by the architect who went on to design Senate House and underground stations for London Transport, as 'virile'. Indeed Holden has here succeeded in making the classic form solid without being overly clumsy and used a variety of classic devices, such as blank arches and columns, to great effect.

However the building is probably more noted for being the sculptor Jacob Epstein's first large commission. The figures that he carved into the Portland stone were highly controversial in that their 'manhoods' were deemed to be excessively large. Such was the offence caused the neighbouring property was obliged to use frosted glass in windows that overlooked Holden's building. It is thought that these figures were mutilated in the 1930s, but frost damage is more likely to have caused the said appendages and heads of the figures to drop off.

Zimbabwe House, 429 Strand, WC2; Nearest transport Charing Cross Rail & LU (Northern and Bakerloo lines); No public access

Edward VII Galleries – British Museum

Sir John Burnet   1904-11

We have considered the familiar front façade of the British Museum in a previous chapter, this is the 'back entrance' in Montague Place. A neoclassical approach to this building was made by Burnet using a giant order of three-quarter engaged Ionic columns. This is of course a nod to Smirke's colonnade and yet its composition as a whole owes much to Burnet's education at the Ecole des Beaux-Arts, and gives the composition an edgy flourish. It's worth having a wander through the museum and out of the rear exit to have a look.

This extension to the museum was part of the plan to clear Bloomsbury of many of its residential properties to create an area that would be associated with scholarship. Within a few years Charles Holden was to build Senate House for the University of London opposite Burnet's work.

Edward VII Galleries, British Museum, Great Russell Street, WC1B; Telephone 020 7636 1555; Nearest transport Holborn LU (Central and Piccadilly lines), Russell Square LU (Piccadilly line); Galleries open Sat-Wed 10am-5.30pm, Thurs & Fri 10am-8.30pm; Round Reading Room open daily 10am-5.30pm and first Thurs in the month until 8.30pm; Great Court open Sun-Wed 9am-6pm and Thurs-Sat 9am-10pm

Methodist Central Hall

Lanchester and Rickards   1905-11

This is one of those buildings that from its exterior is hard to imagine exactly what it is used for as it gives no visual clues as to its purpose. It seems too isolated to be a bank and it certainly doesn't look like a church; the eminent architec-tural historian Nikolaus Pevsner said it could easily be mistaken for a very substantial casino! It is in fact a Methodist hall, like many in Britain's major cities, only on a much grander scale.

It was built on the site of the Royal Aquarium, which had been built as recently as 1876 as a place of entertainment for the London's intelligentsia who stayed away in their droves. Sights had to be lowered to attract a different, hopefully paying, clientele but the tone plummeted so much that the Aquarium was obliged to close and sell-up in 1903. The building was demolished to make way for the Methodist Hall.

Funds to build the Hall were raised by a 'one million guineas from one million Methodists' campaign and building begun in 1905 to a design by Henry Lanchester and Edwin Rickards. They chose the baroque style as a suitable foil to the nearby Gothic Westminster Abbey and Houses of Parliament. However it was not the 'Wrenaissance' baroque influenced by the works of Wren and Vanbrugh being practised elsewhere in London, but an even more flamboyant style from Austria.

The building is framed in concrete and steel with brick arches and the huge main meeting hall is almost square, as is the impressive dome that tops the construction. The interior has a sumptuous staircase, which sweeps visitors up to a spacious landing with smaller meeting rooms off.

There is very impressive sculpture on the exterior by Henry Poole, who collaborated with Lanchester and Rickards on other projects. One contemporary described the architects' work as 'combining opulence and taste with a touch of refined swagger'. No wonder guessing the buildings identity was so hard!

Also see 'Eat and Drink Architecture' p.258.

Methodist Central Hall, Storey's Gate, SW1H; Telephone 020 7222 8010; Website www.chw.com; Nearest transport St James's Park LU (District and Circle lines); Tours of the building are available by booking in advance; Wheelchair access – please telephone for information

Port of London Authority

Sir Edwin Cooper   1912

This is one of those rather imposing buildings on a corner plot that the Edwardian builders seemed to love so much. The columns and indeed the whole building is rather chunky and busy, considering that the obvious influence of the Beaux-Arts is usually expressed in a lighter tone. Six huge Corinthian columns stretch from ground level to the entablature that runs around the whole building. Of interest is the proliferation of sculpture on the exterior from Father Thames lording it in the stepped tower to sea horses and galleons further down. These were designed by Albert Hodge and worked by C Doman.

The Port of London Authority came into being in 1909 by Act of Parliament to control bad practices in the London docks and to oversee physical improvements on the river. By 1971 there were no docks left in London to speak of and the Authority moved to a small office in St Katharine Dock.

The building is now the London office of Willis-Faber. Architecture fans may recall that in 1967 Willis-Faber commissioned Norman Foster to build an office complex in Ipswich, a town not renowned for its innovative architecture. However, thanks to Foster's huge glass fronted reflective block, which is listed, it now enjoys international acclaim.

Port of London Authority, 10 Trinity Square, EC3; Nearest transport Tower Hill LU (District & Circle lines and DLR); No public access to interior

Britannic House

Sir Edwin Lutyens   1921-25

This is one of Lutyens' largest London buildings at seven storeys tall with a lovely curved frontage to Finsbury Circus. A rusticated ground floor and small, very deep set windows give the building a solid appearance with the top three floors flanked by giant Corinthian columns and rounded windows, echoing the ground floor fenestration. This building was made, with almost no expense spared for the British-Persian Oil Company, which later became BP.

Rebuilding of the interior took place in 1987-89 by Inskip and Jenkins but tactfully retained the original marble floors and staircase.

Britannic House, corner of Moorgate and Finsbury Circus, EC2; Nearest transport Moorgate Rail & LU (Circle, Bakerloo, Hammersmith & City and Northern lines); No public access

London Transport Headquarters

Charles Holden   1927-29

For this building, described by one admirer as 'a sophisticated essay in massing', Holden used a clever cruciform grouping to gain optimum natural light. To appreciate this building one must think back to what sort of impact it made at the time of its construction, when its 'step back' form was seen as pure New York.

The HQ was built at a time when small, privately owned transport companies were being consolidated into a London Passenger National Transport Board and it is possible to read the confident, American style architecture of 55 Broadway as propaganda, persuading often reluctant transport companies of the merits of consolidation.

The building boasts fabulous carved statues by Eric Gill, depicting the South Wind (to be found on the north block east side of the building) and the shockingly explicit male and female figures denoting 'Day and Night' by Jacob Epstein.

London Transport Headquarters, 55 Broadway, SW1; Nearest transport St James's Park LU (District and Circle lines); No public access

Victoria Coach Station

Wallis, Gilbert & Partners   1931-32

This, the first large-scale coach station in Britain is a form looking for its medium, in this case by disguising its purpose. As the coaches enter and exit at the rear of the building, the casual observer would be hard-pressed to guess the buildings function. The entrance tower is angled on the corner of the building, which is in Modern style with bands of windows along the two long sides.

Close by is another 1930's building with art deco leanings, the Imperial Airways Office, now occupied by the National Audit Office. Built in 1937-39 by A Lakeman this has a much taller, slimmer central tower that is almost double the height of its wings and does indeed resemble the shape of a bird or plane. Some very good sculpture by E R Broadbent, such as his depiction of 'Speed in the Air'.

Victoria Coach Station, Buckingham Palace Road, SW1; Telephone 020 7730 3466; Transport Victoria Rail & LU (Victoria, Circle and District lines); Unrestricted access; Please telephone for wheelchair access

Imperial Airways Building, Buckingham Palace Road, SW1; Nearest transport Victoria Rail & LU (Victoria, Circle and District lines); No public access

Freemasons' Hall

Ashley and Newman   1927-33

This is the third Masonic Hall on this spot. The first dated from 1776 and was by Thomas Sandby (1721-98), whose Great Hall was much admired and preserved through subsequent rebuilding until irrevocably damaged by fire in 1883. Some remaining sections are held at the British Museum. Sir John Soane designed the second building in 1828 but by the turn of the century its facilities were deemed inadequate.

This late 1920s building by Ashley and Newman, neither of whom are credited with any other London buildings, bears an uncanny resemblance to the Port of London Authority building. Built from Portland stone, the Hall copes well with its awkward corner plot and exudes an air of gravitas, like the head office of a bank. Indeed its entrance façade was used recently in a BBC television series, when the characters, all MI6 intelligence officers, were depicted leaving their place of work. It looks that serious.

The interior is certainly worth a visit with a grand marble staircase, vaulted corridors and exquisite, massive bronze doors that lead to the 62 feet high Grand Hall.

The United Grand Lodge of England, Freemasons' Hall, 60 Great Queen Street, WC2B; Telephone 020 7831 9811; Nearest transport Covent Garden LU (Piccadilly line); Museum and Library open Mon-Fri 10am-5pm; Tours of the building Mon-Fri at 11am, 12noon, 2pm, 3pm and 4pm (tours are free); Admission free; Please telephone for details of wheelchair access

Rudolf Steiner House

Montague Wheeler   1926-37

Expressionism in architecture found a voice in Germany and the Netherlands circa 1905-30 and was the antithesis of Modernism. Expressionism was concerned that buildings should not be merely functional but creative, free and powerful sculptural forms in themselves. Probably the most notable building of this type is the Goetheanum in Dornach, Switzerland built by Rudolf Steiner in 1928.

Rudolf Steiner House near Baker Street is the only example of Expressionist architecture in London, and is a pretty tame one at that. The stone-faced building is perhaps rather inconspicuous but nonetheless it is a well used building with a theatre, bookshop and a particularly good library with a host of archive material relating to the construction of the building. The staff are very friendly and helpful and do not mind the interested having a wander around. Do note the very fine staircase.

Rudolf Steiner House, 35 Park Road, NW1; Telephone 020 7723 4400; Nearest transport Baker Street LU (Metropolitan, Jubilee, Bakerloo, Circle, City & Hammersmith lines); Open Mon-Sat 10.30am-5pm; Library open Tues & Thurs 11am-1pm & 2pm-5pm, Fri 1pm-6pm and Sat 12pm-5pm; Please telephone for wheelchair access information

Bank of England

Sir Herbert Baker   1921-37

Architecturally speaking, the glory days of the Bank of England were from the 1780s to 1808 when Soane's new Banking Halls were the talk of the City. Alas these were swept away in an enlargement programme in the 1920s and 30s with just Soane's retaining wall truly left intact. With the electric light now commonplace, the Bank no longer needed to rely on Soane's ingeniously top-lit halls and could build higher and wider thus creating more interior space, which was at a premium in such a restricted area.

Baker's main entrance sits well with the existing perimeter wall and the ample portico of coupled columns lines up with the colonnade giving the building its familiar form of today.

The most interesting aspect of the building is the Bank of England Museum, which is entered via Bartholomew Lane. The museum is set around a faithful recreation of Sir John Soane's Bank Stock Office of 1792-93 (by Higgins Gardner 1986-88), and it certainly gives the visitor a flavour of what was regarded as the finest neo-classic interior in Europe. This is the only part of the bank that can be entered by the general public.

Bank of England, Bank of England Museum, Bartholomew Lane, EC2; Telephone 020 7601 5545; Nearest transport Bank LU (Central, Northern lines & DLR); Open Mon-Fri 10am-5pm; Admission free; Please telephone for details of wheelchair access

Bank of England

Arnos Grove Underground Station

Charles Holden   1930

When the Piccadilly line was extended south and north in 1930 Frank Pick, the legendary head of London Transport, gave Charles Holden the task of designing the new stations. Pick believed that nothing was too good for the travelling public and he felt aesthetics were as important as the trains and buses running on time. Pick commissioned a calligrapher to give London Transport its own typeface, Johnston Sans, artists to design various posters and, in 1918, a designer to provide a logo. Amazingly this is still in use today – the red circle with the name of the station running through its middle.

'The best' also ran to architecture and Holden's stations are classics. His Piccadilly line extension stations, are all unique and yet are variations on a theme – built from exposed brickwork and concrete, using simple forms such as cylinders and rectangles with ceramic tiles to add colour. Holden designed everything – lighting, kiosks, ticket machines, platform seating and even the clock faces and litterbins.

Holden and Pick had travelled to parts of northern Europe for inspiration. Indeed the Arnos Grove building is reminiscent of the much-admired Stockholm City Library of 1928.

Arnos Grove has a drum-shaped ticket hall, whose large windows let light flood in during the day; at night electric light shines out, making a lovely sight. Southgate station is a rectangular version of this station.

Arnos Grove Station, Bowes Road, N14; Open normal London Transport hours; Wheelchair access on the Underground system is virtually impossible, but there is access to the interior of this station

Unilever House

J Lomax Simpson, with Burnet, Tate and Lorne   1931

This building is on the site of the once renowned De Keyser's Hotel a very successful enterprise started by Sir Polydore de Keyser, a waiter from Belgium who eventually opened his 400 room hotel in 1874. De Keyser became Lord Mayor of London in 1887, the first Catholic since the Reformation to do so and his hotel closed at the end of World War I and the land sold to Unilever in 1921.

Sited on a busy corner where traffic roars along Victoria Embankment and over Blackfriars Bridge this impressive stone building is windowless on the ground floor, presumably to help eliminate some of the noise from the road. From the fourth floor of this lovely curved building is a parapet from which a row of giant Ionic columns stretch upwards. The roots of the design of this building are undoubtedly classical but with more than a hint of art deco.

It is a worthwhile building to contemplate for its form alone, despite the traffic. However the real treat is its display of sculpture with huge figures taming sinuous horses, representing 'Controlled Energy', by William Reid Dick and other figures by Gilbert Ledward and Nicholas Munro. During the evening the façade of the building is particularly well lit.

In a six-year programme of refurbishment that ended in 1983, Unilever House was renovated and expanded by the addition of an eight-storey wing. The new wing had to be low enough so that it did not violate the long-standing edict of London planning authorities that no building should be high enough to block the view of St Paul's Cathedral from Waterloo Bridge.

Unilever House, New Bridge Street/Victoria Embankment, EC4; Nearest transport Blackfriars Rail & LU (District and Circle lines); No public access

St Olaf House

H S Goodhart-Rendel   1932

Built as the head office for the nearby Hay's Wharf in 1931–32; Hay's Wharf itself was started in 1651 by Alexander Hay and claims to be the oldest wharf in London. It certainly was the largest, stretching from London Bridge to Tower Bridge and was noted for its use of cold storage methods as early as 1867, when its principal work was importing cheese and butter from New Zealand.

Hay's Wharf is now a lively place for stopping off on a stroll along the South Bank as there is a choice of cafés and restaurants as well as a selection of shops. When you are there do make sure you check out St Olaf's House which almost abuts London Bridge and is an art deco gem. Faced in Portland stone the building has curved sides and a lively use of windows. The windows of the central four floors have bronze framing and the huge lettering over the entrances on both sides of the building is triangulated art deco.

The staircase is also art deco with a zigzag balustrade – worth pressing your nose against the entrance door to have a peep.

St Olaf's House, Tooley Street, SE1; Nearest transport London Bridge Rail & LU (Northern and Jubilee lines); Private office, no public access

Odeon Cinema

Mather and Weedon   1937

The profile of this building is an art deco dreamscape, built in uncompromising black granite with a huge square tower to one side. Renovations by Stephen Limbrick in the late 1980s have gone a long way to redress the damage caused by a mid-1960s refit, when much of the art deco interior was lost. However, there is still not that much to draw one into the interior unless you want to see the latest Hollywood blockbuster of course.

St Olaf House

This building is at its best in the evening, when it is bathed in blue neon light.

Probably one of the best surviving art deco cinema interiors can be found at the former Hounslow Odeon, now Mecca Bingo, London Road, Hounslow, Middlesex.

The Odeon Cinema, Leicester Square, WC2; Nearest transport Leicester Square LU (Piccadilly and Northern lines); Access as patrons, cinema times vary; Wheelchair access available

Senate House

Charles Holden   1937

It is said that Hitler wanted this building for his London office – if that is correct all one can say is that he had an impeccable eye for architecture for this is a fabulous building, outside and in.

The plan was conceived in 1927 with the purchase of a ten and a half acre site from the Bedford Estate to provide buildings for the University of London, which having been formed in 1836 was in need of more space. The proposal was to build administrative offices, a library, ceremonial hall, students' union, five institutions and two schools; a massive undertaking.

Architect Charles Holden was selected on the strength of his designs for his London Underground stations and 55 Broadway, which had recently opened. His masterplan was duly approved and the start of work on the Senate House and Library was made real by 1937. However lack of funding and the intervention of World War II saw the rest of Holden's plans thwarted.

Holden designed this building with the overall massing based on a pyramidal form for stability. This is what gives Senate House its slight Aztec temple flavour. Holden chose not to use the fairly new technology of steel-framing for his building, although it is used in the floor construction and there is steel framing within the tower to support the many book stacks.

London's first true skyscraper is faced in Cornish granite on the ground floor with Portland stone used on the upper floors. It is thought that the exterior was intended to receive carved figures and ornamentation, but these were never realised and the building is better for that.

Great care has been lavished on the interior. The Ceremonial Hall, where graduates of the University receive their degrees, is double-height and is lined with travertine marble. The same material is used on the exquisite staircase which has a notable wrought iron balustrade.

Senate House, The University of London, Malet Street, WC1;
Telephone 020 7862 8000; Nearest transport Goodge Street
LU (Northern line); No public access, however Senate House
usually participates in the London Open House scheme (see
'Resources' on p.297 for more information)

Senate House

1-3 Willow Road

Erno Goldfinger   1937-39

This small housing project by the Hungarian-born architect Erno Goldfinger is one of the most important examples of the Modern Movement in London. Having worked in Paris, where he mixed with avant-garde artists and architects, he settled in London in 1934.

Goldfinger encountered immense hostility from local conservation groups who saw his proposal for the terrace as being out of step with the rest of Georgian Hampstead. Nonetheless planning permission was eventually granted and the building of the three-house terrace went ahead.

Each of the houses within the terrace has a slightly different internal plan. Goldfinger took the centre house, the largest, as a home for his young family. Mindful of such a family's needs, Goldfinger incorporated a large amount of interior flexibility – whereby walls were moveable so that one large nursery could become two bedrooms when the need arose.

The terrace is three floors high at the front and four at the rear with integral garages, constructed from reinforced concrete with brick-faced walls. Concrete was used for the framing of the first floor windows and for the ground floor columns. Such unifying motifs make this terrace appear to be one large house and thus it fits well with its Georgian neighbours.

Erno Goldfinger was an immensely influential architect and his other London work includes the French Government Tourist Offices at 66 Haymarket (designed in 1958) and their further offices at 177 Piccadilly (built 1963); Alexander Fleming House at Elephant and Castle (1966); Haggerston Girls School (1967) and the much admired Trellick Tower (see details of this building on p.167).

Goldfinger's own house, No 2, has been in the care of the National Trust since 1994 and is open to the public. The house is filled with furniture designed by Goldfinger and his art collection is on display including works by Bridget Riley,

Max Ernst and Henry Moore. There are also some family photographs on show, one particular favourite being a picture of Goldfinger with his aged mother when she came to live in Willow Road – along with her incredibly heavy-looking, solid Hungarian furniture, that looks remarkably at home in such a Modernist setting. There is also an opportunity to see a short film on Erno Goldfinger and his work, which is most worthwhile.

2 Willow Road, Hampstead, NW3; Telephone 020 7435 6166; Nearest transport Hampstead or Belsize Park LU (Northern line); Admission is by timed ticket only; Open Thurs-Sat 12-5pm (April-Oct), and Saturdays only 12pm-5pm (March & November); Admission charge; Wheelchair access limited to entrance hall and cinema only

1945 to the 21st Century

Swiss Re Headquarters

In 1951 Britain set aside post-war austerity for an all too brief moment of celebration and fun. One hundred years after the Great Exhibition, the Labour government, who had ousted Churchill in the general election of 1945, threw economic caution to the wind and decided to allow frivolity and a modicum of excess to replace the rationing and monotonous drabness which had followed in the wake of victory.

The means the government chose was an exhibition which they called a festival, to distinguish it from the instructive exhibitions held during the war which had been deadly serious by necessity.

The primary medium the enlightened socialists chose for their festival was architecture. Every major city in the United Kingdom had been ravaged by the Blitz so the idea of reconstruction and redevelopment was in itself a tonic to the nation. A parcel of land on the south bank of the River Thames between Waterloo and Hungerford Bridges, just north of Waterloo Station, was set aside as the London site of the festival and a young architect, Hugh Casson was appointed Festival Director. Casson recruited a team of his contemporaries to work with him, a majority of whom had served as Royal Engineers during the war, as a result of which they had practical knowledge by the bucket-load, although few, if any, of them, had actually designed a work of architecture before.

The Festival of Britain, ran for five months, attracted almost ten million visitors and was the nursery for all British post-war modern architects. It was here that Casson and his team coined an exceedingly British version of Modernism which drew more strongly on Scandinavian influences than on French or German precedents. The nation loved the whole thing with its bright colours, strange shapes and challenging new ideas about how the British home should be decorated. Sadly, however, when Winston Churchill regained power in the general election of 1951, he in a fit of pique, decided to clear the whole thing away with the exception of the Royal Festival Hall. The Dome of Discovery, the Skylon, the Homes and Gardens Pavilion were all unnecessarily demolished and Britain returned to the realities of austerity.

The architects that had so proved their worth during the Festival now set about the business of rebuilding the country. They designed housing, hospitals, schools and shopping centres. They rebuilt derelict churches and repaired bombed-out houses. Their buildings in the brave new British Modernist style became symbols of the recently established

Welfare State. In time the Festival mood returned as new towns and new housing created new homes that were as different from the pre-war norm as was Dior's 'New Look' from the uniform-like fashions of the 1940's.

Architects could do no wrong. They were social doctors with precisely the right Modernist architectural prescription for the nation. Tower blocks soared into the sky to undreamt of heights, enticingly reminiscent of the land which was the subject of so much admiration, America. Happy children played in the grounds of Scandinavian look-alike schools and doctors preened themselves as they strutted down the squeaky clean corridors of the National Health Service's new cathedrals of well being.

The now monotonously dull buildings in Holborn and public housing such as Powell and Moya's Churchill Gardens estate (1947-62), near Tate Britain, seemed at the time entirely appropriate for postwar Britain. Reinforced concrete replaced brickwork in the same way that steel had replaced timber at the beginning of the century. Government instruction to the architectural profession was quite clear – build, and build fast. But, on a fateful morning in May 1968 this architectural euphoria came to an end, shattered like the pre-cast concrete panels that so dramatically crashed to the ground when the 23 storey tower block of flats that was Ronan Point in Newham, East London collapsed. Clearly it was no longer safe to trust the architectural and engineering vision which housed families in the high-rise apartment buildings that had become symbolic of Britain's post-war renaissance. Critics began to argue that Modernism was a deeply flawed architectural philosophy and that Britain's architecture should return to vernacular roots for safety and sanity's sake. Britain, their reasoning went, was historically a country of brick and stone, not concrete and steel, its buildings in the main were low-rise and had pitched roofs.

The first large local authority housing scheme to be built after the Ronan Point disaster was the high-density scheme at Lillington Gardens on Vauxhall Bridge Road, designed by the young architects Darbourne and Dark. Their solution to housing large numbers of people on a comparatively small site was to build high-density low-rise flats in brick-work and slate hanging tiles. The Government's target for house build-ing could be met and no one would have to live more than five or six storeys above ground. The Lillington Street blocks were linked by walk-ways which, on the drawings at least, were shown as romantic almost pastoral paths through the acres of rippling brickwork.

More incongruously office buildings which since the war had had their steel frames clad in either pre-cast concrete panels or glass were now to be given an unnecessary skin of non load-bearing brickwork. The small hand-sized component that was the British brick was thus forced into service in an inappropriate and meaningless way. However the new vernacular architecture won widespread popular approbation and rumours were rife that tower blocks like Ronan Point were shortly going to be blown up and the sites redeveloped with low-rise brick houses with pitched roofs.

Meanwhile across the English Channel young architects Richard Rogers and Renzo Piano had completed the mind-bogglingly audacious high-tech Pompidou Centre in Paris of 1976 which was immediately voted the 'Most Popular Building in France'. The aspirations of British architecture would not bow down in the face of popular yearning for an unnecessary romanticism. Then in 1978 against all the odds Rogers was appointed by the insurance organisation Lloyds of London, one of the most conservative institutions in the notoriously stuffy City of London, to design their headquarters. This building is considered, to this day, to be one of the most daring and futuristic in the world. This architectural audacity only confused the public mind even more.

The American architect Robert Venturi had published his seminal book 'Complexity and Contradiction in Architecture' in the 1960's when his views suddenly became fashionable. In his so-called Postmodern world, the deep roots of the psyche could only be satisfied by a complex, not rational, environment which carried with it subconscious references to architectural languages of the past. Office buildings built of brick needed to have references to Classical architecture to satisfy the hunger in the human mind for reassurance from the past. The Postmodern architectural movement came with a rich, albeit fraudulent, philosophical system which appealed to a large number of architects. The American Modernist Philip Johnson changed his spots overnight and designed the A T and P building in Manhattan with a Chippendale style split pediment where it reached sky. James Stirling designed the over-complex building at No1 Poultry. The high-tech British partnership of Terry Farrell and Nicholas Grimshaw came to an end. In 1983 Farrell gave a popular twist to Postmodernism with his building in Camden for TV AM with its jokey coloured boiled eggs on the canal elevation and a steel work keystone classical arch over the car park entrance.

No1 Poultry

Terry Farrell went on to complete three grand projects in the Postmodern manner. The MI6 building at Vauxhall, Embankment Place over Charing Cross Station and Alban Gate which spans London Wall in the City. Meanwhile his erstwhile partner Nicholas Grimshaw thumbed his nose at Postmodernism and designed the defiantly high-tech Sainsbury's supermarket in Camden Town. Architecture was clearly at war with itself.

In 1984 Prince Charles, the Prince of Wales, was guest of honour at a dinner hosted by the Royal Institute of British Architects at Hampton Court Palace, to celebrate the Institute's one hundred and fiftieth anniversary. The Prince was there to represent the Queen, the Institute's patron, and to present the Royal Gold Medal. The Prince used the opportunity afforded by his speech to attack British architecture and specifically the proposals for an extension to the National Gallery designed by Ahrens, Burton and Koralek (ABK). The Prince touched a popular nerve and was praised by tabloid and broadsheet alike for taking a brave stand against an arrogant and out of touch profession.

The ABK scheme for the National Gallery was dropped and was eventually replaced with a Postmodern concoction by the ringmaster of the philosophy Robert Venturi, with Denise Scott Brown. And what a baffling building it turned out to be – it was meant to be complex and contradictory and it certainly fulfils these criteria. Classically detailed blind windows at high level feature incomplete mouldings; a couple of cast-iron Grecian columns mysteriously appear in the foyer. Architectural nonsense or a concrete manifestation of a challenging and rewarding philosophy, one way or another the British people seemed to like it.

The early years of Thatcherism at the beginning of the 1980's brought a spectacular renaissance in London's property industry. The derelict docklands in the Pool of London that had been abandoned since the end of the freight handling had lain empty for decades and the Thatcher government began to promote development of the Isle of Dogs. The initial development plans clearly show the Island loosely packed with vernacular buildings, no more than four storeys in height but once the bandwagon was rolling and the American developer G Ware Travelstead had the ear of government the plan was torn up and the seeds for the much larger Canary Wharf development were sown. The message, certainly in central London, was build, build, build – as high as you like provided it was quickly and in almost any architectural style because, after all, the Post-Modern philosophy welcomed diversity Then it all ground to an ignominious and sudden halt.

When Britain left the European Monetary Federation (EMF) in 1991 the country's economy collapsed and with it the British property market. By 1992 45% of all architects in the United Kingdom were either unemployed or seriously under-employed. Canary Wharf was left less than half-complete with Caesar Pelli's old-fashioned pyramid-topped tower standing all on its ownsome. It was a time for deep personal reflection for every British architect – after all there was now plenty of time to think, dream and plan. The profession was in philo-sophical disarray but opponents of contemporary architecture seemed pleased – no buildings least of all ones they could object to, were being built at all. But this dispiriting statement was about to change, rescued by an unlikely change in national affairs.

The Docklands

On Saturday 19 November 1994 the British people experienced their first National Lottery draw. Twenty-eight per cent of the profits from the Lottery are set aside for 'good causes'; to date this has amounted to a staggering £15 billion. The 'good causes' include those which require building. The Arts Council Lottery Fund was to finance art galleries and museums while the Heritage Lottery Fund was there to repair and enhance the nation's historic building stock and the Millennium Fund had bulging coffers to help the nation celebrate a change in date through architecture. The architectural profession had been unprepared for the extent of this new bounty. More by luck than good judgement the 3 years between Britain's departure from the EMF and the birth of the National Lottery had allowed architects to become dab hands at new computer aided design technology. VDU's became standard in architectural practices across the country and drawing boards were carted away for scrap.

Architectural computers did more than replace the T square, set square and Rotring pen. They afforded a new freedom to the architectural imagination liberating it from the previous constraints which were in effect linear geometry. When plans were drawn by hand using the T square and set square, buildings over the fullness of architectural history had tended, in the main, to be rectilinear and right-angular. A computer, however, could turn the strangest lines, shapes and forms into concrete reality. For structural engineers the computer meant more finely honed calculations resulting in new structural systems. Colour photocopying meant that the architect's palette need no longer be monochrome - if Mondrian could paint it, architects could now draw it, reproduce it and specify it. The new language was shape and colour.

Herzog and de Meuron's transformation of the Bankside power station into the Tate Modern and the extension and renewal of Tate Britain were paid for by the Lottery. Outside the capital London architects were busying themselves with Lottery-funded projects throughout the length and breadth of the country. Nicholas Grimshaw designed the spectacularly popular Eden Project in Cornwall, whilst Nigel Coates produced the fatally unpopular Popular Music Centre in Sheffield. Leeds got the Armoury Museum by Derek Walker, and the list continues on, illustrating the Lottery's considerable benefit to British architects and British architecture.

In the main Lottery funded projects are at the forefront of neo-Modernism, a contemporary language that rejects both the vernacular and Postmodernism. Twenty years on the Prince of Wales's "monstrous carbuncle" speech of 1984 seems little but a fascinating paragraph in the history of the British monarchy.

Most of the Lottery funded projects have been immensely popular with one costly exception – the ill-fated Millennium Dome designed by Richard Rodgers. The idea of celebrating a mere change in date was always suspect if, for no other reason than the ludicrous prospect of central government organising a national party! However, the previous, Conservative, government had committed themselves to the Dome and their successors, Tony Blair's New Labour, saw the venture as a symbol of all that the party stood for: new, daring, big and brash. The millennium itself may have gone off like a damp squid with the devastatingly unpopular Dome as its symbol but in fact Richard Rogers structure is as fine a work of architecture as you'll find anywhere in the world.

As British architecture entered the new millennium fuelled by public enthusiasm and the continuing generosity of the Lottery Norman Foster emerged as the most successful architect of his generation. London plays host to dozens of buildings by the maestro including the architecturally challenging Greater London Authority headquarters, on the south bank of the Thames next to Tower Bridge, and the so-called gherkin (the Swiss Re building) in the City of London. Other big names working on big projects in the capital include Renzo Piano (of Pompidou Centre fame) who has received planning consent for 'The Shard' at London Bridge, soon to be the tallest building in Europe. Over at Canary Wharf Caesar Pelli's lonely tower has been joined by another designed by himself and one by Foster – despite its setbacks Canary Wharf is now a thriving neighbour of the City. Another new development at Paddington Basin, north of the railway station, will feature a collection of buildings designed by some of the key names in British architecture today, including Richard Rogers and Terry Farrell.

One strange anachronism which reached completion in 2004 is Paternoster Square, north of St Paul's Cathedral, an area which had been flattened by enemy bombing during World War II. The original buildings were designed and conceived in post-war Modernist enthusiasm, and became the centre of one of Prince Charles's major crusades, fell foul of the economic collapse in the early 1990's and only now can open its doors and be judged as found. Sir William Whitfield, the architect, was the master planner and author of several of the buildings.

British architecture, particularly in London is as strong if not stronger now than it was during the triumph of the Festival of Britain. Architects now seem as unstoppable as were those Victorians who wrought the new London. Below are some of London's most iconic contemporary buildings from The Royal Festival Hall built in 1951 to the gleaming towers of Canary Wharf which are still a work in progress.

Canary Wharf Station

Examples of buildings from this period:

Royal Festival Hall

Martin and Matthew et al   1951

This is one of those building people either loathe or love and its devotees are in the main those who patronise its concert hall, restaurants and shops. Designed in 1948 by a team led by Sir Leslie Martin (1908-2000) and Sir Robert Matthew (1906-75) it was finished in time for the 1951 Festival of Britain, for which it was a showpiece. For visitors to the Festival and passing Londoners this was a taste of what modern architecture could be – solid, functional and accessible.

The exterior is a display of glass and Portland stone, the river elevation having been extended forward during major renovation work in the early 1960s. The interior is a series of intersecting levels with a pleasing use of wood, marble, lighting and textiles throughout. The concert hall is a revelation, Leslie Martin having stipulated from the start that 'the egg of the concert hall should be surrounded by a box of structure'. The acoustics had been taken seriously at the design stage so the problems that dogged the Royal Albert Hall and even the much more recent Barbican Hall were eliminated. The auditorium accommodates 2,600 in seating arranged in one large stalls area, a substantial balcony, and four tiers of boxes. At the hall's opening one critic carped that the boxes looked like 'drawers pulled out in a hurried burglary raid'; now they are seen as amusing, pleasing on the eye and are exceedingly comfortable to occupy.

The architects Martin and Matthew, both employed by the enlightened London County Council at the time of the Festival, went on to enjoy fairly distinguished careers, especially Sir Leslie Martin who was acknowledged as a leading light in the Modern Movement. He designed some quite major additions to various Oxford and Cambridge colleges as well as the celebrated Royal Concert Hall in Glasgow. As well as being a practising architect, he was an academic, and was Professor of Architecture at Cambridge University for over forty years.

The Royal Festival Hall, honoured with Grade I listing, has been the subject of steady, ongoing refurbishment by Allies and Morrison since 1992.

Close by and part of the 'South Bank Centre' along with the Festival Hall are the Queen Elizabeth Hall, the Purcell Room and Haywood Gallery, built in 1964 by Sir Hubert Bennett and Jack Whittle for the London County Council. This group of buildings is a marvellous example of New Brutalism, with its admiration of the work of Le Corbusier and its use of huge blank walls of rough concrete. These buildings have been much criticised not least for their inter-connecting walkways which are difficult for the able-bodied to negotiate and totally impossible for people with any form of mobility restriction and, worst of all, appear to be unnecessary. On paper the design for this group must have seemed bold and exciting but given its location next to a grey Thames and under an often dull London sky its buildings seem out of place.

The interiors of the Queen Elizabeth Hall, seating 1,000, and Purcell Room, seating an intimate 368, feed off the same foyer and whilst they appear to be the smaller siblings of the Festival Hall both are less satisfactory.

Royal Festival Hall, South Bank, SE1; Telephone 020 7960 4242 or 08701 900 901; Website www.rfh.org.uk; Nearest transport Waterloo LU & Rail (Jubilee, Bakerloo and Northern lines); Access to the Festival Hall is open for events; for tickets and wheelchair access please telephone or consult website

The Economist Building

Alison and Peter Smithson   1964

An office block of 1960's vintage which still looks fresh and relevant. The building consists of three towers of differing heights arranged around a shallow pedestrian plaza. The four-storey smallest tower directly faces St James's Street and was originally designed as bank premises. The tallest tower of fifteen storeys is the home of The Economist magazine, the commissioning client of the project, and the third block is an eight-storey residential tower.

The towers are made from concrete with Portland stone spandrels and pilasters with aluminium window frames and the whole building sits well with its neighbours such as Boodles Club of 1765 without a hint of imitation or mockery. This was the first 1960s building to be Grade II listed.

The Economist Building, 25 St James's Street, SW1; Nearest transport Green Park LU (Victoria, Piccadilly, and Jubilee lines); No public access – but the building is part of the Open House scheme (see 'Resources' p.297)

Centre Point

Centre Point

Richard Seifert & Partners   1966

At the time of its construction this building aroused strong hostility and the public was critical of the London County Council's decision to grant planning permission for what was a private speculative project. Concerns regarding the building's intended use as offices rather than as living accommodation were also aired. Ironically in the light of such complaints this particular office block stood unoccupied for nearly ten years until converted to flats in 1975.

The structure's size, at 398 feet high and with thirty-four storeys, was also seen as being out of scale with its surroundings. However, this seems less so with the passage of time. Centre Point is now held in affection, like a much-maligned friend, by most Londoners.

Centre Point, 101 New Oxford Street, WC1; Nearest transport Tottenham Court Road LU (Central and Northern lines); No public access

Trellick Tower

Erno Goldfinger & Partners   1972

This was under construction as Ronan Point tumbled down and indeed Trellick Tower is the last of its breed – but had all tower blocks been like this then maybe the genre would have been more welcome. Commissioned by the Greater London Council for social housing, the 217 flats are arranged on thirty-one storeys with a separate lift and stair tower and bridges to the main block at every three floors à la Le Corbusier's 'Unité d'Habitation' in Marseilles.

Goldfinger's use of high-specification materials, including marble-lined entrance halls, and flexible internal arrangements within the flats, adds to their appeal.

Trellick Tower, 5 Golborne Road, W10; Nearest transport Westbourne Park LU (Hammersmith and City line); No public access – but the building is part of the Open House scheme (see 'Resources' p.297)

Lloyds of London

Lloyds of London

Richard Rogers Partnership   1978-86

In need of further office space to accommodate its growing business, Lloyds sought the talent of Richard Rogers, now Lord Rogers of Riverside, to design a new building which is surely the most striking modern building in London.

Lloyds, a society of insurance underwriters, originated in Edward Lloyd's coffeehouse in Tower Street in the mid 1680s. Ship owners, merchants and ships' captains beat a path to Lloyd's coffee house in order to obtain marine insurance. However, by 1769 new larger premises were established in Pope Head's Alley, but within two years these too had been outgrown. Business growth dictated several further moves to more spacious accommodation until the 1890s when Thomas Edward Collcutt created a bespoke office block at 71 Fenchurch Street. This is now a Grade II listed building and so could not be demolished to make way for the new construction and neither could the façade of Coronation House, the next door building also owned by Lloyds; both had to be incorporated into Richard Rogers' design.

In the early 1970s Richard Rogers and the internationally acclaimed architect Renzo Piano won the commission to design and build the new Pompidou Centre in Paris. Theirs was a radical design, with over half the site given over to a public piazza, and some of the features of the Lloyds building can be traced back to design elements employed in Paris. The most notable feature is that all the vertical structures and services are placed on the outside of the building, thereby leaving uninterrupted floorspace within.

The new Lloyds was designed to make the best possible use of the space available with minimum impact on Collcutt's building and the surrounding streets. Whilst the glass and steel structure soars, when viewed from adjacent streets, it is truly in sympathy with its neighbours. From Lloyds Avenue to the east the building is barely visible and seen from the west the five visible storeys blend harmoniously with other blocks on Fenchurch Place.

With its exterior components and the main lifts and escalators in full view at the front behind full-height glazing there is little need for ornamentation. The ten-storey glazed atrium is a sight to behold and much of this can in fact be seen from the outside.

Just as interesting is the beautifully preserved interior of Collcutt's building, particularly the richly decorated Library, with its sumptuous use of wood and the General Committee Room with its barrel-vaulted ceiling painted by Gerald Moira (1867-1959).

The Link Gallery, originally part of Collcutt's General Office provides a transitional space between the two buildings and is lined with paintings, several of which are by the eminent Sir Frank Brangwyn RA (1867-1956).

It is worth making a visit to the City in the evening just to see this building glowing ingeniously with coloured lighting designed by the Imagination team in 1988.

Lloyds of London, 71 Fenchurch Street, EC3M 4BS; Telephone 020 7709 9166; Nearest transport Monument LU (Circle and District lines); No public access – but the building is part of the Open House scheme (see 'Resources' p.297)

The Circle

CZWG Architects   1987-89

Included here for its striking use of colour – cobalt blue, and lots of it, the project takes its name from the rounded forecourt in front of the flats, of which there are 302. In addition there are eight office suites, a health club with swimming pool, a small restaurant and some retail units. The Circle is part of the now exceedingly fashionable area of Shad Thames.

The blueness of the building comes from glazed tiles used on the entrance façades; the rest of the building is of stock brick. Attention to detailing such as diagonal glazing bars and the deployment of balconies make this an attractive development, there is also a rather splendid statue of a horse in the roadway. Concern as to the Circle's appeal over time has been voiced and suggestions that the use of such a single strong colour was somehow 'gimmicky' are, fifteen years on, as yet unfounded.

The CZWG group have been responsible for some other notable housing projects such as Cascades (built 1987-88) on the Westferry Road and the China Wharf mix of flats and offices (built 1986-88) in Mill Street on the south bank of the Thames.

The Circle, Queen Elizabeth Street, SE1; Nearest transport London Bridge LU & Rail (Northern and Jubilee lines); No public access

The Circle

Imagination

Ron Herron   1989

Originally this six-storey Edwardian building was two schools. Girls occupied the building to the front, whilst the boys were taught in an almost identical one at the rear with a narrow area, open to the elements, dividing the two. Various uses were made of the building after the school closed but it was left in a state of dilapidation until 1988 when the premises was bought by 'Imagination' the design, communications and project management company.

The refurbishment project was handed to architect Ron Herron, who had worked on the conception of the South Bank Centre in the early 1960s and who had been part of the ground-breaking Archigram group of designers who had been responsible for some interesting but unrealised projects. Their vision of disposable, flexible and thus easily extended buildings was very influential from the mid 1960s to mid 1970s. Some of their philosophy can be traced in the Imagination building.

Viewed from the street it's impossible to envisage what lies behind the red brick and hanging green ivy of the façade. The original building space has been given a high-specification and smart appearance, but it is the treatment of the 23 foot wide space between the original buildings that is the most astonishing feature. This once dead-end alley, the walls of which have had their bricks painted white, rises six storeys. White steel and aluminium bridges, link the two buildings and criss-cross the space between them and the whole is roofed by a network of suspension rods and push-up gigantic umbrellas of Teflon-coated PVC fabric.

Throughout the building the predominantly white and natural aluminium decoration has a remarkably calming effect, whilst the use of walkways and the light from the atrium space gives the whole a sense of drama. The refurbishment of the building has won many awards including the 1990 Royal Institute of British Architects 'National Award for Architecture'. In the same year at the BBC Design Awards Sir Norman Foster said of the building "I was so full of enthusiasm, I couldn't stop talking about it. I was stopping people, I was phoning people, I thought it was really wonderful".

The remarkable 'Imagination' building combines the old and new so successfully that it influenced many subsequent buildings, particularly given the stringent new conservation policies and advances in construction technology.

Although this is a workplace with no public access (see below) every year the company 'dresses up' the façade of the building for the festive season. In 2003 some 16,000 twinkling fairy lights were involved, and, along with Regent Street, 'Imagination' has the best Christmas decoration in London and is certainly worth a detour to see!

Imagination, 25 Store Street, WC1E 7BL; Telephone 020 7323 3300; Website www.imagination.com; Nearest transport Tottenham Court Road LU (Central and Northern lines); No public access (apart from occasional exhibitions) – but the building is part of the Open House scheme (see 'Resources' p.297)

Sackler Galleries at the Royal Academy of Arts

Foster Associates   1991

Climb the sweep of glass stairs to the Sackler Galleries, past what used to be the exterior walls of the old building taking in the sheer beauty of the former façade that may have gone unnoticed until given this opportunity to be seen on its own level. This tends to happen with Foster's buildings in that, wonderful as they are in themselves, they also open up the surroundings, whether it be a view, another part of the building or simply the sky.

You may prefer to take the glass-walled lift to the Galleries, but whether by lift or stairs, when you arrive you will be greeted by the bright space and clean lines of the top-lit ante room which beautifully displays some of the Academy's best sculpture, including Michaelangelo's Virgin and Child with the Infant St John. As at the 'Imagination' building, the void between two buildings was used to house new service struc- tures, in the Royal Academy's case providing the space for the stairs, lift and ante-room to the Sackler Galleries (which were formerly the isolated and seldom visited Diploma Galleries).

Norman Foster's fusion of the old and the new here has been universally acclaimed as nothing short of a masterpiece in itself, sitting very well within Burlington House, one of the few surviving 18th century mansions in this part of London. The Royal Academy moved to these premises, so much larger than its cramped quarters in the Old Somerset House, in 1868, the one hundredth anniversary of its foundation.

The eminent architect Michael Hopkins has been commis- sioned to carry out further building work at Burlington House, which includes provision for new gallery space. It is hoped this work will be completed by 2007.

The Royal Academy of Arts, Burlington House, Piccadilly, W1; Telephone 020 7300 8000; Nearest transport Piccadilly Circus LU (Piccadilly and Bakerloo lines) or Green Park LU (Piccadilly and Victoria lines); Open Mon-Thurs, Sat & Sun 10am-6pm, Fri 10am-10pm (closed Christmas Eve, Christmas Day, Boxing Day and Good Friday); Admission free – except for special exhibitions

Sackler Galleries at the Royal Academy of Arts

Vauxhall Cross & Embankment Place

Terry Farrell   1990-93

Seen at its best from across the Thames with one's back to Tate Britain, Vauxhall Cross was designed and built to house the MI6 offices. Gone are the days when Secret Service employees worked in anonymous Government blocks for here we even have a public riverside walkway incorporated into the design. That said, the windows are so incredibly small that peeping in is impossible!

Hungerford Bridge

The whole building has more than a passing resemblance to Terry Farrell's other Thameside building, Embankment Place (1986-91). Offices and public walkways link to Hungerford Bridge and Charing Cross railway station set under a huge curved roof with stone faced towers. The side facing Villiers Street is made of red brick and polished black stone with circular windows breaking up the surface.

Vauxhall Cross, Albert Embankment, SE1; Nearest transport Vauxhall LU & Rail (Victoria line); No public access.

Embankment Place, Charing Cross, Strand, WC2; Nearest transport Embankment LU (District and Circle lines), Charing Cross LU & Rail (Bakerloo and Northern lines); Public access along walkways to Hungerford Bridge and Charing Cross Station but no public access to Embankment Place

Waterloo International Terminal

Nicholas Grimshaw   1991-93

Behind the Edwardian façade of J R Scott's Waterloo Station is the Waterloo International Terminal accommodating trains bound for the Channel Tunnel and Continental Europe beyond. The Eurostar trains are by most standards long at 1312 feet and to protect passengers (boarding and alighting) the platform covers had to stretch out along the track. The roof is what one notices first, and its light and space are most welcome and give the feel of an airport rather than a railway station. From a vantage point outside the terminal, say the London Eye, the whole looks like a giant snake curving its way through the maze of south London buildings.

The two and a half thousand panels of glass contained in the roof are standard size sheets, which overlap where necessary and are bolted with a concertina joint, rather than using bespoke panes. This building has something of the pioneering railway age about it, much like St Pancras and Euston stations over one hundred years before.

Waterloo International Terminal, Waterloo Station, SE1; Nearest transport Waterloo LU & Rail ((Jubilee, Bakerloo and Northern lines); Access for Eurostar passengers only

The Channel 4 Headquarters

Richard Rogers Partnership   1991-94

The Horseferry Road is not an area noted for its innovative architecture and yet, amid a number of bleak buildings stands, bold and brave, Richard Rogers' Channel 4 Headquarters and transmission centre. This was the architect's first work after the success of Lloyds of London. The building project is a mixed-use site with only half the complex being used by Channel 4, the other half, that is the south and east sides, being residential units.

The five-storey office wings extend back at right angles with a glass tower at their centre containing the stairs and external glass-box lifts. The large, rather strange looking objects on the lift-tower are not some avant-garde piece of art but the transmission antennae.

The walls of the building are in the main of glass and grey steel with a surprising use of ochre-red at intervals, which is apparently the same colour as the Golden Gate Bridge in San Francisco. Those passing by can see the curved glass and steel entry atrium without too much difficulty.

Channel 4 Headquarters, 124 Horseferry Road, SW1; Nearest transport St James's Park LU (Circle and District lines), Victoria LU & Rail (Circle, District and Victoria lines); No public access – but the building is part of the Open House scheme (see 'Resources' p.297); Full wheelchair access

Shri Swaminarayan Mandir

Chandrakant B Sompura/Triad Architects Planners 1995

Neasden, in north London, is not the most attractive area in town and yet, turning the corner on Brentfield Road, you will be forgiven for believing your eyes are deceiving you as you behold the most important and spectacular Hindu temple outside of India. The Mandir (the Sandskrit word for temple) has seven white pinnacles and seven white domes, standing out above the neighbouring red brick Victorian terraces.

In the Hindu faith the Mandir is not just a religious building but a part of god manifest on earth. Consequently no man-made materials are allowed in its construction, so the conventional ingredients of a modern building – steel, glass, aluminium, concrete cannot be used. Only natural materials are permitted. Certain types of sandstone were ruled-out because of the English weather conditions and the onslaught of the pollution from the London traffic. The solution was found in 2,828 tonnes of cream-coloured Bulgarian limestone for the outside of the Mandir and 2,000 tonnes of white Carrara marble for the interior – the same type of marble Michaelangelo used for his sculptures.

The stone was shipped to India where 1,500 sculptors worked for two years creating their masterpiece in accordance with the ancient shilpashaastras – a treatise on ancient temple architecture. Their labour was given voluntarily.

All this work was shipped to England and assembled like a massive jigsaw puzzle within three years and at a cost of £12 million; surely one of the new wonders of the western world.

Shri Swaminarayan Mandir, 105-115 Brentfield Road, NW10; Telephone 020 8965 2651; Nearest transport Wembley Park LU (Northern line); Open Mon-Sun 9am-6pm; Please telephone for wheelchair access information

The British Library

Sir Colin St John Wilson   1978-97

The British Library

Originally part of the British Museum, the space given over to the British Library in Smirke's building was totally inadequate by the 20th century. The commission to design a new library was first awarded to Sir Leslie Martin (see Royal Festival Hall p.164) in 1962 when serious consideration was being given to its siting. It took ten years to find a plot of suitable size and a further twenty to construct the library, by which time Wilson, Martin's pupil and eventual associate and who also took over as Professor of Architecture at Cambridge on Martin's retirement, had inherited the project. The delays and hiccups were mostly financial, in 1978 Wilson's plans were to provide storage for 25 million books and seating for 3,440 readers but by 1988 funding for the project was dramatically slashed. As a result what actually is provided is space for 1,176 readers and storage for 12 million books.

Of course, one problem with such a protracted project is that tastes change. During the decades of implementation and what looked fresh on paper in the late 1970's now resembles an out-of-town shopping centre with its red bricks and pitched roof, chosen initially to blend with its neighbour Gilbert Scott's Midland Hotel. Even the brave attempt at a city piazza in front of the library somehow fails to entice the unsuspecting passer-by, it is not a universally loved building.

However the fact that the exterior leaves a lot to be desired is a shame for it detracts from the interior space which is worth seeing by the casual visitor and is a joy to use for the hundreds of readers who pass through the building every day. It is perhaps the finest public space created in the 20th century, with tall, square pillars faced with white Travertine marble and the floor paved with Portland and Purbeck stone. The foyer displays some fine modern works by British artists such as R B Kitaj's tapestry inspired by T S Eliot's 'The Waste Land'. The exhibition galleries are comfortable to use and have such gems on display as a copy of the Magna Carta and the lyrics of a Beatles song written on the back of an envelope.

There is a pleasing use of light from clerestory windows incorporated wherever possible throughout the building and the reading rooms are calm, light spaces with well-crafted furniture of American white oak. Books are stored and retrieved, via motorised rollers and paternosters, from the four-storey basement. However, a large section of stock is still held off-site because of the already inadequate facilities at the library.

The British Library, 96 Euston Road, NW1; Telephone 020 7412 7332; Website www.bl.uk; Nearest transport Euston LU & Rail (Northern and Victoria lines) and King's Cross/St Pancras LU & Rail (Northern, Victoria, Circle and Metropolitan lines); Open Mon, Wed-Fri 9.30am-6pm, Tues 9.30am-8pm, Sat 9.30am-5pm, Sun and Bank Holidays 11am-5pm; Wheelchair access available; See also 'Eat and Drink Architecture' p.258.

Sadler's Wells Theatre

Arts Team @ RHWL with Nicholas Hare Architects   1998

This is the sixth theatre on the site. The last was built in 1931 and was fondly remembered but not easy to use with cramped facilities. However with a Grade II listing most people assumed that little could be done, but when pressed English Heritage confirmed that Sadler's Wells was listed for its historical significance rather than its architectural merit and therefore what we have now is an almost brand new theatre.

Technical and operational facilities were given a badly needed update and an 85 foot fly-tower was built and stands proud – in both senses of the word – above the rest of the theatre. The bar, ticketing and ladies WC facilities are all excellent, as is the provision for wheelchair users. The auditorium has one of the best dance stages anywhere and one only has to note the amount of world-class companies who include Sadler's Wells on their performance itineraries since refurbishment for evidence of its success.

Importantly the whole foyer area, now feeling like one single space from the ground floor almost to the roof with its exciting use of light and sheer glass front wall, makes the theatre feel accessible to those who might otherwise find a visit to such a temple of culture rather daunting.

The whole project cost a cool £30 million, funded from the National Lottery.

Sadler's Wells Theatre, Roseberry Avenue, EC1R 4TN Telephone 020 7863 8198; Website www.sadlers-wells.com Nearest transport Angel LU (Northern line); Public access 9am-11pm; Excellent wheelchair access

Sadler's Wells Theatre

The Great Court, The British Museum

Foster and Partners   2000

When the British Library moved to its new premises in St Pancras in 1998, the Round Reading Room and its surrounding space was taken into use by the British Museum. Before the Reading Room had been built by Sidney Smirke in 1855, the area had been an open court-yard, albeit not one that had been held in affection, having been called a 'miserable-looking space'. Norman Foster and his team have given the courtyard back to the public in spectacular fashion.

The Round Reading Room forms the core of the space, retaining its original function but now serving as a public reference library, whilst a staircase wraps around its exterior giving access to the restaurant (some of whose tables have fabulous views into Smirke's Reading Room) and to the upper galleries via a short walkway.

The Great Court has a well-stocked bookshop, a gift shop, lecture theatres and WCs as well as two cafés and improved access to galleries on the ground floor.

The whole Great Court area is covered by a lightweight roof with 3312 glass panels – each one a different size! The roof structure rests on the perimeter walls and slender columns hidden beneath the skin of the Reading Room. The area feels somehow lighter than out of doors (in England, anyway!) with the only slight irritation being the noise-level. However, even that cannot spoil the overall effect, especially when one can look up and see clouds scudding across the London sky or when the sun shines through the glass and casts shadows on the creamy marble beneath.

Judging by the crowds of people who now use this piazza this must be one of the most successful and universally popular architectural and engineering feats of the modern age, even at a cost of £98 million.

The Great Court, British Museum, Great Russell Street, WC1; Telephone 020 7636 1555; Nearest transport Russell Square

LU (Piccadilly line) Tottenham Court Road LU (Northern and Central line); Galleries open Sat-Wed 10 am-5.30pm, Thurs & Fri 10am-8.30pm; Round Reading Room open daily 10am-5.30pm and First Thurs in the month until 8.30pm; Great Court open Sun-Wed 9am-6pm and Thurs-Sat 9am-11pm; Fully wheelchair accessible

The Great Court, The British Museum

The Wallace Collection

Rick Mather Architects   2000

The Wallace Collection is home to one of London's best preserved art collections. It used to be possibly one of the city's best kept secrets – no matter when one visited it was never crowded and yet it all felt a bit stuffy and overbearing.

Rick Mather's work at the Collection, in celebration of its Centenary, has magically opened up the heart of this Georgian house, allowing in light and space to brighten the whole experience of this unique place.

Expansion beyond the walls of the museum was logistically impossible so the architect opened up former basement levels as galleries, spaces for storage, lecture theatre and education centre.

The use of glass for the sides of staircases and roofing works well with the fabric of the original building. The central courtyard has also received a glass roof and is now home to a splendid café, an oasis of calm in the West End. Among the treasures on display are works by Rembrandt, Joshua Reynolds, Romney, Gainsborough, Van Dyck, Titian, Poussin and Frans Hals.

Wallace Collection, Hertford House, Manchester Square, W1; Telephone 020 7563 9500; Nearest transport Bond Street LU (Central and Jubilee lines); Open Mon-Sat 10am-5pm, Sun 2pm-5pm; Admission free; Please telephone for wheelchair access information

Royal Opera House

Dixon and Jones Building Design Partnership   2000

By the closing years of the 20th century, the facilities at E M Barry's 1858 Opera House had become totally inadequate for both audience and performers alike. Refurbishment of this Grade I listed theatre and an increase in the general arts space to advance the Opera House as both a national and internationaly renowned facility was seen as vital. Public access was also an issue and the powers that be at the Royal Opera House wanted to exorcise the myth that their building was only for the elite. The whole scheme also needed to take into consideration the replacement of the long-lost façades of Inigo Jones's Covent Garden piazza at the rear of the Opera House and to this end the architects created a stripped-down classical reinterpretation, rather than a mere replica, of what was there before.

The focus of this notion of public access was the restoration of the 1860 Floral Hall, using a clever combination of clear glass and mirrors to cultivate a feeling of light and space which was to be enjoyed by ticket-holders and casual visitor alike. The need for a major service entrance on Bow Street meant that the Floral hall had to be elevated above its original position and however stunning this new space undoubtedly is, trying to access it is not for the unadventurous. This has been the main criticism of this particular project.

Nonetheless the rest of the Royal Opera House has benefited greatly from the £140 million spent. The Grade I listed auditorium has far better acoustics and sightlines. The backstage technology, scenery storage, workroom and dressing room space has been improved and the addition of a much needed 400-seat Studio Theatre used for rehearsals, chamber concerts and educational projects has been a success.

The Royal Opera House, Covent Garden, WC2E 9DD; Telephone 020 7304 4000; Website www.royalopera-house.org; Nearest transport Covent Garden LU (Piccadilly line); Public access to Floral Hall Mon-Sat 10am-3.30pm; Wheelchair access available

City Hall

Foster and Partners   1998-2002

Part of the 67 acre development in the area to the west of Tower Bridge on the south bank of the Thames, known as More London. The City Hall provides 4 acres of space on ten levels to house the offices of the Mayor of London, 500 staff members and the assembly chamber for the 25 elected members of the London Assembly.

The curiously shaped glass building is entered either at the ground level or, better still, through a large, slightly sunken amphitheatre, paved with rather nice blue limestone and the focus of outdoor events. The amphitheatre entrance leads the visitor into a public café and on to an elliptical exhibition space where a dramatic, yet gently rising, ramp takes visitors up through the building affording fantastic views of London out of the windows or should we say walls? Visitors can see into the assembly chamber, which is also open to the public, and which provides 250 seats for visitors and members of the press.

Beyond the assembly chamber level the ramp curls on past the Mayor's Office to the public space at the top of the building. This area is known as 'London's Living Room' with an external terrace encircling the whole of City Hall.

The form of the building is derived from a geometrically modified sphere which provides the greatest volume with the least surface area, thereby minimising heat loss and thus saving energy. The building leans back towards the south where the floor plates step inwards to provide natural shading for the offices beneath. Energy saving schemes are employed throughout the building such as the cooling system which uses cold ground water pumped up from the water table which is then passed through beams in the ceilings, reducing, by approximately one quarter, the annual energy consumption.

The City Hall was the first building to be finished in the 'More London' scheme which on completion will include other office blocks, shops, and cafés, with over half the total site area being given over to public space.

City Hall, The Queen's Walk, SE1 2AA; Telephone 020 7983 4000; Website www.london.gov.uk/gla; Nearest transport London Bridge LU & Rail (Northern and Jubilee lines); Open Mon-Fri 8am-8pm (some weekend openings please telephone for details); Wheelchair access

Swiss Re Headquarters

Foster and Partners   1997-2004

When the architecturally noted Baltic Exchange in the heart of the City was damaged beyond repair by an IRA bomb in 1992, those with an interest in such matters waited with bated breath to see what would replace it. What Norman Foster and his team have produced exceeds expectation for amid the rectangular and pointed City skyline emerged this rounded bullet-shaped building. This 41 storey, 10 acre construction has been described as 'London's first ecological tall building'. Part of the low-energy environmental strategy is the provision for air conditioning whereby stale air will be drawn into green garden spaces integrated into the workplace and re-oxygenated by the dense planting. Mechanical air conditioning will only be used in a 'back-up' role and, joy of joys, the windows will be able to be opened! The building services, lifts and stairs are concentrated in a central core leaving the rest of the floor space free of intrusions.

The first two floors of the building are given over to retail use and the top two levels will accommodate bars and restaurants, with the rest of the building being used for offices.

Opinion is mixed on this building's appearance – it is called the 'gherkin' by some, even worse names by others. However in an age of computer-aided design, architecture does not have to conform to what went before. More importantly, there are sound ecological reasons for curves (see City Hall on the opposite page). Such thought has been put into this structure, including the painstaking aerodynamic modelling of the tower so as to avoid down draughts thereby ensuring the enjoyment of those using the piazza outside. A fabulous building and one that gives us hope for the future of modern architecture.

Swiss Re Headquarters, St Mary Axe, EC3; Nearest transport Liverpool Street LU & Rail (Central, Circle and Metropolitan lines)

Swiss Re Headquarters

Canary Wharf

Skidmore, Owings & Merrill Inc   1988 +

During the 1980s financial boom Canary Wharf was conceived as a major new location to complete the golden triangle of world-class financial centres along with New York and Tokyo. It was felt that the buildings of London's traditional financial centre, the City, would not be able to cope with the rush of new technology that was going to be needed to compete in the new age money market.

Canary Wharf, built in 1880, had been one of the largest and busiest docks in Europe, but just one hundred years later it lay abandoned. The area then became the focus of the government's Urban Development Corporation and the marriage of business and property developers was blessed. Originally conceived by the American developer G Ware Travelstead in the early 1980s the whole area still retains a flavour of Chicago and New York from an architectural point of view. Indeed American architects dominated the whole project.

The first building to be completed at Canary Wharf was No1 Canada Square by Caesar Pelli (1926-), an Argentine-born American, who had been responsible for the huge skyscraper and plaza at the World Financial Centre in New York. This steel-clad building is a true landmark, and is readily identifiable looking east from many parts of London by the flashing red light on its pyramidal top. The light is not for decoration but because the Wharf is under the flight path of the City Airport. Pelli's obelisk like building sets the tone of what was to follow: tall, slim and with framed windows rather than strip glass.

After the financial slow down of the 1990s Canary Wharf is once again experiencing the good times. Transport links, once the subject of much frustration, have almost been solved by the services of the Docklands Light Railway and the Jubilee Line extension, with its fabulous Canary Wharf station by Norman Foster. Architecturally speaking there is, as yet, not one building which merits special attention but Canary Wharf is certainly worth a visit to see as a whole.

A shopping mall, a plethora of bars and restaurants, summer open air concerts and an impressive display of public art go some way to providing a quality environment for those who work, live and visit the area.

Canary Wharf, Isle of Dogs, E14; Nearest transport Canary Wharf LU & DLR (Jubilee line); Public access is open

Canary Wharf Station

Walking London's Architecture

Bartholomew Walk

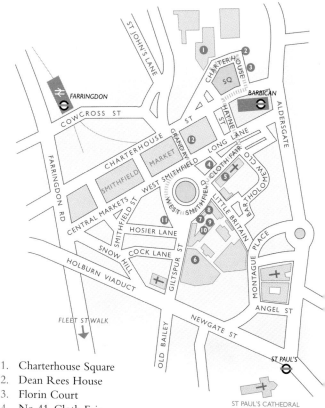

1. Charterhouse Square
2. Dean Rees House
3. Florin Court
4. No 41, Cloth Fair
5. St Bartholomew the Great
6. St Bartholomew's Hospital
7. Gatehouse of St Bartholomew's Hospital
8. St Bartholomew the Less
9. St Bartholomew's Hospital Museum
10. Great Hall (St Bartholomew's Hospital)
11. Haberdashers' Hall
12. Smithfield Market

A fairly short walk, in terms of distance, but one which takes in the variety London has always offered. Choose any area in the capital and the curious will find all sorts of half-hidden nuggets of history and architectural gems.

We start this walk in the corner of **Charterhouse Square (1)** by the entrance gates to **St Bartholomew's and Royal London School of Medicine and Dentistry**. Where you are standing was once part of the thirteen acres purchased in 1348 by Sir Walter de Manny, a loyal knight to King Edward III, having fought for his monarch against the Scots and the Flemish.

The purpose of the land purchase was to provide a burial ground for the many victims of the 'Black Death', the term given to a particularly vicious epidemic of bubonic plague that ravaged London and the rest of Europe during the 14th century. Thought to have reached London in September 1348 it had petered out by 1350, but in that short period between 50,000 and 100,000 Londoners suffered an agonising, but blessedly swift, death. Whole families were wiped out and commerce and manufacturing came to a halt when entire workforces perished. In one month alone in 1349 the Abbot of Westminster died along with twenty-seven monks.

De Manny's act of piety did not end there for in 1370 he founded the Charterhouse, a Carthusian Priory. Building work began in the following year by Henry Yevele (c1330-1400) who was considered to be the most gifted master mason of his day. Yevele had worked extensively for the King, especially at Westminster Abbey and he was also charged with the design of royal tombs, such as that for John of Gaunt who died in 1399. Work on the Priory was finished in about 1414.

Life was hard for the brothers in the Priory, living and eating alone except for Sundays and feast days, and where speaking to one another was only allowed after the Sunday meal when they were also allowed a walk outside the priory grounds.

The Priory closed at the dissolution of the monasteries in the 1540s and the land was given to Lord North, who destroyed the church and much else in order to build himself a fine mansion house. This was bought in the early 17th century by Thomas Sutton who used the premises as a school for forty-four poor boys and as a 'hospital' for eighty elderly poor gentlemen. This formed the basis of the famous Charterhouse School, which enjoyed a chequered history until its move to larger premises in Surrey in 1872. Famous pupils of the school include John Wesley, Robert Baden Powell (founder of the Boy Scouts movement) and the writer William Thackeray.

For a short while the premises were used by the Merchant Taylors' School, which soon found larger accommodation in Hertfordshire. The site became the Medical College of St Bartholomew's in 1933, but suffered extensive bomb damage during World War II. It is not possible to visit the remains of the Priory on a casual basis, but tours are organised between April and August. For information please telephone 020 7251 5002 - but be warned these tours get filled very quickly and must be booked in advance.

As you are standing by the gates of the School of Medicine, the last house in the square closest to you is the **Dean Rees House (2),** which dates from 1894; it is quite an ornate building for its size and has French overtones. The house was actually built for the Headmaster of the Merchant Taylors' School when they had their short stay here and Merchant Taylor motifs are in evidence on the building. The Merchant Taylors were one of the many lively and prosperous Livery Companies of the City of London (see p.13).

Walk along the east side of Charterhouse Square, and at numbers 6-9 you will find a block of flats named **Florin Court (3)**. This lovely, curved building, recessed at the centre, opened in 1936 and was designed by Guy Morgan. The residents of this handsome ten-storey block enjoy a roof garden with wonderful views and there is a swimming pool in the basement. The architectural historian Nikolaus Pevsner aptly described Florin Court as being 'poised between modernism and art deco'.

Moving on, cross **Charterhouse Street**, bear right and take the narrow **Hayne Street**, cross **Long Lane**, and take the narrow alleyway next to the 'Red Cow' public house. This brings us to **Cloth Fair (4)**.

Building first took place on this land when it passed from nearby Bartholomew's Priory to Lord Rich at the dissolution of the monasteries. Although the Priory was not completely closed, much of its property was confiscated. Until the mid 20th century, houses were packed

St Bartholomew The Great

on both sides of this fairly narrow street, giving a flavour of how much of London looked at the time of the Great Fire. Take a look at the red brick, four storey **No 41**, which is a private residence, an almost unique example of a 17th century City merchant's house. The house is hard to date precisely and it could be as early as 1614 when the first land lease was released although the building conforms to post Great Fire regulations. **Nos 39-40** date from about 1830.

The curious name of the street is derived from the cloth merchants who settled here and because of the area's association with the Bartholomew Fair, an annual three day affair that always started on the feast day of St Bartholomew, 24th August. Begun in 1133 this fair was an important source of income for the Priory of St Bartholomew, whose canny founder Rahere had instigated the Fair as a way of making money for his hospital. A Royal Charter authorising the Fair had been granted by Henry I to Rehere, whom, it is believed, was at one time minstrel to the King.

The Fair soon became a cloth specialists' market, where merchants from all over England and from the Continent would flock to sell and buy their wares. During the 17th century wrangling arose over who was to receive the largest portion of the Fair's revenue and the Fair was threatened with closure. Nonetheless diversions - fire-eaters, magicians, tight-rope walkers - abounded here for a good many years more until 1855 when public disorder, probably related to the vast quantity of drink consumed, was blamed for its eventual closure. Ben Jonson's play 'Bartholomew's Fair' is an apparently accurate vignette. This street was also the birthplace of the architect Inigo Jones, his father being a cloth merchant.

 After exiting Cloth Fair at West Smithfield bear left where you will shortly arrive at the **Tudor gatehouse** of the church of **St Bartholomew the Great (5)** (see p.23 for more details).

On leaving St Bartholomew the Great, walk through the gatehouse again and along **West Smithfield**, past the entrance to **Little Britain** and along the perimeter wall of **St Bartholomew's Hospital (6)**.

Often as not there are bunches of flowers left on the ground under the plaque on the wall commemorating the three hundred or so Protestants burned at the stake near this spot between 1553 and 1558, during the reign of Queen Mary, a deed which earned her the nickname of 'Bloody Mary'.

The name 'Smithfield' is probably a corruption of 'smooth field', meaning flat land. Jousting tournaments took place here as did public executions until about 1400 when they were moved to Tyburn.

Now we move onto the **Gatehouse of St Bartholomew's Hospital (7)**. This nice little building dates from about 1700 and has a bust of Henry VIII in a niche at the centre of the pediment. The carved figures representing Lameness and Disease are contemporary with the building.

Walking past the gatehouse into the Hospital grounds on your left is the church of **St Bartholomew the Less (8)**. Some of the church dates from the 15th century, namely the south tower and the vestry but the rest dates from 1823-25 and is by Thomas Hardwick to a plan by George Dance the Younger. This is a lovely little octagonal, brick-built church with small windows placed high up to give a dramatic light effect. Although the church is now parochial, rather than exclusively for the Hospital, the link can be seen in its early 20th century stained glass window, depicting a nurse and which was the gift of the Worshipful Company of Glaziers.

This building suffered severe bomb damage during World War II but was sympathetically restored by Lord Mottistone of Seely and Paget, who was responsible for much of the post-war restoration work in the City. The church is open every day from 7am to approximately 8pm.

When you have finished at the church make your way to the '**North Block**' where sign posts will direct you to **St Bartholomew's Hospital Museum (9)**. This small museum has a collection of surgical instruments and illustrates the fascinating history of the Hospital and the changing roles of the staff. Make your way through the museum to the door that leads to the **Great Hall (10)**.

This building was designed by James Gibbs (1682-1754), also responsible for St Martin-in-the-Fields and St Mary-le-Strand, in about 1730. Gibbs gave his services to the Hospital for free. Security will not permit you going very far into the Hall, but far enough to allow a look at the wonderful murals painted on the walls of the staircase by William Hogarth in 1735-37. The paintings represent Christ at the Pool of Bethesda and The Good Samaritan. The figures are larger than life size and the artist is said to have used hospital patients for his models. Hogarth did this work without charge, perhaps as an act of pure charity for he had been born nearby and his sister and mother still lived there. He may also have seen the gesture as an opportunity to show that British artists could paint as well as the Italians whose work was being brought home as souvenirs by the wealthy from their Grand Tours. Indeed it is rumoured that an Italian artist had been offered the commission at the Hospital, for which a large fee would have to have been paid, when Hogarth stepped in. To get a better look at the whole thing join one of the Friday tours (see p.203 for more information).

Many historic events are associated with the hospital, which is not surprising given its location. One of the most famous was in 1381 when Wat Tyler, leader of the Peasants' Revolt, was brought to St Bartholomew's Hospital having been stabbed in the back by the Lord Mayor of London, William Walmouth, as Tyler went to speak peaceably to the King. However before he could be treated he was dragged outside and beheaded by the King's men.

After visiting the museum you may like to walk through to the Court, also designed by James Gibbs as are the buildings to the left and right. The impetus to build separate ward blocks was justified by Gibbs as a precaution against fire, but the elimination of the risk of cross-infection may have been a factor.

Go out of the Hospital grounds and to your left follow West Smithfield, crossing **Guiltspur Street** and **Hosier Lane**. Still in West Smithfield, at number 18 is **Haberdashers' Hall (11)**.

The Worshipful Company of Haberdashers is one of the 103 City Livery Companies. These City Companies are in many ways like clubs. Their members are called freemen or liverymen and officers are elected to a committee or court chaired by the Master, usually for one year. Livery companies date back to the middle ages, when they were founded to promote and protect the crafts which their members practiced. The livery companies probably had their origins in this country before the Norman Conquest of 1066 and are similar to the fraternities and guilds (or mysteries) that flourished throughout Europe for many centuries. The term 'mystery' is still in use and derives from the Latin 'misterium' meaning 'professional skill'.

Livery was the term used for the clothing, food and drink provided for the officers and retainers of great households, such as those of bishops, barons, colleges or guilds. The term then became restricted to mean just the distinctive clothing and badges which were the symbols of privilege and protection. Since the members of each guild were distinguished from one another in this way, the guilds gradually became known as livery companies. It is still their custom to wear ceremonial dress on official occasions.

The earliest record of livery activity is a Royal Charter granted to the Weavers' Company in 1155. Members paid to belong and the word 'guild' is derived from the Saxon 'gildan' meaning 'to pay'. These guilds controlled services and the manufacture and selling of goods and food within the City of London. This prevented unlimited competition and helped to keep wages and working conditions steady. Customers, employers and employees were protected by checks for inferior work that did not meet the guild's standards; the term 'baker's dozen' originated during this time of strict regulations. Fines and other penalties could be severe – including expulsion, which meant the loss of livelihood. Disputes were settled by arbitration at the guild's hall, which also served as a meeting place for their particular trade.

Many street names within the City of London have trade-derived names, such as Bread Street, Milk Street, Ironmonger Lane and, of course, Cloth Fair. Many of the trades and crafts have now diminished in importance and the modern livery company concentrates its energies on charitable and educational activities.

The first Haberdashers' Hall was built in 1458-61 in Maiden Lane, later re-named Staining Lane, in the City and was destroyed in the Great Fire. The second Hall was built 1667 on the same spot but was destroyed during enemy bombing in World War II and the last was built 1954-56 as part of an office complex. In April 2002 the Company moved to its new bespoke premises here in West Smithfield. Her Majesty the Queen attended the opening ceremony.

The West Smithfield façade of the new building is made up of shops and residential units with offices to the rear. The Livery Hall, associated offices and meeting rooms are arranged on two floors around a central courtyard. **The Livery Hall**, where the official business takes place, has a high vaulted ceiling and oak panelled walls. Designed by the eminent architect Michael Hopkins, it has modern stained glass and bespoke furniture by David Linley (the son of the late Princess Margaret). This is a lovely, light, modern, yet classic building. Tours of this building are rare, only four per year at the moment (telephone 020 7246 9975 for further details).

Walking on, past the interestingly named Bishop's Finger pub, cross the road and head for **Grand Avenue**, which dissects **Smithfield Market (12)**.

A cattle market was formally established on this site in 1638, and during the early 18th century tales of unruly cattle and even more unruly herdsmen abounded. The beasts were herded into conditions that were totally inadequate and were slaughtered in the market with blood and waste running into the nearby Fleet River. Some of the streets about the market bear witness to this market, such as **Cowcross Street**.

Sir Horace Jones (1819-87), City architect, was charged with designing a building that would be suitable as the chief meat market for London. The site was enlarged to about ten acres to accommodate Jones's huge building, 631 feet in length and 246 feet wide. Nikolaus Pevsner, said of the building that 'it is of an uncertain style', but without any architectural precedent, finding a suitable 'style' must have been a nightmare for Jones!

Jones used red brick with Portland stone decorations and cast iron – lots of it. As you stand in the Grand Avenue note the cast-iron railings, gates and decorations. Also of note is the rather touching war memorial. The market has recently undergone a £70 million renovation in which all the paintwork has been restored to its original colours, these are unexpectedly vibrant deep blue, red and green with a lavish sprinkling of gold stars!

Sir Horace Jones went on to design Leadenhall Market, parts of the Guildhall and Tower Bridge.

In order to see Smithfield Meat Market in full working mode one has to get up very early as the trading 'day' finishes by 8am! Some pubs in the area have a 6am licence, the only place in London where this is so. Obviously it must be thirsty work!

When the market is at rest, the many cafés, bars and restaurants in the area come alive, and a lovely view of the illuminated dome of St Paul's can be enjoyed from many of the establishments.

More Information:

St Bartholomew's Hospital Museum
West Smithfield, EC1
Tel: 020 7601 8152
Transport: Barbican LU, Blackfriars LU, Farringdon LU, St Paul's LU
Open: Tues-Fri 10am-4pm, Tours 2pm on Friday only
Admission free
For details of the tours and wheelchair access information please telephone
020 7601 8033

War Memorial, Smithfield Market

Fleet Street & Beyond Walk

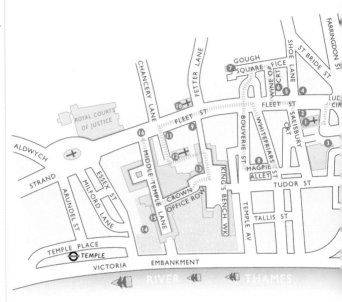

1. St Bride's Church
2. Reuters building
3. St Bride's Printing Library
4. Daily Express building
5. Daily Telegraph building, (now Peterborough Court)
6. The Cheshire Cheese (public house)
7. Dr Johnson's House
8. Whitefriars Monastery
9. Hoare's Bank
10. St Dunstan's in the West
11. Prince Henry's Room
12. Temple Church
13. Inner Temple
14. Middle Temple
15. Middle Temple Hall
16. Temple Bar

e start our walk at the **Ludgate Circus** end of **Fleet Street**. The street is named after the River Fleet which once flowed down what is now Farringdon Street and New Bridge Street and on into the Thames. What is left of the river today trickles through pipes under the road.

Our first stop is Sir Christopher Wren's beautiful church of **St Bride (1)**– note the magnificent steeple (see p.55). As you leave St Bride and rejoin Fleet Street note the building to your left, the **Reuters Building (2)** (85 Fleet Street). This is the former Headquarters of Reuters and The Press Association and was designed by Sir Edwin Lutyens in 1935. One may be forgiven for thinking the three-storey 'pavilion' was an afterthought, but it was very much part of Lutyens' plan.

The building is no longer occupied by Reuters, whose recent departure from the area marked the end of the news-paper publishing era in Fleet Street. Since the time of Wynkyn de Worde, about 1500, the street and the surround-ing alleyways have had an association with the printed word. During its early days the Crown and the Church viewed the printed word with suspicion and strict censorship prevailed and an unsuspecting printer could find himself in prison.

If you are particularly interested in the printed word there is a superb little library, **St Bride's Printing Library (3)** tucked away behind St Bride's church. This is a good source of books and periodicals relating to the history and techniques of printing (for details see p.211).

The first London newspaper, the Daily Courant, was published on 11 March 1702 and others followed such as The Morning Chronicle and The Diary, all published in Fleet Street. Until recently Fleet Street, and the surrounding area, was primarily concerned with the publication of daily national and provincial newspapers. Even now people of a certain age refer to the press as 'Fleet Street', long after the newspapers had decamped to more convenient premises in Canary Wharf.

However, the departing newspaper industry has left behind a couple of fabulous buildings, the first of which you will see now. Having crossed Fleet Street opposite the **Reuters Building (2)** you should now be on the corner of **Shoe Lane**, in front of you will be the gleaming,

unmistakable rounded form of the former **Daily Express Building (4)**
Designed by Sir Owen Williams and built 1930-33, this was the first
curtain walled building in London, with distinctive banding in glass and
black Vitrolite set in chromium strips. The printing of the newspaper
took place in the basement and at the rear of the building (this part was
demolished in 1990). As it is now a private office there is no public
access, but by pressing your nose against the reception door you will be
able to see into the fabulous Reception Hall, note the ceiling and the
concealed lighting arrangement – pure art deco. The building is part of
the 'Open House' scheme (see p.297 for more details).

Daily Express Building

Just a few paces on is the former **Daily Telegraph
Building, (now Peterborough Court) (5)** built
1928-31 by Elcock and Sutcliffe . This massive stone
building with six vast columns from the third storey
and stepped-back roofline exudes confidence and self-
importance, but must have felt old-fashioned within just a couple of

years on the opening of the Daily Express building. The huge projecting art deco clock is somewhat of a landmark. This building is now a private office and there is no public access.

Now we can take a diversion from Fleet Street. Stay on this, the north side of the road and you will soon find yourself at a narrow alley way called **Wine Office Court** and, on entering, you will see to your right **The Cheshire Cheese (6)** public house. Parts of this building date back to 1667, the original pub having perished in the Great Fire. This very atmospheric building still has its 18th century room arrangement intact, so there are lots of cosy corners to hide in! This was the haunt of Dr Johnson and his circle which in turn made it a focus of pilgrimage for writers such as Mark Twain and Charles Dickens.

Further on along Wine Office Court and to the left is **Gough Square**. One of the first things you will see is a small statue to a cat called 'Hodge', the companion of Dr Samuel Johnson who lived in the Square for a number of years. His house, number 17, is his only surviving home and is particularly significant in that it was here, in the attic, that he wrote his Dictionary of the English Language. **Dr Johnson's House (7)** is open to the public and a visit is a most worthwhile experience and gives a good flavour of 18th century life (see p.100 for details).

Make your way back to Fleet Street and cross to the south side into **Bouverie Street** and then left into **Magpie Alley**; this will bring you to the rear of the offices of the prestigious City law firm **Freshfields**. Have a look over the railings into the glass-clad basement where you will see the preserved remains of a tiny fraction of **Whitefriars Monastery (8)**. The Whitefriars were so called because they wore a white mantle over a brown habit, but were really Carmelites, named for Mount Carmel where their mother church was located. A priory had been built for them in this area in the mid 13th century. On the dissolution of the monasteries all the buildings were confiscated, the hall being made into a playhouse.

Back to Fleet Street, turn left and walk on until you arrive at number 37, **Hoare's Bank (9)**. One of the last remaining private banks in London, it has been in business for over four hundred years and is therefore older than the Bank of England! Hoare's have occupied this

Daily Telegraph Building

building since 1830. The bank took the then unusual decision to trade from a bespoke building rather than a converted house, as was the custom. Having said that, this building also has accommodation to enable a Director of the bank to be always in residence.

The building is made from Bath stone with a wrought-iron balcony, which is a 1930s addition. The Banking Hall has a circular bronze stove at the centre and polished wood counters.

Just a few yards along Fleet Street, on the opposite side (north) of the road is the church of **St Dunstan's in the West (10)**. Not surprisingly there is another St Dunstan's in the City, to the east. The foundation of St Dunstan's in the West can be traced back to the 13th century but this present building dates from 1830-33. The plan of the church is a Gothic octagon, unusual for such a late building. The number of interesting external features go some way to compensate for very restricted public access opportunities (see p.211). To the right of the church, as you are viewing it, is a statue of Elizabeth I, dating from 1586. As she died in 1603, this statue was made in her lifetime and the question arises whether it is an accurate likeness? It was made to stand at Ludgate (demolished in 1760) as were the statues of King Lud and his sons, which are inside the church. The Northcliffe monument on the exterior of the church commemorates the life of Alfred Harmsworth, 1st Viscount Northcliffe, the journalist and newspaper magnate. He started his career by editing his school magazine and went on to found such publications as Comic Cuts (1890), the Daily Mail (1896) and the Daily Mirror (1903). The huge clock dates from 1671 with two figures, sporting gold loincloths, who strike the quarter-hours with their clubs; they could well be Gog and Magog, the giants of legend who roamed the City.

Proceed along the south side of Fleet Street, until you arrive at the alleyway named **Inner Temple Gate**. There you will find the building known as **Prince Henry's Room (11)**. One of the last remaining timber-framed houses in London, it dates back to at least 1610 and therefore survived the Great Fire of London which ended its path of destruction only a few yards further down the road. The building also survived the threat of demolition in the late 19th century and the Blitz of 1940-41. The building contains interesting interior wooden panelling contemporary with the building and further 18th century panelling and fireplace. There is also a very nice plaster ceiling decorated with motifs including the Prince of Wales's feathers. The building probably takes its name from its time as a tavern rather than with any royal associations (for more information see p.211).

Walk down Inner Temple Lane and you will arrive at the west end of one of the most exquisite churches anywhere. This is the **Temple Church (12)** (see p.24).

When you exit the Temple church, look around at the buildings in the immediate vicinity. These buildings make up the **Inner Temple (13)** and the **Middle Temple (14)**(see p.211 for details), which represent two of the four **Inns of Court of London** – the others being **Gray's Inn** (entrance in Gray's Inn Road, telephone 020 7458 7800 for information) and **Lincoln's Inn** (accessed from Lincoln's Inn Fields, telephone 020 7405 1393 for information).

The four Inns, or Honourable Societies of Barristers, each fulfil the same function but have different traditions, rather like collegiate universities. According to custom, which dates back many hundreds of years, any law student training to be a barrister in England must join one of the Inns of Court and dine there at least twenty-four times, as well as passing written exams, before becoming officially qualified.

The maze of courtyards and buildings that make up Inner Temple and Middle Temple seem like something from another era, especially in the evening when the area is still lit by gas light. With your back to the Temple Church make your way right towards **Middle Temple Hall (15)**. Built between 1562-73 this Hall saw the first performance of 'Twelfth Night' in February 1602 and it is thought its author, William Shakespeare, acted a small part in it. Note the magnificent hammer-beam ceiling and the 29 foot table, made from a single oak tree from Windsor forest and presented as a gift by Elizabeth I.

Follow **Middle Temple Lane** back out to Fleet Street and look for the **Temple Bar (16)** in the road. This marks the boundary between the City of London and London general. When the reigning sovereign wishes to enter the City permission is sought from the Lord Mayor, who will greet His or Her Majesty at this point.

Until its removal in 1878, the old Temple Bar was a stone tri-arched affair thought to have been designed by Wren. It had to be taken down and something a little more modest put in its place to ease the flow of the ever-increasing traffic. Since its placement in the 1670s the Temple Bar had seen a lot of activity, not least the custom of displaying the heads of executed traitors on it, the last being that of Francis Townley the Jacobite, in 1746.

 The present **Temple Bar** is made of granite and coloured stone with statues of Queen Victoria and the future Edward VII, topped by a fierce looking griffin rampant. Sir Horace Jones, City architect, who was also responsible for Leadenhall Market, Smithfield and Tower Bridge and other projects, designed the Bar in 1880.

This is where the City and this particular walk ends. If you are feeling energetic you could carry on with the Strand walk which, quite conveniently, starts right here.

More Information:

St Bride's Printing Library
St Bride's Institute, Bride Lane, EC4
Telephone: 020 7353 460
Transport: Blackfriars or Aldwych LU
Open: Mon-Fri 9.30am-5.30pm
Admission free
Wheelchair access (telephone for details)

Dr Johnson's House
17 Gough Square, EC4
Telephone: 020 7353 3745
Transport: Chancery Lane, Aldwich or
Blackfriars LU
Open: Mon-Sat 11am-5pm
(Oct to April),
Mon-Sat 11am-5.30pm (May-Sept)
Admission charge, concessions available
Wheelchair access (telephone for details)

St Dunstan's in the West
Bride Lane, EC4
Open: Tues 10am-2pm, Sat 2pm-6pm
& Sun 9am-2pm
Transport: Blackfriars or Aldwych LU
Admission free

Prince Henry's Room
17 Fleet Street, EC4
Open: Mon-Sat 11am-2pm
Telephone: 020 7953 4522
Transport: Temple or Aldwych LU
Admission free
Wheelchair access (telephone for details)

Middle Temple
Middle Temple Lane, EC4
Open: Mon-Fri 10am-12pm & 3pm-4pm
Telephone: 020 7427 4800
Transport: Temple or Aldwych LU
Wheelchair access (telephone for details)

Inner Temple
Middle Temple Lane, EC4
Transport: Temple or Aldwych LU
Open: Wed-Fri 10am-4pm, Sun
12.30pm-4pm

Strand Walk

1. Royal Courts of Justice
2. St Clement Danes
3. 'Roman Bath'
4. St Mary-le-Strand
5. Somerset House
   Courtauld Institute of Art
   Courtauld Institute Gallery
   Gilbert Collection
   Hermitage Rooms
6. King's College London
7. Australia House
8. Bush House
9. India House
10. Savoy Chapel
11. 6–10 Adam St
12. Royal Society of Arts

This is a particularly good walk on a wet day as there are lots of buildings to disappear into. We start this walk where the Fleet Street Walk finished, at the Temple Bar. We are now out of the City of London and Fleet Street has become the Strand. The street is named so because until the 19th century and the embankment of the river Thames, the Strand was very close to the river. The first building we stop at is the **Royal Courts of Justice (1)** on the north side of the road (stand with your back to the Temple Bar – the monument with the griffin on the top – and the building will be on your right).

The Royal Courts of Justice, often referred to as the 'Law Courts', stand on a seven acre site which was cleared of its festering slum-dwellings in the mid 19th century to make way for a new Court of Justice. The Courts deal with civil cases, that is not criminal cases which are heard at the Old Bailey (see p.136).

The Royal Courts were conceived in the wake of the success of the Parliament building in Westminster, with the consequence that every submitting architect put forward plans in the Gothic Revival style. The design of George Edward Street (1824-81) was chosen and work began in 1871. Street had previously built many churches and looking at the Royal Courts of Justice one could be forgiven for thinking the building was actually a cathedral! By the time the construction was underway Gothic Revival was going out of fashion and on its completion the reception the building received was cool to say the least. This is particularly sad given that the architect died the year before it was finished – the stress of the project was said to have been a large contributory factor in Street's relatively early death.

The façade, so familiar as the background to reports from the Courts on television news programmes, is complicated: bay after bay of free design with pinnacles and towers stretching up and a rose window over the main entrance. The whole is brick built (an estimated 35 million were used) faced in Portland stone, and contains one thousand separate rooms, eighty-eight of them court rooms, served by an estimated 3.5 miles of corridors. Immense care was taken over detailing, such as the metal work on the exterior, and this attention to detail extends to the interior.

The public is allowed into the court rooms to watch proceedings, and there is a small exhibition of legal dress. A good diversion from the walk is just to wander in and admire the splendour of Street's work (see p.219 for more details).

We now walk on to the church whose rear can be seen as we leave the Court. This is **St Clement Danes (2)**, one of the two small churches which sit on traffic islands in the middle of the Strand's heavy traffic, and whose name derives from the Danish settlers who came to the area in the 9th century.

The present church was built by Sir Christopher Wren in 1680-82, with additions to the tower and the provision of a spire by James Gibbs in 1719 but the extensive restoration work was carried out in 1955 by Anthony Lloyd, who faithfully reproduced Wren's beautiful interior.

If the church is open and you have time, do go in and look at the plasterwork, particularly that on the barrel-vaulted ceiling and at the east end of the church. There is also a very good dark stained wooden gallery. This is the place to contemplate the immense task of the renovator, in this case Anthony Lloyd studied photographs and drawings to re-create Wren's church and his work here is considered to be his most successful.

In 1958 the church was adopted by the Royal Air Force, hence the proliferation of RAF badges and rolls of honour (see p.219 for more details).

On leaving St Clement Danes cross to the south side of the Strand and proceed west. Make your way to **Surrey Street**, just off the Strand, and look for the entrance to the **'Roman Bath' (3)**, which will have a National Trust sign pointing you in the right direction.

Whilst known as a 'Roman Bath', there is certainly nothing to suggest that it is anything of the sort; the bricks are not Roman and there is no evidence of Roman settlement in the area. However, this was the site of a grand house owned by Thomas Howard, Lord Arundel (1586-1646). He had a passion for paintings, antiquities and travel and had been in Rome during the excavation of the Forum, so it is quite feasible that he would have returned with the idea of a Roman bath, perhaps with genuine decorations. The surrounding street names, Arundel and Surrey (he was also Earl of Surrey) commemorate the site's history. Dickens mentions this bath in his novel 'David Copperfield'. The 'Roman Bath' can be viewed through the window from the pathway at any time.

Back to the Strand and we can now cross the road to the other church that sits in the middle of the road. This is the church of **St Mary-le-Strand (4)**, details of which can be found on p.85.

Return once more to the south side of the Strand to **Somerset House (5)**. This was the site of a palace built 1547-52 by Edward Seymour, Duke of Somerset who foolishly fell out with his monarch Henry VIII and was duly executed in 1552 and the building passed into royal hands. The palace was the domain of the monarch's consort until

the reign of George III and Queen Charlotte, who preferred Buckingham House. The buildings were demolished in 1775 and the architect William Chambers set about designing the first purpose-built office block in Europe. The offices were used for the Navy Board and the newly-formed Royal Academy of Arts and the Society of Antiquaries. Over the intervening years the buildings also housed the Registry of Births, Deaths and Marriages and the head office of the Inland Revenue.

Completed first were the buildings we come to first, those that face the Strand. As you pass through the entrance arch the building to your left is the **Courtauld Institute of Art** and, apart from those attending lectures or wishing to use one of the two art libraries, is not open to the public. The building to your right is the **Courtauld Institute Gallery**.

The Courtauld Gallery moved to Somerset House in 1990 and occupies rooms which were once home to the Royal Academy of Arts. Here is one of the best collections of art anywhere in Europe, particularly strong in major works by the Impressionists and Post-Impressionists – Degas, Cézanne, Manet, Renoir, Gauguin, Van Gogh and more. Other periods are well represented in the collection, particularly early Flemish and Italian painting (for more details see p.219).

After the Gallery continue further into the courtyard of Somerset House – looking to your left through a gap in the buildings you will see the rear of **King's College London (6)** and the building designed by Robert Smirke in 1829. So much better than the unfortunate 1960's front of the College which faces the Strand.

The courtyard of Somerset House used to be a car park for the Inland Revenue but has been transformed into a new space for cultural events.

Now known as **Fountain Court**, its new name is not misleading as there is indeed a charming group of fountains which magically turn into a skating rink during the winter months.

The rest of Somerset House is ahead of you and what was once the Navy Board building now houses two more collections, one of which is the **Gilbert Collection**. One of London's newest museums this displays the life-long collection of Sir Arthur Gilbert, who made his vast wealth from real-estate and making evening gowns! Pieces range from exquisite little jewelled boxes to a lavish silver 'howdah' which is a seat one places on an elephant in order to ride it and a pair of wrought-iron gates commissioned by Catherine the Great (see p.219 for details).

The other collection in this south block is the **Hermitage Rooms** which house a changing exhibition of pieces from the vast State Hermitage Museum in St Petersburg. These five rooms, opened to the public in 2001, are very plush with splendid chandeliers (see p.219 for details).

Bush House

It is possible to walk through the south buildings of Somerset House and out onto the **River Terrace**, where you can take coffee, lunch, afternoon tea or supper during the summer months. A steel and glass walkway connects to Waterloo Bridge here.

Its interesting to remember that until the 19th century and the embankment of the Thames, the river lapped against the terrace immediately below the building. Can you see where boats would have sailed into the basement of Somerset House? This is still called the Water Gate.

After looking around William Chamber's magnificent neo-classical complex, we rejoin the Strand. Next stop on our walk are three of the buildings that languish between the Strand and Aldwych and are so often passed by when travelling by car or bus. All three buildings are of the early 20th century and were built as part of a town-planning scheme by the London County Council, rather in the mood of Nash and his Regent Street plan, but not nearly so ambitious. Slum dwellings were cleared and the tenants re-housed in blocks of flats on Drury Lane. Aldwych was to be the culmination of the widening and re-building of Kingsway and the architecture had to be fairly monumental. Unfortunately, as a group the buildings look rather over-the-top, some might even say vulgar. It is most likely you will not be able to enter the buildings for security reasons, but the exteriors of Australia House and Bush House are worth looking at and are best viewed from the north side.

The first building of the group is **Australia House (7)** and is on the extreme right of the group when you are looking at them with your back to Somerset House.

Australia House is the oldest of the trio, built 1913-18 and designed by Marshall Mackenzie and was the first in a series of large buildings in London associated with Commonwealth countries such as India House nearby and South Africa House in Trafalgar Square (see Whitehall Walk p.220). Fittingly for a High Commission the building is very grand in a Beaux Arts-ish design.

Some excellent sculpture is incorporated within the building, as with all the buildings in this group. To the left and right of the main entrance is the monumentally-sized 'Awakening of Australia' and 'Prosperity of Australia' by Harold Parker, a British born, Australian trained sculptor of note. Above and central to the entrance is a sculpture in a heroic vein, a bronze male nude wearing just a cloak and crown with four horses entitled 'Phoebus Driving the Horses of the Sun' by Australian-born Bertram Mackennal. All the sculpture dates from the early 20th century.

The centre building, **Bush House (8)**, designed by the New York architects Helme and Corbett in 1920-23, was named for its first owner Irving T Bush, an American. His vision was that the building would be a large, grand show-case for manufactured goods and the interior decoration reflects this, with ample application of marble. Alas the economic climate changed and the luxury goods market that Bush had his sights set on faltered so the building was bought by the Church of Wales. They in turn sold it to the Post Office Pensions fund who lease it to the British Broadcasting Corporation and since 1940 it has been the home of the BBC's World Service.

The building is big and bold with two huge columns and two male figures, both twelve feet tall representing England and America each with an outstretched hand holding a torch between them in the arched area above. Bush House looks very impressive from Kingsway during the evening when the façade is illuminated.

India House (9), by Sir Herbert Baker and Alexander Scott, was built in 1928-30 and its rather forgettable exterior belies its wonderful interior, mainly executed by Indian artists. If you are ever fortunate enough to be invited to tea by the Indian High Commissioner, do accept and take in the lovely carved jali-type open work decoration.

Cross back over the road to the south (Somerset House) side and negotiate the traffic at Lancaster Place to continue along the Strand. On your right you will find **Savoy Street** and from there you will find **Savoy Hill** which is the location for the **Savoy Chapel (10)**.

This very simple chapel dates back to the Savoy Palace of John of Gaunt, who was the younger son of Henry III and was born in Ghent (hence 'Gaunt'). The palace was razed to the ground during the Peasants' Revolt of 1381.

The present building dates back to the early 16th century but a fire in the 18th century destroyed much of the original decoration, which has since been reconstructed. Note the nice heraldic details. In 1936 this became the chapel of the Royal Victorian Order and is now a private chapel of the present Queen. However visitors are most welcome to this relatively unknown little gem (for details see below).

Further west along the Strand you will come across Adam Street which has several excellent examples of Robert Adam's work (see p.93 for further details) **(11)**. Another good example of his work is to be found just around the corner at the **Royal Society of Arts (12)** (see p.93 for further details).

This concludes our walk but if you would like to look at some more architecture, and you have the energy, you could continue west along the Strand to Trafalgar Square which is easy to find with Nelson's Column at its centre. Now you are ready to start the 'Whitehall Walk' (see p.220).

More Information:

Royal Courts of Justice
Strand, WC2
Telephone: 020 7947 6000
Transport: Temple LU
Open: Mon-Fri 9.30am-4pm
(closed public holidays)
Telephone for details of wheelchair access

St Clement Danes
Strand, WC2
Transport: Temple LU
Open: daily 8am-4.30pm,
service on Sunday at 11am

The Courtauld Gallery
Somerset House, Strand, WC2
Telephone: 020 7848 2646
Transport: Temple or Covent Garden LU
Open: Mon-Sat 10am-6pm,
Sun 2pm-6pm
Admission charge, concessions available
Free entry for visitors Mon 10am-2pm
(this does not apply on Bank Holidays)
and after 5pm daily
Telephone for details of wheelchair access

Gilbert Collection
Somerset House, Strand, WC2
Telephone: 020 7845 4600
Transport: Temple or Covent Garden LU
Open: Mon-Sat 10am-6pm,
Sun 2pm-6pm
Admission charges apply
Telephone for details of wheelchair access

The Hermitage Rooms
Somerset House, Strand, WC2
Telephone: 020 7845 4600
Transport: Temple or Covent Garden LU
Open: Mon-Sat 10am-6pm,
Sun 2pm-6pm
Admission charges apply,
Telephone for details of wheelchair access

The Savoy Chapel
Savoy Hill, Strand, WC2
Telephone:020 7836 7221
Open: Tues-Fri 11.30am-3.30pm,
service on Sunday at 11am
(closed during August and September)
Telephone for details of wheelchair access.

Whitehall Walk

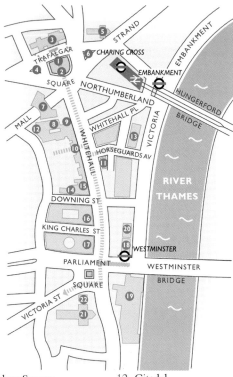

FThis walk starts and finishes at two world famous landmarks, Nelson's Column and the Houses of Parliament respectively and takes in fine examples of work by some of the best architects that Britain has produced. If started early enough in the day, the walk could culminate in a visit to Westminster Abbey.

Trafalgar Square (1) The recent re-routing of traffic from the north side of the square has given London an impressive new public space with a new café and plenty of places to sit and contemplate the surrounding buildings. The most famous landmark at the heart of the square is **Nelson's Column (2)**. This monument together with the naming of the square commemorates the British naval victory over the French at the Battle of Trafalgar on 21 October 1805. However it was forty years after the event before it was decided to build some sort of memorial to the occasion and the man.

The site on which Trafalgar Square now stands has a long history of use. From at least the early 13th century it had been the Royal Mews; mews being a corruption of the French verb 'muer' meaning to moult, being the place where royal hawks were confined whilst moulting their feathers. During the 14th century the area was part of a pleasure garden and from the time of Elizabeth I it was the home of the royal stables. William Kent (1685-1748), architect responsible for Horse Guards Parade, built the Crown Stables here in 1732. The plot became vacant when the stables were re-located to Buckingham Palace since when it was decided that it should become a public area, open to all.

The first square on this site had been designed and built by John Nash in the 1820s but this was remodelled in the 1840s by Charles Barry when it was decided to honour Nelson and his victory. The memorial to Nelson is probably better appreciated from a distance, being 185 feet in the air, but is nonetheless impressive from any angle! The statue of Nelson itself stands at 17 feet, weighs 18 tons and was designed by E H Baily. The Corinthian column on which the statue stands is by William Railton. The lions who lie at the bottom of the column are by Sir Edwin Landseer, who was one of Queen Victoria's favourite artists. The whole project was completed in 1868.

Trafalgar Square

To the north of the Square stands the **National Gallery (3)** built by William Wilkins between 1832-38, and to which the newly pedestrianised north terrace provides direct access. Built to house the nation's blossoming collection of publicly-owned art, it now ranks alongside the Louvre, the Prado and the Uffizi as one of the world's great art collections. Much criticism has been levelled at Wilkins' design, whose brief was to produce a crowning effect for the square, in that the building was seen to lack impact. Wilkins favoured, whenever possible, keeping his design 'pure' in the classical sense and perhaps lacked the ability to assimilate and to synthesise. The architect's decision to place a dome over the portico, with its eight columns, and turrets over the outer wings, whose Ionic columns came from King George IV's Carlton House in Pall Mall, attracted much derision. One critic likened the effect to a clock and two vases on a mantelpiece – but of less use! Wilkins also designed University College, in Gower Street in a similar classical fashion.

As the collection grew so the building has been extended, three times during the 19th century, twice in the early 20th, and a further addition at the rear of the building added in the 1970s. However the latest extension is the very substantial 'Sainsbury Wing', designed by the architectural partnership of Venturi, Rauch and Scott Brown, built between 1987-91. The rather sober exterior, incorporates echoes of Wilkins' Corinthian orders but takes nothing away from the main buildings façade. The rather restrained and muted galleries inside are the perfect foil for the highly coloured collection of Italian and Northern European early Renaissance paintings displayed here.

Standing in Trafalgar Square with your back to the National Gallery you will find to your right **Canada House (4)**, built by Robert Smirke between 1822-25 (see also the entry for British Museum p.98). This building was originally shared between the Royal College of Physicians and the Union Club. Smirke was a dedicated Greek Revivalist and this style is reflected in the unified Grecian Ionic order of this building. In 1924 the interior and some of the exterior was remodelled for the Canadian High Commission.

Still with your back to the National Gallery, to your left is the unmistakable frontage of James Gibb's church of **St Martin-in-the-Fields (5)**. Unmistakable that is, unless you live in parts of Ireland or Northern America where this was the prototype for 18th and 19th century church building. Constructed under the New Churches Act of 1711,

Gibb took the unusual step of placing a tower and steeple almost over the portico. The interior is really not to be missed – very Wrenesque with huge columns and a balcony to three sides. Its nave is noticeably wide but not overly tall and surmounted by an interesting barrel vaulted ceiling. The interior was renovated and altered in 1887 by Sir Arthur Blomfield.

One famous incumbent vicar of St Martin's was Dick Sheppard, who later became Dean of Canterbury Cathedral. Whilst at St Martin's he opened the crypt as a retreat for homeless soldiers returning from the 1914-18 war and thereafter for anyone homeless. In 1924 he also conducted from here the first church service to be broadcast on the radio. Concerts are performed at St Martin's on a regular basis and the crypt has a very good café and shop.

Still to your left, but further down from St Martin's is **South Africa House** (1935) **(6)** by Sir Herbert Baker. Designed to be in keeping with the National Gallery and St Martin's – its porticoes have been placed at the same level as Gibb's church.

Walk down through Trafalgar Square, taking in the wonderful view stretching away down Whitehall towards the Houses of Parliament as you do so, and on reaching Whitehall to your right you will see **Admiralty Arch** **(7)** designed by the respected architect Sir Aston Webb in 1908-11. The arch is part of a memorial to Queen Victoria (the other part being her statue outside Buckingham Palace). The building is in fact three archways, all of equal height, with offices on either side, and makes a pleasing entrance to the Mall.

Continue along on the right hand side of Whitehall and you will find yourself outside **Admiralty House (8)** built 1786-88 by S P Cockerell. Two and a half storeys tall, its most redeeming feature is its interior – which is sadly not open to the public. The house has been home to the First Lords of the Admiralty of whom Earl Grey (1806) of tea fame and Winston Churchill (1911-15 and 1939-40) are but two. Built as an extension to the Admiralty (built 1722-6 by Thomas Ripley) next door, the rear of this whole complex can be viewed from Horse Guards Parade slightly further down Whitehall. In front of these buildings, facing Whitehall, is Robert Adam's **Admiralty Screen (9)** made in 1760-61 when Whitehall was subject to a road-widening scheme.

This is the first work Adam completed in London on his return from an extensive trip to Rome. The row of ten Tuscan columns against a blank wall hides the rather dour buildings behind and give a glimpse of Adam's blossoming genius.

Just a little further down Whitehall you will come to two finely – dressed mounted guards (members of the House-hold Cavalry the Life Guards or the Blues and Royals) and usually surrounded by picture-snapping tourists! You have arrived at **Horse Guards Parade (10)**. This was at one time the site of the tiltyard of Whitehall Palace, where in 1540 Henry VIII presided over a huge tournament with knights jour-neying from all parts of Europe to attend. In 1650 a guardhouse was erected but after much enlargement and re-building, finally fell into decay. It was decided the whole building needed re-designing and this was done by William Kent in 1748. Construction was undertaken after Kent's death and was finished in 1760. The result is not only one of the best and most accessible buildings in Whitehall, but perhaps one of the finest examples of Georgian architecture in Britain. In contrast to Inigo Jones's flat-fronted **Banqueting House** (see later), Kent manages to create a quite dramatic Palladian-inspired building, using projection and recession and without a single column in sight! The building is surmounted by a cupola containing a clock, to which the 18th century Londoner looked for the correct time. Note that there appears to be a black circle around the Roman numeral II (two o'clock) which is prob-ably a reference to the time at which King Charles I was executed just across the street, outside the Banqueting House some one hundred years earlier in 1649.

Walking through the arches of the building you will arrive at the **Horse Guards parade ground**, which leads on to the Mall and St James's Park. It is here in the parade ground that the Trooping the Colour takes place every year in cele-bration of the Queen's official birthday on 10 June. The rather curious, creeper-clad building at the north-west corner of the parade ground is the **Citadel (12)**. Built in 1939 from blocks of compressed pebble and flint, it is the entrance to a series of deep underground shelters designed to house the country's political leaders during the air raids of the Second World War. It seems far too modern for its surroundings and yet it is a strangely attractive building and one of the few remaining examples of its type.

Return to Whitehall, and with your back to William Kent's magnificent building, almost directly opposite is Horse Guards Avenue. This short thoroughfare leads to **Whitehall Court (13)** which, built by Archer and Green and completed in 1887, is an eight-storey block of very superior flats, faced with Portland stone in an almost French Renaissance style.

Back on Whitehall stands the magnificent **Banqueting House (11)**. This building formed just a small part of a complex of buildings known as Whitehall Palace, from which the road and indeed the whole area, takes its name. The story of Whitehall starts in 1514 when Cardinal Wolsey, then Archbishop of York, rebuilt the existing London house of the Archbishopric known as York Place. He built York Place in the grandest manner and in the latest fashion, but later fell foul of the Henry VIII being dismissed in 1529. Henry lost no time in occupying York Place. The building was renamed Whitehall Palace and became the monarch's principal London residence until William III (1650-1702). Henry acquired the land roundabout (what is now Horse Guards Parade) and had a tiltyard, four tennis courts and a cockpit built – truly a 16th century leisure complex!

Banqueting House, Inigo Jones's addition to Whitehall Palace, was finished in 1622 in the reign of James I and may have been the intended start of an improvement plan for the whole site, but nothing further was built. Whatever architectural merit the building exudes (see p.38 for further details), its popular fame rests on its association with the execution of Charles I.

On the morning of Saturday 27th January 1649 in Westminster Hall, the clerk of the court read to the King his fate that 'this court doth adjudge that he the said Charles Stuart…shall be put to death by severing his head from his body'. The King was not allowed to speak but taken back to Whitehall and later the same day transferred to St James's Palace. Over the next two days workmen were busy setting up the scaffold against the walls of the north side of the Banqueting House facing Whitehall, and the building which epitomised the spirit of the Stuarts, with flamboyant masques and sumptuously painted ceiling, was now to be the backdrop for the dynasty's darkest hour. The King was executed at noon on January 30th, having been led from the private chambers through the hall of the Banqueting House and on to the scaffold via one of the large windows, which had been removed for the purpose. Charles won sympathy by his display of dignity at his trial and execution.

On 5th January 1698 Whitehall succumbed to a terrible fire which destroyed practically all the Palace except the Banqueting Hall which miraculously escaped. The Court moved to St James's (see p.33) and Whitehall was never re-built.

Proceed south along Whitehall and on the same side of the road as Horse Guards Parade we arrive at the security gates that prevent entry to **Downing Street (14)**, the official London residence and office of the Prime Minister (Number 10) and of the Chancellor of the Exchequer (Number 11). If you are able to stop and peer through the gate note the modest Georgian façade of number 10 which is misleading as the original house now connects with a much larger and grander house, which looks onto the Horse Guards parade ground. Downing Street dates from the late 17th century when it was developed by Sir George Downing, a speculative builder, after whom the street was named. Between 1766 and 1774 many alterations were made, but the street's façade has changed little since then. Number 10 was gifted to the country's first 'Prime minister' Sir Robert Walpole, by King George II in 1732.

In Whitehall on either side of Downing Street are government offices dating from the 19th century. To the north, that is the side closest to Trafalgar Square, stand the **Privy Council Chambers (15)** designed by Sir Charles Barry and built between 1844-5. On the south of Downing Street is the **Foreign and Commonwealth Office (16)**, designed by Sir George Gilbert Scott and constructed between 1862-75. The conception and birth of this building is steeped in controversy, an episode in the history of London architecture known as 'the Battle of the Styles'. Changes in government during the planning meant Gilbert Scott had to modify his plans for a Gothic construction to something more Italian. The final result, as we can see, is every inch a neo-Renaissance palace that would not look out of place in Florence!

In the centre of the busy Whitehall roadway at this point is the Cenotaph, a word that means 'empty tomb'. This is the national memorial to those who lost their lives in both World Wars and was originally a simple wooden affair used as the focus of the 1919 victory parade. The Portland stone Cenotaph we see now was designed by the architect Edwin Lutyens and was in place by 1920.

Continuing towards Parliament Square, the very last buildings on this side of Whitehall are the **New Government Offices (17)**, which primarily house HM Treasury. Designed in 1898 by J M Brydon in a Neo-Baroque style these were finally completed in 1915. The basement of this building contains the **Cabinet War Rooms** used by Winston Churchill during the 1939-45 war. These once top secret rooms have been preserved in their original state since 1948 and are now open to the public.

In our journey down Whitehall we have arrived at Bridge Street and if you look to your left you will see **Portcullis House (18)**. Completed in 2001 this building is the outcome of a very long, drawn-out process to consider development of the area. Michael Hopkins and Partners were commissioned to design office and committee room accommodation for Parliament in 1989, the same year it was mooted that an extension of the Jubilee line of the London Underground should be routed to include a station at Westminster. The need for total security of the Houses of Parliament ruled out the station being placed below Parliament, so it was incorporated into Michael Hopkins and Partners

brief for the office site, work on which started in early 1994. Portcullis House not only had to fit in with the Gothicised-Classicism of the **Houses of Parliament (19)** over the road (see p.110) but also Norman Shaw's much admired **Scotland Yard (20)** building next door. Indeed the new building strongly echoes the sloping roof and tall chimneys of Shaw's building.

Portcullis House, and Scotland Yard House, which is also used as Parliamentary offices, can accommodate 450 Members of Parliament and their administrative staff. Within the new building there are seven Select Committee rooms, two TV interview studios, a post office, café and eight meeting rooms arranged on seven floors around a central courtyard. The building is highly efficient and uses only approximately one third of the fuel of conventionally air-conditioned offices, being heated by recycled exhaust heat from the system and cooled by groundwater from deep bore holes. The cost of the building was a cool £231 million.

Westminster Underground (21) station below Portcullis House is a modern miracle of engineering. Its design had to take into consideration the existing District and Circle lines (which had to remain open and fully

Portcullis House

operational during the building work); care had to be taken with regard to the foundations of the nearby Houses of Parliament and Westminster Bridge; provision had to be made for the six massive column foundations of Portcullis House above. The result is a bold statement which celebrates these engineering feats – a 130 feet deep, 72 feet wide space which contains a series of intersecting escalators capped with a glass roof. The decoration is subdued, granite grey and steel. A fantastic piece of architecture!

The walk can end here but if time permits the delights of **Westminster Abbey (22)** can be explored (p.16) passing the **Church of St Margaret (23)** (see p.32) and the **Houses of Parliament** (see p.110) on the way. Note the bust of Charles I placed on the church wall, he gazes over towards the Houses of Parliament and the statue of Oliver Cromwell in front, with his head bowed.

John Nash Walk part 1
John Nash and the Via Triumphalis – from Regent's Park to Park Cresent

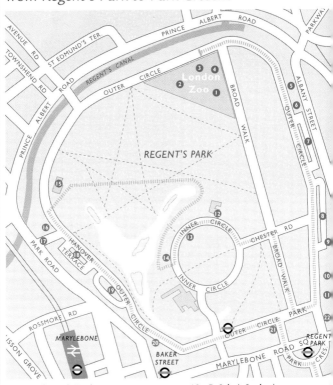

1. Zoological Gardens
2. The Round House (part of Zoo)
3. The Penguin Pool (part of Zoo)
4. Snowdon Aviary (part of Zoo)
5. Gloucester Lodge & Gloucester Gate
6. Danish Church
7. Cumberland Terrace
8. Chester Terrace
9. Chester Gate
10. Cambridge Gate
11. Royal College of Physicians
12. St John's Lodge★
13. Open Air Theatre★
14. The Holme★
15. Winfield House★
16. London Central Mosque
17. Hanover Gate
18. Hanover Terrace
19. Sussex Place
20. Cornwall Terrace
21. Ulster Place
22. Park Square (number18)
(★ No access / limited view)

This route takes you from Regent's Park down through the heart of the West End to the monarch's residence, Buckingham Palace. Due to the length of the walk it has been divided into two maps, which could be walked over several days. The time taken to cover both maps will depend very much on the temptations the walker gives into en route. Distractions such as the zoo, the Royal Institute of British Architects' bookshop, fashion stores, cafés and restaurants may add an hour or three to the time taken! The buildings around Regents Park's inner circle are difficult to see and can easily be missed if time is short.

The 550 acres of Regent's Park at one time formed a small part of a huge forest and was the property of the Abbess of Barking. At the dissolution of the monasteries in the 16th century the land was appropriated by the Crown and used as a hunting ground; Elizabeth I entertained the Duke of Anjou here in 1582. After the execution of Charles I in 1649 the land was sold only to be handed back to the Crown at the Restoration in 1660. Gradually most of the sixteen thousand trees were felled to make way for the farms that would flourish here for the next two hundred years or so. This bucolic scene lasted until 1811 when the farm leases became due for renewal and it was seen that the land could be developed for prestigious housing, enhancing the area and adding to the royal coffers.

The architect chosen to oversee the whole project was **John Nash** (1752-1835), a favourite with the Prince Regent after whom the park was named. Nash's grand design, the only one London has ever had, started to the north of Regent's Park with a new canal which linked London to the Midlands; fifty-six large houses within the park and a triumphal way' down to Carlton House, the home of the Prince Regent, then on to Bloomsbury and the British Museum, then under construction. Most of the plan did not materialise, with other events intervening such as the Prince Regent's ascension to the throne in 1820 as George IV and his decision that time, effort and money should be spent on providing a grand palace in which he could reside.

Regent's Park

As we will see as we walk on, Nash took inspiration for the circuses and curves for his design from the naturally round boundary of this park, which today is just under 500 acres in total area. It is quite easy to spend a whole day here, just wandering and watching, as there always seems to be something going on! Conversely, if you just want some quiet, the park can provide that too.

Before Nash suggested a change of name to honour the Prince Regent, the area had been called Marylebone Park, that is 'place by St Mary's stream' ('bone' being a corruption of burna meaning stream or water). At the top of the park, on the north edge, is the **Zoological Gardens (1)** (Regent's Park Zoo). The Zoological Society was founded in 1824 and four years later the first 'Zoo' in the world was opened to the public, with the aim of encouraging an interest in the scientific study of animals. Set in a 20 acre site the layout is still, more or less, in its original form as set out by the eminent architect Decimus Burton, who also designed the first house in the park, The Holme (see p.235). Also to his design are – the East Tunnel, the Clock Tower, Ravens Aviary, the West Tunnel and the original Giraffe House, all of which are Grade II listed.

The Round House (2), originally the Gorilla House, of 1932-33 was one of the first buildings in the Modernist style in Britain. Its design-ers, from the innovative architectural team known as Tecton, were led by the brilliant Berthold Lubetkin and was so successful that it was followed in 1934 by a commission for a new **Penguin Pool (3)**. Now an icon of modern architecture, the Penguin Pool has a series of inter-locking ramps and is so stark and minimalist that it could be easily taken for a piece of constructivist sculpture, were it not for the presence of the penguins! So iconic is Lubetkin's work considered to be that both the Round House and the Penguin Pool are Grade I listed.

Look out for the **Snowdon Aviary (4)** built 1962-64 and designed by architects Cedric Price and Frank Newby with Tony Armstrong-Jones (now Lord Snowdon) the society photographer who was once married to the late Princess Margaret. The aviary is a huge aluminium wire tetrahedron cage where the birds are free to fly and which one walks through to observe them. This construction proved that even aviaries could be sexy in London's 'Swinging Sixties'! (For details on London Zoo see p.249)

The Outer Circle
- on leaving the Zoo take the **Broad Walk** southwards through the park. On your left you will see **Gloucester Lodge and Gloucester Gate (5)**, our first encounter, on this walk, with the architecture of John Nash. The Lodge is a pleasingly symmetrical house with a large portico with fluted Ionic half columns. Gloucester Gate, the most northerly of Nash's eleven terraces, sports huge Ionic pilasters (these are the flat representations of a classical column usually placed against a wall). Both buildings date from 1827.

Cumberland Terrace

Next to these buildings, to the south, is the stock brick church of St Katherine built in 1826 by Ambrose Poynter, an early example of the Gothic Revival movement, a style which grew in popularity in Britain until about 1870. The church was built as the chapel of the Royal Foundation of St Katherine's when a move from its site next to the Tower of London was necessitated by the construction of St Katherine's Dock. St Katherine's was the only religious house to survive the dissolution of the monasteries in the 16th century. After World War II St Katherine's moved to another new site in Shadwell, east London and this church is now used as the **Danish Church (6)**.

We now come to perhaps the grandest and the most flamboyant of all Nash's terraces, **Cumberland Terrace (7)**. Built 1826-27 it is 800 feet long, an essay in symmetry with the centre portion projecting forward and having ten great Ionic columns and an enormous pediment filled with sculpture. It looks every inch a palace rather than a set of apartments. If you only have time to look at one of Nash's buildings, this is probably the best example.

Further on is **Chester Terrace (8)**, again by Nash, dating from 1825. This building has the longest unbroken terrace of all, with ninety-nine bays in a complicated but symmetrical system of division, around a central section of seven bays and with a similar number of bays at each end, (interspersed with the odd huge Corinthian column for decoration). Contemporary complaints were that Nash's workmanship was shoddy and rumours of rubble behind the stucco and other slapdash practices prevailed. Indeed this building was in such a bad state of repair that demolition was seriously contemplated after World War II. **Chester Gate (9)** is the two storey building here, again by Nash and with Doric detailing.

The next building we come to is faced in Bath stone, so its skin looks rather different to Nash's stuccoed houses. This is **Cambridge Gate (10)**, built in 1875 by Archer and Green on the site of Decimus Burton's 'Colosseum'. The Colosseum was a huge rotunda, which once housed a panorama of London's buildings sketched by a 'Mr Horner', who had spent weeks recording the capital's architecture for the project. The initial popularity of the attraction waned and the building was closed and demolished to be replaced by the current grand building.

We complete this side of the park with a look at the **Royal College of Physicians (11)**, designed and built 1961-64 by Sir Denys Lasdun. Pevsner called this 'one of the most distinguished buildings of the decade', praise indeed from this most fastidious of architectural arbiters. The College moved here from its previous premises in Canada House, Trafalgar Square (see Whitehall Walk p.220). Lasdun's building is made from concrete with white mosaic tiling for the façade and brick elsewhere, the overall shape being reminiscent of Lasdun's slightly later work at the National Theatre. Not usually open to the public the College is normally part of the 'Open House' scheme (see p.297).

We are now going to look at some of the buildings within the Park and then briefly examine the other side of the Outer Circle. If you wish to move on please skip this next section and rejoin at **Park Crescent**.

Buildings within the Park

Nash's plan to build fifty-six large villas within their own substantial gardens was, mercifully, not fulfilled and only eight were actually built. One of these is **St John's Lodge (12)**, the large white house situated between Broad Walk and the Inner Circle (before reaching Chester Road). It was started in 1818 by John Raffield, who had been working with the Adam brothers, but who appears to have done nothing else in London. St John's was originally the gatehouse for the Inner Circle but has been altered many times over the years.

The **Inner Circle** was to have been a circus of terraces, much like the Outer Circle but this plan was felt to be too overwhelming. The land here was leased in 1839 to the Royal Botanic Society, and from 1932 made into a public garden in which the **Open Air Theatre (13)** was built. The Theatre is only open during the summer months and is perhaps the most magical of places to see a musical or a play. This is especially so for Shakespeare and particularly his 'A Midsummer Nights Dream', with the rustling trees of the park providing a perfect backdrop for the play (telephone 020 7935 5756 for details).

From the Inner Circle, walking west towards the Boating Lake we arrive **at The Holme (14)**; the first villa to be built in the Park. Constructed in 1816-18 by the 18-year old Decimus Burton, for his father, the villa exhibits a central Corinthian portico supported by four columns. The house is in an idyllic spot with gently sloping gardens looking towards the lake. The wings were added in 1911 and the house has received substantial renovation in recent years. The house is now privately owned and with security gates and a well planted garden is very difficult to see from anywhere in the park.

Walking north from The Holme, past the lakes and looking towards the west side of the Outer Circle you may see **Winfield House (15)**, dating from 1937, in brick with stone dressings. The house is used as the residence of the United States Ambassador. Beyond this house you will see the unmistakable outline of the **London Central Mosque (16)** and Islamic Cultural Centre. Designed by

Sir Frederick Gibberd and Partners, 1972-78 this building is an exciting one, if only because it lends a certain exoticism to the Nash terraces with its gleaming copper dome and minaret. The main hall of the mosque is designed to accommodate 1,800 people (for more information see p.249).

In the shadow of the Mosque sits **Hanover Gate (17)**, a small octagonal lodge house with a pitched roof and a sweet central chimney stack, forming a traffic island and marking the western entrance to the park. Designed by Nash 1822-23 it had additions made by Lutyens in 1909

Slightly further south is **Hanover Terrace (18)**. Again by Nash and built 1822-23 the Terrace is one of the shorter, 460 feet in length with four Doric columns at each end and six at the centre. Further south is **Sussex Place (19)** and here

Nash adds to a grand terrace of some 650 feet in length, steep-sided octagonal domes – which, as Pevsner notes, are most 'unclassical'.

The last terrace we come to is **Cornwall Terrace (20)**, but the first, in fact, to be built in 1821. Although attributed to Nash and Decimus Burton, the design was probably more the latter's work. Burton was the precocious pupil of George Maddox (1760-1843), noted more as architectural drawing master than for any notable projects. The young Burton was also a pupil at the Royal Academy School, where his professor was John Soane.

Decimus Burton was the tenth son of James Burton (also known as James Haliburton), a successful speculative builder and wealthy enough to have a grand London house (see The Holme, p.235) and a large country house in Tonbridge. Burton senior was employed extensively by John Nash and much of what will be seen on this walk is his building work. For Decimus, his father's work with Nash was a golden opportunity to obtain further commissions for himself amongst which were the Athenaeum Club, Waterloo Place (see p.244) and the Ionic Screen at Hyde Park of 1823-27. Some of his most notable work was with glass and iron such as conservatories at the Botanical Garden in Regent's Park (now demolished) and the fabulous Palm House (built 1844-48) still very much in use at Kew. These pre-dated Paxton's Crystal Palace by at least three years (see p.109).

Making our way to the **Ulster Place (21)** exit of Regent's Park, this terrace, named for George IV's younger brother, Frederick, Earl of Ulster and Duke of York, is an unusual Nash design in that it is devoid of columns and pilasters. However each of the end two bays has bay windows for emphasis.

In **Park Square (22)**, just before crossing the busy Marylebone Road, look out for **number No 18** (on the east side). This was the entrance to a large polygonal building at the back of the terrace which was home to the Diorama. Constructed in 1823 by the architect Pugin, the engineer James Morgan and James Arrowsmith who was related by marriage to Daguerre, a name synonymous with early cinema, the dark circular auditorium, could hold 200 people and was revolved by a boy working a ram engine. The audience was thereby able to view two stages alternately – with one being changed whilst the other was being viewed. Each view was lit from the front as well as the back giving each picture a mysterious atmosphere. In 1851 the Diorama closed, the equipment dispersed and the building used as a Baptist chapel, but from 1922 the old auditorium had a large skylight and therapy pool installed as part of its further metamorphosis as Institute of Rheumatic Diseases.

If the first part of the walk has not quenched your thirst for Georgian architecture, continue south across the busy Euston Road. It is here that you will find one of the finest examples of Nash's work – Park Crescent. Refer to John Nash Walk II map and the proceeding text for further details.

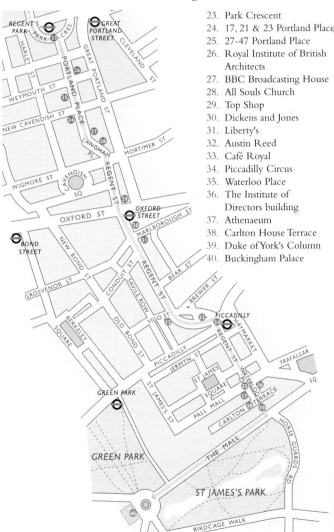

John Nash Walk part 2
from Park Crescent to Buckingham Palace

Cross the Marylebone Road and we arrive at **Park Crescent (23)** – Nash designed this to be a circus, which would have made it the largest in Europe, but only the southern half was realised. Nevertheless the crescent makes an impressive statement and it is probably more recognisably 'Nash' than any of the Outer Circle terraces. A single storey colonnade runs the length of each of these curving terraces which makes for simply elegant architecture. The generally pristine exterior decoration and stucco work are the result of a total renovation in the early 1960's when most of the houses were turned into offices.

Between the two terraces of Park Crescent is the start of **Portland Place (24)**. Originally laid out by the Adam brothers in 1773 as a speculative building adventure, the street was the widest in London at the time as the scheme was intended for superior housing only. Nash did not need to make any changes to this arrangement as it suited his Via Triumphalis project beautifully. However within a relatively short time one of the finest Adam houses in London, Foley House, built in 1758, was demolished in 1864 to make way for the huge **Langham Hotel**. This was one of the first super-large hotels in Britain with some 600 rooms and a 100 feet dining room. Unfortunately, this was the beginning of the end and now little evidence of Adam's work at Portland Place remains. However what has survived can be seen on the exteriors of numbers **17, 21** (with Ionic pilasters and pediment), **23 (24)** and, best of all, numbers **27-47 (25)** (the centre of which was unfortunately lost in World War II enemy bombing).

On the east side of Portland Place, at the corner with **Weymouth Street**, is the **Royal Institute of British Architects (26)**, built 1932-34 by Grey Wornum. Designed in total sympathy with the Adam remains, it is no taller than any of the 18th century houses yet it is instantly recognisable as a very modern piece of architecture. Made from Portland stone, everything about the outside of this building is crisply cut with square or rectangular windows and huge bronze entrance doors. The flat roof and corner plot exaggerate this.

On entering the building, the first thing one notices is the superb wide staircase and the impressive use of materials such as marble, wood and ornamental glass. Take the stairs, or the mirror-interior lift, to the first floor and enjoy coffee or lunch in the café surrounded by finely engraved glass panels by Raymond McGrath and revel in this Art Deco delight (for more information see p249).

Walking south along Portland Place and still on the east side is **BBC Broadcasting House (27)**. This is one of those buildings which provokes strong feelings – people either love it or loathe it. Likened to a huge ship, the Tower of Babel and hated by the doyen of architectural writers Nicholas Pevsner, Broadcasting House was designed by G Val Myers and completed in 1931. It is perhaps unfortunate that not only is the building out of sympathy with **All Souls Church** (see below) which is so close by but also only makes the slightest of nods towards its Georgian neighbours with fleeting recognition in the shape of the windows, a detail which is lost on such a solid, heavy mass. However, the one redeeming feature is the series of superb sculptures on the building's exterior, carved by Eric Gill.

John Nash very cleverly placed the church of All Souls in **Langham Place** at a point were his Via Triumphalis needed to change direction at the top of Regent Street from Portland Place. He did this at the other end of Regent Street too, by gently taking one's gaze onto another vista. Nash, being the first architect to apply 'town-planning' on such a massive scale in London is often compared with Haussmann, the man who re-organised so much of Paris in the late 1840's. Nash however was able to create his little tricks on the eye with twists and turns accommodating any awkwardness in the lay of the land unlike Haussmann who had to build in straight lines for purposes of security in post-Revolution Paris. Furthermore, Nash was only building for certain groups of society, his scheme envisaged 'a boundary and complete separation between Streets and Squares occupied by the Nobility and Gentry, and the narrow Streets and meaner houses occupied by mechanics and the trading part of the community'.

Nash designed **All Souls Church (28)** in 1822-24 with a large, circular portico and pillars of the Ionic order with the roundness softening the corner into Langham Place. Atop the portico is a rather curious smaller version of itself from which rises a pointed spire. The inside is light and airy with galleries carried on Corinthian columns. The church is often used for services and concerts broadcast by the BBC. There are, additionally, occasional free lunchtime concerts (for more details see p.249).

Walking from Langham Place, down Regent's Street towards Oxford Circus, on the east (left hand) side of the street is **Top Shop (29)**. This is the site where in 1833, as part of Nash's scheme, Peter Robinson set

Royal Institute of British Architects

up his linen drapery shop. The present shop dates from 1925 and its large windows and general appearance is based on the New York 5th Avenue store of Lord and Taylor. Peter Robinson's shop was taken over by the Burton menswear group in the late 1940's.

Cross Oxford Circus and carry on walking down Regent Street. Among the shops on the east side is the department store **Dickens and Jones (30)**. Built slightly earlier than Liberty's, in 1919, Pevsner describes the building as being a mix of 'Beaux-Arts classical with a slight Egyptian admix- ture'. The shop was founded by a Mr Dickens and a Mr Smith in 1790 in Oxford Street 'at the sign of the Golden Lion', who appears to have eaten Mr Smith because nothing further is heard of him. The business moved to the newly fashionable Regent Street in 1835 and became known as Dickens and Jones in the 1890s when Mr John Prichard Jones became a partner.

The shop's reputation rested on its supply of fine fabrics and in 1901, on the announcement of the death of Queen Victoria, the shop had to dye all of its white cloth black in order to meet the demand for black material for mourning clothes. At that time the staff numbered approx- imately 200, most of whom lived in the store's lodging house behind the shop in Argyll Street.

 Continuing to walk in a southerly direction you will pass **Liberty's (31)**, or more properly Liberty and Co Ltd. As a young man Arthur Liberty worked for Farmer and Roger's Great Cloak and Shawl Emporium but ambition very soon led him to open his own store at 218a Regent Street in 1875, calling it 'East India House' and selling exotic silks and Japanese goods. By 1925 the shops along this stretch of the road were seen as too small and outdated for the modern customer's needs, and were thus demolished.

A new store was commissioned by Liberty's, who, extraordinarily, decided to look backward rather than forward in their chosen design of a timber-framed 'Tudor' department store which rounds the corner into Great Marlborough Street. The timber used in the building came from two redundant ships, HMS Hindustan and HMS Impregnable; with the abundant stained glass and lovely carving coming from the store's own workshop. The interior is arranged around three balconies on consec- utive floors made of sumptuous wood, which always seem to smell of polish and to creak although this is strangely reassuring rather than alarming! This part of the store is linked to the Regent Street façade by a quaint covered bridge decorated with the Liberty coat of arms and a clock showing St George and the Dragon – lest you forget you are in England!

Walking on towards the south end of Regent Street but on the opposite side of the road, on the corner of Vigo Street, is the menswear shop **Austin Reed (32)**. The company was originally founded in 1900 in Fenchurch Street in the City, and its Regent Street shop has the most delightful tonsorial parlour in the basement. Completed in 1930 and recently renovated it is a barber's shop like no other – pure Art Deco with the most wonderful huge, curvy, corona ceiling light (telephone 020 7734 6789 for enquiries).

Back on the east side is the **Café Royal (33)**, opened in 1870 as a café-restaurant. Between 1890 and 1920 it was the haunt of London's most famous actors, writers and artists such as Oscar Wilde and J A M Whistler. The premises were re-built in the early 1920's as part of an attempt to bring conformity to this part of the street. By the 1930's the Café was once again fashionable amongst writers such as T S Elliot and J B Priestley. The Grill Room still has some of the old Cafés atmosphere as well as some gilt caryatids and mirrors from the 19th century building (telephone 0870 400 8686 to book a table and for general enquiries).

We arrive now at **Piccadilly Circus (34)**, formed when Nash needed to curve his Via Triumphalis into Piccadilly from Regent's Street. It is quite difficult to imagine – standing in the hubbub of people, traffic, and flashing advertisement hoardings – that this was once an elegant oasis of calm! Nash had placed a circle of stuccoed buildings here, not unlike Park Crescent. Unfortunately in the 1880s this arrangement was spoilt by the demolition of the north east quarter of the circle to accommodate the formation of Shaftsbury Avenue. By 1910 the trend for bright, electrically lit advertisements had been started by Bovril and Schweppes and a decade later even larger ones were in place and had become a successful tourist attraction.

Another familiar landmark within Piccadilly Circus is the statue of **Eros** – the winged boy. However, he is not really Eros, the god of love, but the Angel of Christian Charity and is a memorial to the philanthropist

Anthony Ashley Cooper, 7th Earl of Shaftsbury (1801-1885). The Earl was a successful social reformer having led the campaign to restrict the hours women and children worked in factories to ten hours a day in 1850. He also secured the Mines Act of 1842 which forbade women, girls and boys under the age of ten years from working underground.

 The last stretch of Regent Street culminates in **Waterloo Place (35)**, named after the then recent battle against Napoleon. This is where Nash's Via Triumphalis was to terminate, at the entrance of **Carlton House**, the home of the Prince Regent. It was mooted that the most appropriate buildings for this area should be gentlemen's clubs and that their façades should be identical, however this latter stipulation was unpopular and not enforced. For The United Services Club of 1826-28, on the east side of Waterloo Place, south of **Pall Mall**, now **The Institute of Directors building (36)**, John Nash designed a masculine building with just more than a hint of Rome, with a broad two-storey portico consisting of double Doric columns at the lower level and Corinthian columns above.

Additions by Deciumus Burton in 1858-59 include new window surrounds at the ground floor and do not miss the rather good frieze by John Thomas just below the cornice. However attractive this building is, it really does not compare with the all-Decimus Burton **Athenaeum (37)**, also in Waterloo Place, on the west side, and also south of Pall Mall. Built in 1827-30 it is much more of a coherent whole with a very fine Doric frieze running on three sides, carved by John Henning junior. Above the entrance is a large gilt copy of the Pallas Athene of Velletri by E H Baily.

Heading straight on to Carlton House Terrace, we come to the beginning, or end, depending on which way the Prince was travelling, of Nash's 'Triumphant Route'. This street is named for the very large house that once stood on the spot, built originally in 1709 for Henry Boyde, the first Lord Carlton. In 1732 the house was bought for George II's son Frederick, Prince of Wales, who employed William Kent to re-design the garden. Unfortunately Frederick, who had never enjoyed a good relationship with his family, died in 1750, a year before his father's death, and thus never became king. Carlton House was then remodelled by Sir William Chambers for the Princess Augusta, Frederick's widow, and on her death in 1772 the house became the residence of the Prince of Wales, the future Prince Regent.

The Prince was noted for his extreme extravagance in all matters so it is perhaps no surprise that he engaged the eminent architect Henry Holland to turn Carlton House into a sort of 'Golden House of Nero'. The Prince also employed an army of French decorators and his painted rooms were the talk of the town as was the debt he was running up – a cool £640,000 by 1795. Even so, the Prince was unstoppable, adding a Gothic conservatory, with cast iron fan vaults. The employment of the services of John Nash in 1813, initially to design a Gothic dining room for the Prince was the beginning of a very long association and friendship.

By 1820 the Prince of Wales had become King George IV, and having no further use for Carlton House ordered its demolition, saving just a few of his favourite fittings and determined to make his mark on Buckingham Palace. Our walk will finish at the Palace, but let us first look at what replaced Carlton House.

Carlton House Terrace (38) was designed by John Nash 1827-33 and the whole is pleasing on the eye – giving its best side perhaps to the view from St James's Park. The two long ranges, nine houses in each, are reminiscent of his work around Regent's Park and were the last of Nash's grand designs as he was to die not long after their completion in 1835. Although built as terraces each individual house is different and Nash was perfectly happy to allow other architects to embellish his basic work here. **Numbers 7-9**, until World War II, made up the German Embassy with the interior having been remodelled by Albert Speer, Hitler's favourite architect. This is the only example of Speer's work in London (this building is not open to the public).

The terraces form a rather good frame for the **Duke of York's Column (39)** and the powerful granite flight of steps down to St James's Park. The Column is in honour of Prince Frederick Augustus, Duke of York and Albany (1763-1827), the second son of King George III and the Prince Regent's brother. The Duke had been groomed for a military career, commanding the British expeditionary forces to Flanders in 1793 and it was his habit of marching and counter-marching his troops that gave rise to the nursery rhyme 'The Grand Old Duke of York'. The Column was erected 1831-34 and is loosely modelled on Trajan's Column in Rome. The drum and dome at the top are based on Hooke/Wren's Monument in the City. Designed by B D Wyatt the whole column stands at 137 feet tall, including the bronze statue of the Duke dressed in his Garter robes.

Although Nash's Via Tiumphalis finished at the Duke of York's Column we can take in one more London gem, **Buckingham Palace (40)**, a project in which John Nash became heavily involved. Go down the steps into The Mall, turn right and walk along to the Palace. There has been a house on the site since at least the mid 17th century, and it was John Sheffield, 1st Duke of Buckingham who built his country house here in 1702-05 partly on land owned by himself and partly on Crown land. During the reign of James II the land had been planted with one thousand mulberry trees in an effort to start a silk industry – unfortunately this venture did not take off, rumour has it that the wrong kind of trees had been bought.

In 1762 George III purchased the house. The official residence of the monarch was St James's but the young King found the rambling and ramshackle apartments unsuitable for his new wife. Indeed the Royal couple, who had fifteen children, were very content with Buckingham House, also known at this time as the Queen's House and most of the initial building work was for the enlarging of the King's library, as he was a keen bibliophile. However over time the private apartments were extended and, following a serious fire at St James's in 1809, state ceremonies were performed here. It was still, however, very much a house and not yet a palace.

It was on the succession of George IV that things changed dramatically. Carlton House was swept away and the Prince turned his attention to making Buckingham House into something truly palatial. Against advice he employed his trusted architect friend John Nash and between them they spent colossal amounts of money remodelling the building. Within three years, 1825-28, the exterior alterations had been completed except for the entrance arch, the Marble Arch, which now stands in Hyde Park.

When the King died suddenly in 1830, Nash was immediately sacked from his post. The thrifty, reliable architect Edward Blore was given the task of completing the work which was to take many years yet. Indeed George IV's successor, his brother William IV died in 1837 without ever living at the Palace. The first reigning monarch to do so was Queen Victoria where she was said to have been 'most happy' and it has been the London residence of the royal family ever since. The sale of the Royal Pavilion in Brighton financed a further major extension between 1853-55.

The last major alteration to the building took place in 1913 when Sir Aston Webb added the east wing façade. This is the 'side' of the Palace which is most familiar, made from Portland stone in a neo-classic style but which has received much criticism most usually because the façade is seen as 'predictable' and 'boring'.

During the summer months of August and September, when the royal family are on holiday elsewhere, the state rooms of the Palace are open to the public; a scheme that was started in the early 1990's to help raise funds to repair the fire damage at Windsor Castle.

The Ticket Office itself is a little gem designed by Michael Hopkins and Partners. The small timber cabin has a tensile fabric canopy which covers the whole structure, which is erected at the beginning of the tourist season and taken down at the end of it.

Eighteen state rooms are usually available for viewing during the period of opening. Visitors enter through the **Ambassador's Court** and take the very grand staircase to the set of rooms created by Nash, which, despite all the past controversy, are the highlight of most people's visit! These rooms are on the west side of the Palace overlooking the magnificent gardens, which stretch to some forty-five acres. Visitors can enter the Throne Room and marvel at the seven magnificent chandeliers before moving on to the baroque Ballroom where investitures and banquets are held. The spectacular white and gold Music Room can also be visited as can the Picture Gallery with paintings by Rubens and Rembrandt.

The Queen's Gallery, accessed from the rear of the Palace in Buckingham Gate, has been the subject of a recent major overhaul by John Simpson and completed in 2002. The theme here is Greek Classicism, complete with Homeric friezes and all done within the bounds of excellent taste.

Visitors can watch the Changing of the Guard in the Palace forecourt. This famous ceremony takes place at 11.30am daily from April to July and on alternative days from August to April. This is a colourful ritual when the scarlet clad Guard march from Wellington Barracks (accompanied by a Guard band) to relieve the previous Guard.

John Nash's **Marble Arch,** designed in 1825-26 as a magnificent entrance to Buckingham Palace now sits sadly amid the roaring traffic where four major roads intersect in the area named after it. Partly based on the Arch of Constantine, it is in fact three arches flanked by Corinthian columns and the whole is clad in Carrara marble – the first piece of architecture in Britain to use this material. It has been sited here since 1908 waiting for members of the Royal Family or the Royal Horse Artillery, the only people who are allowed to pass through the Arch.

John Nash Statue

More Information:

London Zoo
Outer Circle, Regent's Park, NW1 4RY
Tel: 020 7722 3333
Transport: Regent's Park LU (Bakerloo)
Open: Daily 10am-5.30pm (Mar-Oct), 10am-4pm (Nov-April)
Admission: £13.00 adults (concessions and family tickets available)
Visitors with disabilities: Parking bays, wheelchair and electric buggy hire,
large print guides available (please telephone for details)

London Central Mosque
146 Park Road, NW8
Tel: 020 7724 3363
Open: Daily dawn until dusk
Please telephone for details and wheelchair access information
Note: All visitors must remove their shoes before entering the building and
women must cover their heads

Royal Institute of British Architects (RIBA)
66 Portland Place, W1
Tel: 020 7580 5533
Transport: Regent's Park LU (Bakerloo line) or Great Portland Street (Circle,
Metropolitan and Hammersmith and City lines)
Open: Mon-Fri 8am-6pm and Sat 9am-5pm
Admission free; wheelchair access

All Souls Church
Langham Place, W1B 3DA
Tel: 020 7580 3522
Transport: Oxford Circus LU (Bakerloo, Central and Victoria lines)
Open: Mon-Fri 9.30am-6pm, Sun 9am-9pm
Admission free
Please telephone for wheelchair access information and times of services

Buckingham Palace
The Mall, SW1A 1AA
Tel: 020 7799 2331 (information line)
Transport: St James's Park LU (Circle and District lines)
Website: www.the-royal-collection.org.uk
Open: Daily 9.30am-4.15pm (Aug-Sept)
Admission charge (telephone for details and wheelchair access information)

Greenwich Walk

"On Thames's bank in silent thought we stood:
Where Greenwich smiles upon the silver flood:
Pleased with the seat which gave Eliza birth,
We kneel and kiss the consecrated earth."
Samuel Johnson, 1763

1. Greenwich Foot Tunnel
2. Cutty Sark
3. Gypsy Moth IV
4. St Alfege's
5. Ranger's House
6. Royal Observatory
7. Flamsteed House
8. Queen's House
9. National Maritime Museum
10. Royal Naval College
11. King Charles Block
12. The Painted Hall –
    King William Block
13. Chapel – Queen Mary Block

As much as you will enjoy this part of London there is no need to kiss the ground as Johnson and his friend James Boswell did! Arrive by Docklands Light Railway at the Cutty Sark station to start the journey or alight a stop earlier, at Island Gardens station and take the **Greenwich Foot Tunnel (1)** and have the unique experience of walking under the Thames.

This tunnel is 1,217 feet in length and is the only tunnel under the Thames built exclusively for pedestrians. Opened in 1902 the tunnel replaced the ferry which had been in operation since the mid 17th century and allowed workers from south London to walk to work in West India and Millwall Docks.

With an internal diameter of only 11 feet this is not an experience for those who suffer with claustrophobia! At each end of the tunnel there are circular shafts with domed glass roofs that house stairs and lifts (for more details see p.257)

Royal Naval College

On arrival at Greenwich a small diversion can be made by taking a look at the **Cutty Sark (2)**, the world's only surviving tea clipper from the 19th century. She was launched in 1869 and won the prestigious clippers' Shanghai to London race in 1871 making the voyage in only 107 days. Her last voyage was in 1938 and she has been here in dry dock since 1957.

Close by is the yacht **Gypsy Moth IV (3)** in which Sir Francis Chichester made the first single-handed circumnavigation of the world in 1966-67, a journey that took nine months and one day to complete. Both vessels can be inspected at close range (for more details see p.257).

The first building we are going to look at is **St Alfege's (4)** at the junction of Church Street and Greenwich High Road. This splendid Georgian church is named after the Archbishop of Canterbury who was murdered near this spot by Danish invaders in 1012 and stands in replacement of a much earlier church in which the future King Henry VIII was baptised in 1491.

This church is by Nicholas Hawksmoor and was built between 1712-18 after the old church had collapsed in a storm and was the first church to be built under the Fifty New Churches Act of 1711, funded from a coal tax. Hawksmoor's church is rectangular with a flat ceiling and the east façade, which faces Greenwich High Road, has a shallow apse behind which rises the main portico with four Doric pilasters at the sides and two massive columns in the middle supporting a pediment surmounted by three huge urns. The south and north sides carry giant pilasters and on the west end sits the tower. Designed in the manner of James Gibbs, the tower and steeple were in fact added by John James in 1730.

The interior of the church suffered extensive damage in the Second World War, restoration of which was carried out by the eminent, if somewhat eccentric, architect Sir Albert Richardson, who faithfully reproduced Hawksmoor's work. The beautifully coffered ceiling at the apse and other decoration are in fact trompe l'oeil paintings.

Famous people associated with this church include General James Wolfe, who defeated the French at Quebec and was buried here in 1759 and General Charles Gordon, hero of Khartoum, who was baptised here in 1833. Thomas Tallis, the 16th century composer was buried in the previous church on the site where he had been the organist. He is commemorated in a south aisle window. The church is open to the public at varying times – please telephone 020 8853 2703 for details.

On leaving the church head for Stockwell Street, which forms a three-way junction with Greenwich High Road and Church Street. Walk the length of Stockwell Street which becomes Croom's Hill and at the end of which take the left-hand fork to arrive at Chesterfield Walk. Half way along Chesterfield Walk is **Ranger's House (5)**. This is one of three houses built in the 1680s by Andrew Snape, the King's Sergeant Farrier, as a speculative venture. One of the houses was demolished in 1815 but the other remaining house of this trio is **Macartney House** which you would have passed at the start of Chesterfield walk and which had additions in 1802 by Sir John Soane. It was converted into flats in 1925.

Ranger's House has been the subject of additions over the years to form a very substantial domestic dwelling, one of its owners being Philip, 4th Earl of Chesterfield (1694-1773). The house is seven bays wide of red brick with a stone centre frontispiece, in which sits the main doorway flanked by Ionic columns with a Venetian window above. The wings of the house are in yellow brick and the south wing had a gallery added in 1750. The house has recently been refurbished by English Heritage and is now home to the Wernher Collection, an eclectic collection of more than 700 works of art purchased by mining magnate Sir Julius Wernher 1850-1912 (for more information see p.257).

When you have finished at Ranger's House make your way across into **Greenwich Park** and head for the **Royal Observatory (6)** with its distinctive dome. Greenwich Park itself consists of 163 acres set on a hill between Blackheath and the River Thames. King Henry VI enclosed the park in 1433, with its perimeter wall built during the reign of James I. The land is still owned by the Crown. Directly across from Ranger's House and situated in the top of the park in the far corner is a 13 acre enclosure known as '**The Wilderness**' in which deer roam – having first been introduced to the park in 1515 for the purpose of hunting.

The name Greenwich is derived from the Anglo-Saxon 'green port' and Saxon remains have been found in the area. From the top of the hill one can take in the splendid views across the Thames towards the skyscrapers of Canary Wharf. If the weather is pleasant you may wish to wander in the park or just sit by the pond, a popular haven for wild-fowl. You may also be lucky enough to be serenaded by music from the decorative cast-iron bandstand that dates from 1880. The park is open to pedestrians every day from 6am to dusk, with traffic permitted from 7am to dusk (telephone for further information 020 8858 2608).

King Charles II founded the Royal Observatory at the instigation of the influential Royal Society. The original part of the building dates from 1675 and was designed by Christopher Wren and Robert Hooke, both of whom were active members of the Royal Society. **Flamsteed House (7)**, as the more 'domestic' part of the Observatory is known, is named after the first Astronomer Royal John Flamsteed who lived and worked here. This was the first purpose-built scientific research establishment in Britain.

Built from red brick with some nice exterior detailing that Wren called 'a little for pompe', Flamsteed House has one of the best-kept Wren interiors, the splendid Octagon Room and apartments. Flamsteed lived in the four rooms of the ground floor, and worked in the Octagon room above until his death in 1719. The house now contains displays telling the story of time and astronomy. The 28-inch Refracting Telescope in the onion-shaped dome is the largest in Britain and is still used for occasional night viewing. The whole project cost the Crown only £500, but there appears to have been a little 'scratching around' for materials and, splendid as the building is, it does not compare with Perrault's very grand Observatoire in Paris, which Greenwich was trying to emulate.

In 1948 it was decided that the lights of London were too bright and were interfering with accurate readings so the astronomers moved to darkest Sussex and today the Astronomer Royal is based in Cambridge.

The **Greenwich Meridian**, Longitude 0, an imaginary line joining the north and south Poles, passes through the dead centre of a specialised telescope installed at the Observatory in 1851. A line in the ground marks the position of the meridian. It is a famous feature in the courtyard and it is from where all time zones around the world are measured since international agreement in 1884. This is your opportunity to stand with one foot in each hemisphere of the East and West – everyone does it!

Above Wren's Octagon Room, on one of the two turrets is a ball on a rod. This Time Ball has been dropped at 1pm every day since 1833 so that passing sailors could set their clocks by it (for more details see p.257).

From the Observatory, walk on down the hill towards Inigo Jones's splendid **Queen's House (8)** (see Chapter 1.2, p.36). Flanking the Queen's House, attached by colonnades are the long rooms, added during the 19th century and now forming the **National Maritime Museum (9)**.

 The National Maritime Museum was formally established by Act of Parliament in 1934 and was opened to the public in 1937. The museum has displays of boats, real as well as models, including Prince Frederick's state barge of 1723 and the largest collection of marine art in the world. There is also a permanent exhibition entitled 'Maritime London' that uses prints and video installations to present the history of the capital's shipping industry.

At the heart of the museum is **Neptune Court** a glass-roofed former open courtyard which had previously lain unused but which now houses large display items. It is claimed that this is Europe's largest free-span glazed roof and it is certainly impressive. Rick Mather, an exciting young architect, masterminded this project between 1996-99 and the general overhaul of the museum and its facilities, which was funded by the National Lottery (for more details see p257).

Royal Naval College

After leaving the museum we can now walk down to the buildings of the **Royal Naval College (10)**, crossing the busy Romney Road directly in front of the Queen's House. Enter the gates immediately in front and you will have arrived at the group of four buildings known as the former Royal Naval College. The College moved from Portsmouth to occupy these buildings in 1873. Its four main blocks were built from 1696 to 1751 to the plan of Sir Christopher Wren and were used from 1704 to 1869 as the Royal Hospital for Seamen.

Greenwich Hospital, as it was universally known, was the naval equivalent of the Royal Hospital Chelsea (see p.77) – a home for needy veterans of the service. The idea was originally mooted by King James II, himself a naval officer at one time, and was developed by his daughter Queen Mary who founded the Hospital by Royal Charter in October 1694.

The group of buildings stand on the site of the demolished Tudor palace of Placentia and is set around a Grand Square with a 115 foot wide vista towards the Queen's House.

King Charles II had wanted to live at Greenwich and the eastern half of the **King Charles Block (11)**, the building nearest to the river towards Greenwich pier, is the only part of his planned 'King's House' to be realised. It was built in 1664-69 to the design of John Webb, pupil and son in law of the late Inigo Jones. Economic factors prevented further building; eventually the money ran out.

When Queen Mary rededicated the unfinished palace as a hospital Sir Christopher Wren was asked to devise a plan that would accommodate her wish to preserve the King's and Queen's Houses. This he did in his usual brilliant manner in what has been called 'the most stately procession of buildings we possess' and after 1703 he was assisted in his work here by a series of outstanding architects including Sir John Vanbrugh and Nicholas Hawksmoor. Colen Campbell and James 'Athenian' Stuart also worked here.

After 125 years of residence in these splendid buildings the Royal Navy vacated the site in 1998 and they now house the University of Greenwich.

There are two areas of the College open to the public and both are a treat to visit. **The Painted Hall (12)** completed to Wren's design in 1707 was decorated by Sir James Thornhill between 1708 and 1727. For nineteen years he worked for a flat rate of pay, £3 per square yard of ceiling, £1 per square yard of wall. His subject matter ranged from the triumph of the reign of William and Mary, who are portrayed surrounded by the four cardinal virtues to portraits of the great and good such as John Flamsteed, the first Astronomer Royal.

The other area available to visit is the **Chapel (13)** in the Queen Mary block, which is diagonally across the courtyard to the King Charles block. The original chapel interior was burnt out in 1779 and the present one is the work of James Stuart. The domed tower sits over the chapel entrance and a run of double pillars is reminiscent of Perrault's colonnades at the Louvre in Paris. Light floods into the building from the three tiers of windows on the east wall.

More Information:

The Cutty Sark
Tel: 020 8858 3445 for enquiries
Open: Mon-Sun 10am-5pm

Gypsy Moth IV
Tel: 020 8858 2698 for information

Greenwich Foot Tunnel
Greenwich Pier, SE10 and
Isle of Dogs, E14
Transport: Island Gardens or
Cutty Sark DLR
Public access: Open all day, lifts in
operation daily 7am-7pm

National Maritime Museum
Romney Road, SE10
Tel: 020 8858 4422
Open: Daily 10am-5pm (until 6pm
during summer months)
Admission free
Telephone for wheelchair access details

Royal Observatory
Greenwich Park, SE10
Tel: 020 8312 6565
Open: Daily 10am-5pm (until
6pm during summer months)
Free admission, charge made for
special exhibitions
Wheelchair access

Painted Hall & Chapel of the former Royal Naval College
King William Walk, SE10
Tel: 020 8858 2608
Open: Mon-Sat 10am-5pm and
Sun 12.30pm-5pm
Telephone for wheelchair access details

Ranger's House
Chesterfield Walk, SE10
Tel: 020 8853 0035
Open: Wed-Sun 10am-5pm
(June-Aug)
Adults £5 (concessions available)
Wheelchair access

Eat and Drink Architecture

Vertigo - Tower 42

The George Inn

C1676+

A unique survivor this is the last galleried inn left in London, where they were once commonplace. Inns have occupied this site since medieval times, this building dating from about 1676. The coming of the railway to the area in 1899 resulted in the demolition of the north wing and centre of the original inn, so we are left with just one third of the original. Charles Dickens mentions this inn in Little Dorrit (1857) – and we can still sup here today!

Bar and bar food available daily. A la carte restaurant open Monday to Saturday. Please telephone for reservations.

The George Inn, George Inn Yard, 77 Borough High Street, Southwark, SE1; Telephone 020 7407 2056; Nearest transport London Bridge LU (Northern and Jubilee lines); Open year-round normal licensing hours; Telephone for wheelchair access information

St John's, Smith Square

Thomas Archer 1713-28

St John's is considered to be one of the finest examples of English Baroque architecture to be found anywhere. Built as part of the 'Fifty Churches' scheme (see page 67) during the reign of Queen Anne, to a Greek-cross plan, the north and south 'arms' of the building have enormous Doric columns and these mark the two entrances. The east and west ends each have a large Venetian window and Doric pilasters. However, on first seeing the church, one's eye is immediately drawn to the four corner towers – circular with short Doric columns set diagonally and each topped by a small pineapple ogee lantern. It is from this endearing roofline that the building gets its nickname 'Queen Anne's Footstool' because it does indeed resembles one that has been upturned!

The church was severely damaged by enemy bombing in 1941 and was restored by Marshall Sisson 1965-69 as a concert hall. With its excellent acoustics and varied programme of classical music, St John's is now a much-valued venue in the heart of Westminster.

However, one does not need to attend a concert to savour the delights of the interior of St John's for in the brick-vaulted crypt there is the superb Footstool restaurant. An a la carte British menu, light buffet, drinks and snacks are available weekday lunch times and from 5.30pm onwards on concert evenings (which happens to be most days of the week!) For anything other than a drink and snack it is recommended that you book a table.

Around the walls of the restaurant is a display of artwork that is changed monthly and is always a delight.

The Footstool Restaurant, St John's, Smith Square, London SW1; Telephone 020 7222 2779; Nearest transport Westminster (Circle, District & Jubilee lines) and St James's Park (Circle & District lines); Open weekday 11.30am–2.45pm and from 5.30pm on concert evenings; telephone above number to reserve a table and for details of wheelchair access

Tate Britain

Sidney R J Smith et al   1893+

A visit to Tate Britain is always a treat, discovering new works of art and revisiting favourites. The architecture is of interest in itself. The main building was built with money donated by the sugar tycoon Sir Henry Tate on the boggy site of a miserable prison known as Millbank Penitentiary. A large projecting portico and fairly shallow dome give this building a classical air, but with a little Victorian over-enthusiasm.

The recent extension to the Tate, the Clore Gallery added in 1987, is the only completed London work of the eminent architect the late Sir James Stirling. This was built to house the Tate's wonderful collection of paintings by J M W Turner.

The restaurant at the Tate is a very grand affair, decorated with murals executed by a young Rex Whistler in 1926-27. Appropriately he took as his subject 'The Expedition in Pursuit of Rare Meats'. The medium-priced à la carte menu, (a set menu is available), and an extensive wine list make dining here an enjoyable experience. Booking ahead is almost essential.

Tate Britain, Millbank, SW1; Telephone 020 7887 8000 (reservations 020 7887 8825); Website www.tate.org.uk; Restaurant open daily Mon-Sat 12pm–3pm, Sun 12pm–4pm

The Black Friar

H Fuller Clark   c1905

First built in 1873, this is a typical London-pub-on-the-corner wedge shaped building. Of earlier pedigree than those of the 1890s pub boom, the Black Friar was given a new ground floor sometime at the turn of the last century. The interior was completely redecorated by Herbert Fuller Clark and his colleague artist Henry Poole and what was accomplished needs to be seen to be believed. The entire bar area is decorated with red and green marble depicting the activities of the monks who lived on the site when the land belonged to the Dominican, or Black Friars, monastery. The whole work was executed in an art deco manner and it is a truly unique experience to come and sip a beer in this pub.

The Black Friar, 174 Queen Victoria Street, EC4; Telephone 020 7236 5650; Nearest transport Blackfriars Rail & LU (Circle and District lines); Open daily lunchtimes to mid evening (this is a City pub so has shorter opening hours); Please telephone for current opening times and for wheelchair access information

Café at the Methodist Central Hall

Lanchester and Rickards   1905-11

The café in this splendid Edwardian baroque building is a bit of a secret in this café/restaurant free zone of Westminster. There is an opportunity to see the inside of the beautiful dome, so take your camera!

Methodist Central Hall, Storey's Gate, SW1; Telephone 020 7222 8010; Website www.chw.com; Nearest transport St James's Park LU (District and Circle lines); Open for morning coffee, light lunch and afternoon tea Mon-Sat 10 am 4pm; Wheelchair access – please telephone for information

The Ritz

Charles Mewes   1903-06

Whether taking tea or propping up the bar in the Ritz do take a closer look at the first steel-framed structure in London. This lovely building looks as though it strayed in from Paris and indeed the architect did design the Paris Ritz in 1899, very wisely repeating all the successful parts here.

If you are unable to venture in through lack of time or short-age of funds, stay outside and admire the ground floor arcade, again very French. The whole building is faced in Norwegian stone at the ground floor with Portland stone above.

Tea at the Ritz costs just over £30 per person, but is truly a treat you will not forget in a hurry. You will need to book at least six weeks ahead.

The Ritz, 55 Piccadilly, W1; Telephone 020 7493 8181; Nearest transport Green Park LU (Piccadilly, Jubilee and Victoria lines); Please telephone for restaurant and bar opening hours and wheelchair access information

Bibendum Oyster Bar and Restaurant

François Espinasse   1909-11

The style of this building hovers between art nouveau and art deco – with colourful decorations and motifs playing on the theme of wheels and tyres as befitting the former British Head Office of the Michelin Tyre Company. Built 1909-11, this is a very early example of what could be achieved with reinforced concrete. 'Bibendum' is the name of the Michelin Man, (who is surely Bertie Bassett's Gallic uncle), hence the name of this very stylish bar and restaurant.

Bibendum, Michelin House, 81 Fulham Road, SW3; Telephone 020 7581 5817; Nearest transport South Kensington LU (Piccadilly, Circle and District lines); Please telephone for opening times, reservations and wheelchair access

Renaissance London Chancery Court Hotel

Moncton and Newman   1912-19

A rather slick, comfortable hotel, restaurant and bar in a lovely building that still oozes Edwardian grandeur. Built 1912-19 by Moncton and Newman and converted in 1998 by Bennett and Son. A baroque-style dome sits over the entrance – walk through to the Lobby Lounge to enjoy coffee or afternoon tea whilst you recline in the ample upholstery, or sip a champagne cocktail in the marble lined bar. All in the name of architectural interest, of course!

Renaissance London Chancery Court Hotel, 252 High Holborn, WC1V; Telephone 020 7829 7000; Nearest transport Holborn LU (Central and Piccadilly lines); Please telephone for opening times, wheelchair access and disabled facilities

Oxo Tower

Albert W Moore   1928

The Oxo Tower was built in 1928 as an art deco addition to a meat manufacturer's London base. At this time there was a ban on any form of neon lit advertising in the area, so one bright spark thought of picking out the name OXO in coloured glass windows at the top of the tower and placing a strong light behind it which shone out into the London night!

The Tower, which sits equidistant between Blackfriars Bridge and Waterloo Bridge and long abandoned by its originators, is now part of the Coin Street Housing Association. Shops, galleries and small workshops occupy the first three floors, the next five floors consist of affordable-housing while the top floor is devoted to the restaurant, brasserie and bar.

Both the restaurant and brasserie are modern and spacious and lack any form of cosiness, but the views over the Thames are spectacular, especially in the evening.

Oxo Tower Wharf, Barge House Street, SE1; Telephone 020 7803 3888; Nearest transport Blackfriars Rail & LU (Circle & District lines); Open daily for lunch and dinner – telephone for reservations and information about wheelchair access

Blueprint Café at the Design Museum

Sir Terence Conran   1988-89

Built on the site of a disused warehouse on the banks of the Thames in 1988-89 before the area became truly fashionable. One could be forgiven for thinking they had stumbled upon something that had strayed from the Bauhaus! On a particularly sunny day with the proximity of the water this building has something of a seaside promenade about it too.

The building is of white painted and rendered brick and its primary purpose is to house a museum dedicated to all aspects of 20th century design from kitchen appliances to chairs, from packaging to computers. Terence Conran and Stephen Bayley founded the museum in an attempt to highlight the need for good design at every level.

The glazed balcony overlooking the Thames is a spectacular setting for the Blueprint Café, which serves good modern European fare.

Blueprint Café, The Design Museum, Shad Thames, SE1; Telephone 020 7378 7031; Nearest transport London Bridge Rail & LU (Northern and Jubilee lines); Open for lunch daily 12pm-3pm; dinner Mon-Sat 6pm-11pm; Please telephone for reservations and information about wheelchair access

Vertigo – Tower 42

Seifert and Partners   1970-81

Champagne and seafood bar located 590 feet up the famous Tower 42 (formerly known as the NatWest Tower) in the heart of the City. Built 1970-81 by Seifert and Partners, it has a stabilising concrete service core with floors cantilevered out from it, with the whole enclosed in a glass sheath. For ten years this was the tallest building in London, indeed in Britain, until the towers of Canary Wharf sprang up.

The views from this bar are the best in London and the food and drink is outstanding too!

Vertigo – Tower 42, 25 Old Broad Street, EC2N; Telephone 0207 877 7842; Nearest transport Bank LU (Central, Northern lines & DLR); Open Mon-Fri 12pm-3pm and 5pm-10pm; Telephone for reservations (at least 24 hours in advance) and wheelchair access

Pizza Express – Alban Gate

Terry Farrell   1988-92

An opportunity to eat lunch or supper inside a piece of very modern architecture. The Pizza Express chain has always, wherever possible, sited their restaurants in architecturally interesting places and this is one of the latest. The Alban Gate complex spans the busy London Wall roadway at Wood Street and Terry Farrell, its architect, likens it to a gigantic gatehouse. Completed in 1992 Alban Gate provides 8.6 acres of office space in granite of differing colours and glass.

There are in fact two Pizza Express restaurants here, almost side by side and mirror images of each other. Although it's almost impossible to see out of the windows whilst dining, it is fun to contemplate the glass and steel and wonder what is holding it all up!

Pizza Express, 125 London Wall, Alban Gate, EC2; Telephone 020 7600 8880; Nearest transport Moorgate Rail & LU (Northern, Circle & Metropolitan lines) St Paul's LU (Central line); Open Mon–Fri 11.30am-10pm, Sat & Sun 11.30am-8pm; Please telephone for wheelchair access information

Ondaatje Wing, National Portrait Gallery

Dixon and Jones   1994-2000

The main body of the Gallery is the original 1896 building by Ewan Christian and was designed to blend with its neighbour the National Gallery - indeed perhaps a little too successfully as many people miss the National Portrait Gallery altogether believing it to be part of the huge Gallery next door. Despite its excellent collection of portraits of the great, the good and the interesting the National Portrait Gallery was never particularly busy and rarely did visitors venture further than the first floor; if they entered at all. The site was cramped and there was little chance of expansion.

In 1994 the then director, Charles Saumarez, and the Gallery trustees appointed Jeremy Dixon (who also worked on the

Covent Garden refurbishment) and Edward Jones to conjure up some space from seemingly nowhere! Miraculously a three-storey atrium was gleaned from an old, narrow service yard and a long escalator now whisks visitors up to the top floor, where the earliest portraits are hung. The visitor can then percolate down through the collection enjoying a gallery that now feels spacious and light. However, the charming front façade of the building is unchanged so the unsuspecting visitor gets quite a surprise on entering.

As with nearly every new building extension, provision was made for a public restaurant. At 92 feet above ground level on the fifth floor of this new Ondaatje Wing it has spectacular views over Nelsons Column down Whitehall and on to the Houses of Parliament. The 80 seat restaurant and 25 seat bar area is under the care of Searcy's catering, with eminent chef Brendan Fyldes in charge.

The Portrait Restaurant, National Portrait Gallery, St Martin's Place, WC2H 0HE; Telephone 020 7312 2490 (Restaurant), 020 7306 0055 (Gallery); Nearest transport Charing Cross Rail & LU (Bakerloo, Northern, Jubilee lines), Embankment (Circle & District lines); Restaurant open Sat-Wed 11.45am–2.45pm, lounge and bar open Wed–Sat 10am –5pm, restaurant open Thurs & Fri 11.45–2.45pm and 5.30pm-8.30pm, lounge and bar open Thurs & Fri 10am–10pm; Table reservations are almost essential for the restaurant; Wheelchair access is excellent throughout the new wing

British Library Coffee Shop

Colin St John Wilson & Partners   1997

The impetus to form the British Library came from the donation of his father's book collection by George IV to the British Museum. The library moved from the British Museum to new premises in 1999 and the King's Library is now attractively displayed in the Tower of Books which can be seen by all in the entrance hall, but which can be contemplated more closely from the comfort of the Coffee Shop.

Open to the public in general as well as library users the self-service coffee shop offers coffee, pastries, light lunches and afternoon teas. The café is open during the library's opening hours.

The British Library, 96 Euston Road, NW1; Telephone 020 7412 7332; Nearest transport Euston Rail & LU (Northern and Victoria lines) and King's Cross/St Pancras Rail & LU (Northern, Victoria, Circle and Metropolitan lines); Open Mon, Wed-Fri 9.30am-6pm; Tues 9.30am-8pm, Sat 9.30am-5pm, Sunday and Bank Holidays 11am-5pm; Wheelchair access available

Tate Modern

Sir Giles Gilbert Scott 1947-63/Herzog & de Meuron 1994-2000

This building should be intimidating. After all it is huge, new and displays modern art! However it is one of the most successful National Lottery funded projects. All sorts of people come here and are not necessarily those who would frequent, say, the Royal Academy. Part of this popularity is due to the building itself – £134 million was lavished on its conversion from disused power station to vibrant modern art venue and its spaces, from the vast Turbine Hall and user-friendly galleries have proved a real hit, attracting in excess of five million visitors a year since its opening in 2000.

The architects, Herzog and de Meuron, made plenty of provision for dining within the building. The top floor (level 7) restaurant is fun and has good views – but only from a very few tables; it is always busy but worth queuing for. However the best treat is coffee, lunch or tea in the Friends Room on level 6. This enjoys fabulous views to the Thames side but equally interesting views to the south of London from the rear terrace. Not so many landmark buildings maybe but a wonderful panorama nonetheless.

Tate Modern, Bankside, SE1; Telephone 020 7887 888; Website www.tate.org.uk; Nearest transport Southwark LU (Jubilee line); Open Sun–Thurs 10am–6pm, Fri–Sat 10am–10pm; Admission is free (charge payable for special exhibitions); Wheelchair access to all parts of the building

View from the Tate Modern

Shopping & Architecture

Barkers

A s if one needs an excuse to go shopping, here is a short list of some of the architectural gems in London which just happen to be retail outlets too.

Burlington Arcade

Samuel Ware   1819

One of three shopping arcades off Piccadilly, the other two being the Princes and the Piccadilly, both of which are on the opposite, south side of the road. Burlington Arcade was built in 1819 by the architect Samuel Ware (1781-1860) for Lord George Cavendish, who owned Burlington House. The arcade formed the western boundary to Cavendish's property and it is said that the impetus behind its construction was to stop passers-by flinging rubbish into his Lordship's garden, not because he wanted to make money from this piece of speculative building!

The arcade consists of two rows of small, bow-fronted, shops with rooms above, set in a narrow passage, some 585 feet long, which becomes wider and one-storey taller in three places. At every fourth shop a cross arch rests on Ionic pilasters, thereby adding variety and the whole passage is top lit from windows in the roof.

The shops cater for the luxury end of the market; cashmere, pure Irish linen, leather goods, Penhaligon fragrances, Mont Blanc pens, items by Theo Fabergé, and jewellery. Security is provided by the frock-coated, top-hatted Beadles who are instructed to eject anyone running, carrying large parcels, whistling or generally causing a nuisance – you have been warned!

The Burlington Arcade, Piccadilly, W1; Nearest transport Green Park LU (Piccadilly, Jubilee and Victoria lines) and Piccadilly Circus LU (Piccadilly and Bakerloo lines); Open Mon-Sat 9am-6pm (closed Sundays); Wheelchair access is possible

Royal Exchange

Sir William Tite   1841-44

This building is often mistaken for the Bank of England, which is just over the road in Threadneedle Street. With its massive portico supported by huge Corinthian columns, the front of the building is much wider, at 175 feet than the back 119 feet. This is the third Royal Exchange building on the site, the others having burned down in 1666 and 1838; the present building was declared open by Queen Victoria in 1844.

The 'Exchange' was established by Sir Thomas Gresham, a successful merchant and favoured courtier, in 1565. Prior to this City merchants and traders had carried out their business in a fairly informal way, gathering together in the street twice a day, but after visiting the Antwerp Burse Gresham decided that a more formal setting was needed for business in London. The first building was opened in 1570 by Elizabeth I, who gave it its Royal title and it is from the steps of the Royal Exchange that new monarchs are announced to the City.

The Royal Exchange ceased to be a business institution in 1939 and since then the building has been occupied by various organisations including the Guardian Royal Exchange Assurance offices until 1991. Disused and neglected after this time it was decided to breath new life into the place by turning it into a retail and restaurant complex.

The interior of the Exchange forms a covered quadrangular surmounted by colonnades, with a statue of Queen Victoria by Thornycroft at the centre and a series of paintings around the walls of the courtyard by artists such as Lord Leighton, Frank Brangwyn, and Stanhope Forbes.

The shops within the Exchange are bordering on the luxury end of the market with Tod's, Agent Provocateur, and Jo Malone amongst them, and they are fun to browse. The restaurant at the centre of the building is the Grand Café and Bar, a Conran venture, which offers sustenance of the highest quality from breakfast to dinner. The Mezzanine Bar serves champagne wines, beers and cocktails and is a super place to take in the architecture!

Royal Exchange, between Threadneedle Street and Cornhill, EC3; Nearest transport Bank (Central and Northern lines and DLR); Shops are open Mon-Fri 9am-6pm (closed Sat & Sun); Grand Café and Bar open Mon-Fri 8am-11pm (closed Sat & Sun); Grand Café and Bar telephone 020 7618 2480

Leadenhall Market

Sir Horace Jones   1880-81

The name 'Leadenhall' comes from a large medieval house which once stood close by to this site, which apparently had a lead roof, the market being established on adjoining land. The house, its estate and the market were sold to the City Corporation at the beginning of the 15th century. House and market both perished in the Great Fire of London but were quickly rebuilt on a plan around three courtyards.

The present market, designed by City architect Sir Horace Jones, in 1880-81, is a lovely structure built on the cross-plan of the old street configuration. The main entrance, off Gracechurch Street, has engaged, fluted columns in dark-red and cream paintwork with gilded capitals. These appear to support a stone pediment with carved decorations and a fairly small, simple clock.

The market still sells fresh meat and fish but is mainly given over to fashion, with shops such as Jigsaw and Hobbs doing a brisk trade during the City lunchtime.

Leadenhall Market, Gracechurch Street, EC3; Nearest transport Bank LU (Central, Northern lines & DLR); Open Mon-Fri 7am-4pm; Wheelchair access

Harrods

Stevens and Munt   1901-05

The store's motto is: 'omnia, omnibus, ubique' (everything for everyone, everywhere) and Harrods could indeed at one time brag that they could supply anything from a packet of pins to an elephant! Henry Charles Harrod began this retail legend as a tea merchant in the early 19th century at Eastcheap in the City, moving to Knightsbridge in 1849. It stayed a thriving, family-run shop until 1889 when it became a public limited company and between 1901-05 its present building was under construction. Additions were made to the building up until the 1930's.

The building, with its famous terracotta façade, was designed by the architectural practice of Stevens and Munt and at its completion, was declared the largest department store in Europe, occupying a site of some 4.5 acres, with a total retail space of 13.5 acres over five floors. The tilework in the magnificent Food Hall on the ground floor is alone well worth the trip to Knightsbridge as is the art deco ladies' restroom on the first floor and the gentlemen's hairdressers in the basement. The 1997 addition of the imposing Egyptian Halls pays tribute to the heritage of the store's current owner Mohammed Al Fayed.

The store is particularly attractive at Christmas while the Toy Department is famously comprehensive and is where A A Milne purchased the original Pooh bear for his son Christopher.

Harrods, 87-135 Brompton Road, Knightsbridge, SW1; Telephone 020 7730 1234; Nearest transport Knightsbridge LU (Piccadilly line); Open Mon-Sat 10am-7pm (closed Sundays); Telephone for information on wheelchair access

Selfridges

David Burnham et al   1906+

Arguably London's most popular department store since it was first opened in March 1909, Selfridges was the brain-child of its owner, Henry Gordon Selfridge (1858-1947), who was American-born and learned the business of retail in Chicago. He brought the art of browsing to the London shopper who up until this point was used to simply being shown items selected by the shopkeeper – this was a radical departure.

Selfridge bought the huge plot in 1906 and set about creating a building the likes of which Londoners had not seen before. Massive shop windows separated by short pillars dominate the ground floor while gigantic Ionic columns stretch up from the first floor to the exquisitely carved attic floor balustrade. Over the central entrance recess is an 11 feet figure named 'Queen of Time' as well as a huge clock, both of which were installed in 1931. The whole project took nearly thirty years to complete and a number of architects were involved, the most prominent being Daniel Burnham of Chicago.

Major refurbishment started in 1995 and has given the interior of the store a much lighter, more modern feel with a huge atrium accommodating a series of escalators from which all floors can now be accessed.

Despite the serious effort of other retailers, Selfridges still remains the largest store in the West End of London.

Selfridges, 400 Oxford Street, W1A; Telephone 0870 837 7377; Nearest transport Bond Street LU (Central and Jubilee lines); Open Mon-Fri 10am-8pm, Sat 9.30am-8pm and Sun 12pm-6pm; Wheelchair access via Duke Street (Spirit fashion department entrance is best), wheelchair-friendly toilets for both sexes on 3rd floor, if using the car park use the ground or second floor for ease of access to the store

Fortnum and Mason

Wimperis, Simpson and Guthrie   1926-29

This enterprise was started in the 1770s by Charles Fortnum, who, as a former footman in the royal household of George III knew a thing or two about service, and his friend John Mason, who owned horses and a yard close-by and who dealt with the deliveries. They made their reputation by importing exotic foods and supplying such to the gentlemen's clubs of London.

In the late 19th century Fortnum and Mason took the radical step of stocking Heinz canned food, becoming one of the first stores in the world to do so.

The shop now sells a range of goods including clothes and giftware, as well as supporting some very nice in-store restaurants, but is still famous for being the Queen's grocer. Indeed the emporium has received royal warrants from most members of the royal family. The array of cheeses, smoked salmon, teas, breads, not to mention the display of chocolates and candied fruit, are always presented in a tempting way.

Fortnum and Mason started their business in premises close to their present shop in Piccadilly, which was built in 1926-29 by Wimperis, Simpson and Guthrie who, given the shop's pedigree, chose a Georgian style. The fussy automated clock by Eric Aumonier was made in 1964, but appears to come from an earlier era.

Fortnum and Mason, 181 Piccadilly Circus, W1; Telephone 020 7734 8040; Nearest transport Green Park LU (Piccadilly, Jubilee and Victoria lines) and Piccadilly Circus LU (Piccadilly and Bakerloo lines); Open Mon-Sat 10am-6.30pm, Sun 12pm-6pm (Food Hall & Patio Restaurant only); Telephone for information on wheelchair access

Peter Jones

W Crabtree et al   1936-38

Peter Jones is part of the John Lewis Partnership chain and one can purchase almost anything in the way of household, electrical, sports goods and fashion. This was one of the first uses of the glass curtain wall in Britain and was heavily influenced by Mendelsohn's designs for the Schoken department stores in Stuttgart and Chemnitz. The concept of curtain walling in modern buildings is a thin subordinate wall, usually made of glass or metal, held between piers or other structural members but which are not load-bearing.

A fine building, which has something of the ocean-going liner about it. The building has been the subject of a recently completed £100 million renovation programme which has added air conditioning, new restaurants, over 20% extra retail space and a dramatic central atrium in which escalators to all floors are sited.

Peter Jones, Sloane Square, SW1; Telephone 020 7730 3434; Nearest transport Sloane Square LU (District and Circle lines); Open Mon-Sat 9.30am-7pm (closed Sundays); Wheelchair access is good but telephone for further details

Barkers

Bernard George   1937-38

It was during the heyday of the department store, that is the first sixty or so years of the 20th century, that Bernard George was given the brief to remodel the highly successful Barkers store. The building he was to re-vamp had originally been designed by the much respected architect Sir Reginald Blomfield in 1912-13.

Bernard George presented Kensington High Street with an outstanding example of Art Deco. The unmistakable outline of the building owes much to the twin glass towers which soar above neighbouring rooflines. The facade has some remarkable ornamental stonework and do note the exquisite murals celebrating the art of chic shopping.

Alas, unlike its contempories Harrods and Selfridges, Barkers succumbed to the economic downturn of recent decades and is no longer a department store but a collection of retail units – mainly fashion shops such as Monsoon. Nonetheless the splendour of its architecture has not been diminished.

It is interesting to contrast the splendour of Barkers with the nearby building which houses Marks and Spancers at Nos 99-121 Kensington High Street – this was also designed by Bernard George in a 'Moderne' style, and looks rather subdued compared with its neighbour. This too was originally built as a department store in 1935 for Derry and Toms, another victim of changing economic fortunes. What is remarkable about this particular building is that unknown to most of the shoppers, the building has a truly spectacular one and a half acre roof garden! Created between 1936-38 by the landscape architect Ralph Hancock, the garden contains over 500 species of shrubs and plants and is divided into three themed areas – the Spanish, the Tudor and the English Woodland gardens. So important is this garden that during the 1970s the Council applied a Tree Preservation Order on much of its contents.

Since 1981 the top floor of the Derry and Tome building and its amazing roof garden has belonged to the business enterpreneur Sir Richard Branson and is the home of his private members club and restaurant 'Babylon'. The latter is open to the public, and although perhaps quite expensive (about £350 per 3-course dinner without drinks) it is, nevertheless, an absolute treat, overlooking the gardens and the rest of London beyond.

Barkers, 63-97 Kensington High Street, W8; Open daily, usual shop opening hours.

Babylon Restaurant, Kensington High Street, W8; Telephone 020 7368 3993 for information and reservations

Barkers

Waterstones (formerly Simpsons of Piccadilly)

Joseph Emberton   1935-36

It is easy to walk by or into this building and not realise its significance for 20th century architecture. This was the first shop in Britain to have an uninterrupted curved-glass front made possible by arc-welding the wide-span steel-frame, rather than using bulky bolted joints. The method had been pioneered the year before at the renowned De La Warr Pavilion in Bexhill-on-Sea by Mendelson and Chermayeff, who were members of MARS (Modern Architecture Research) set up in 1933. Notable among the group were Walter Gropius, Marcel Breuer, Ove Arup, Hugh Casson, and John Betjeman.

The interior was designed to domestic proportions as a series of rooms with an open-well staircase (there is an apologetic notice explaining why the handrail appears to be a little short for today's customers); note also the original hanging light fitting.

The shop was originally commissioned by Alexander Simpson for his quality menswear store. The move to Piccadilly was prompted by success of the DAKS brand of trousers with their patented self-supporting waistband. During the very early 1970s the writer Jeremy Lloyd was employed as an assistant and it from his short spell at Simpsons that the idea of a television sitcom blossomed into 'Are you Being Served?' which in 1979 was turned into an American version called 'Beanes of Boston'.

In 1999 the shop was sold to Waterstones and is now their flagship store, on the top floor of which is a bar conveniently located next to the 'Art and Architecture' section. From the comfort of the bar there is a wonderful view south, over the rooftops towards the Palace of Westminster. Do you need any more excuse to pay a visit?

Waterstones, 203-206 Piccadilly, W1; Telephone 020 7851 2497 (main shop) 020 7851 2433 (bar); Nearest transport Piccadilly Circus LU (Piccadilly and Bakerloo lines); Open Mon-Sat 10am-10pm, Sun 12pm-6pm; Wheelchair access – please telephone for details

Architecture with a View

The London Eye

Many of the buildings already mentioned afford great views across London, particularly some of those in the 'Eat and Drink Architecture' section. Don't forget places such as the dome of St Paul's Cathedral (Golden Galleries) welcome visitors (see p.49).

Any bridge that crosses the Thames offers splendid views, but some are better than others and a few favourites are:

Tower Bridge

Sir Horace Jones   1886-94

Architect Sir Horace Jones collaborated with engineer Sir John Wolfe Barry to design this definitive London landmark. Victorian technological wizardry hides behind architecture which was designed to be in keeping with the Tower of London nearby, the architect calling it 'a steel skeleton clothed in stone'

At the time of its construction the Thames and the Pool of London was used intensively, with the bascules of the bridge being raised many times during a working day. A walkway was needed so that pedestrians were able to cross the river even when ships were passing underneath. This was done by means of a high walkway – which was not popular with those who suffered from vertigo! However, the whole walkway has now been glassed in and some of the best views in London can be taken in from here.

The Tower Bridge Exhibition, on the south bank of the Thames just by the bridge is a well thought out presentation of the bridges history and engineering.

The Tower Bridge Exhibition, Tower Bridge, SE1; Telephone 020 7403 3761; Nearest transport Tower Hill LU (Circle and District lines and DLR); Open daily 9.30am-6pm (last admission 5pm) (until 6.30pm April–Oct); Admission £5.50 (concessions available); Please telephone for details of wheelchair access)

Tower Bridge

Waterloo Bridge

Rendell, Palmer and Tritton   1937-42

All those of a certain age will remember the song 'Waterloo Sunset' by the Kinks and think of Julie and Terry meeting here! Who could blame them, the views are splendid. The river frontage of Somerset House is particularly interesting; from here you can see the water gate that allowed boats into the complex although it's somewhat land-locked now since the embankment of the river.

The bridge was built in 1937-42, with Gilbert Scott acting in an advisory role to the architects. This bridge replaced the much-loved one of 1811 by Rennie, the foundations of which were considered unstable.

The artist Barbara Hepworth was asked to submit plans for sculptures which it was hoped would adorn the finished bridge, but the scheme did not materialise.

Waterloo Bridge, approached from Lancaster Place on the north bank or Waterloo Road on the south; Always open and no charge to cross

Millennium Bridge

Sir Norman Foster   2000

Unfortunately, this will always be known as the 'wobbly bridge' since its unfortunate swaying episodes at its first opening. It's perfect now. The architect collaborated with the sculptor Anthony Caro to produce this 'blade of light'. Traffic–free bliss and the best view of St Paul's and the rest of London. Fantastic! Check out the website for interesting technical bits about the bridge: *www.arup.com/millennium-bridge/*

Millennium Bridge, spans the Thames from St. Pauls Cathedral to the Tate Modern, Bankside, SE1; Nearest transport Bank LU (Central, Northern lines & DLR), Blackfriars Rail & LU (Circle and District lines), Southwark LU (Jubilee line)

The Monument

Sir Christopher Wren and Robert Hooke   1671-76

This work is often attributed to Wren alone and yet it has all the hallmarks of a Robert Hooke project, particularly given that the basement was arranged so that he could carry out his experiments and observations with the aid of the column itself, which he used as a sort of telescope.

Erected as both a memorial to the devastated City of London after the Great Fire of 1666 and as a morale-booster to those who were struggling to put the City back together, the Monument stands at 202 feet, taller than Trajan's Column in Rome, and is still believed to be the tallest isolated stone structure in Europe. There are 311 steps to the top, but the view is certainly worth the climb, despite the amount of tall buildings around.

Made from Portland Stone, this fluted Roman Doric column is topped with a bronze urn with flames licking the sky.

The Monument, Monument Street, EC3; Nearest transport Monument LU (Circle and District lines); Open daily 10am-5.40pm; Admission charge

The London Eye

Julia Barfield and David Marks   1993-2000

One of the most popular structural projects ever carried out anywhere was conceived at the kitchen table of architects Julia Barnfield and David Marks in 1993. This was the year that marked the centenary of the unveiling of the 'Big Wheel' at Chicago's World Columbian Exposition designed by George W Ferris. The Ferris Wheel became the main attraction of the fair – just as the London Eye was to become the 'hit' of millennium celebrations in London when it first took paying passengers in January 2000.

The wheel of the London Eye is the largest of its kind ever built at a height of 450 feet. The foundations consist of 44 concrete piles, 110 feet deep, sunk in by 2,200 tonnes of concrete. The holding backstay cables are held in place by 1,200 tonnes of concrete and about 1,700 tonnes of steel was used in the construction – the statistics are mind-boggling!

Each of the 32 capsules gently glide the visitor up into the air above the buildings of London and provide a panorama of up to 25 miles in all directions – with the whole trip taking 30 minutes. This is an experience not to be missed, even if you normally do not like 'heights,' and the ride feels as though you are hardly moving. It is difficult to recommend the best time of day to enjoy the trip – but a particular favourite is dusk when the lights are coming on all over London; sheer magic! The whole of the capital city stretches out before you and the higher you rise the smaller and more model village-like it becomes – the perfect way to appreciate London's fabulous architecture.

The London Eye, Jubilee Gardens, Embankment, London SW1. Telephone 0870 5000 600 (Booking line). Transport LU Westminster (Jubilee, District and Circle line) and Waterloo (Jubilee, Bakerloo and Northern line). Opening times vary, depending on the day and the time of year, and are subject to change – however currently the Eye is in operation every day, all day (up to 9pm or 10pm). Booking is highly recommended but it is possible to purchase tickets at County Hall (next to the London Eye) but be prepared to queue. There is a charge for tickets with concessions available. Full wheelchair access.

The London Eye

Area Maps

BLOOMSBURY

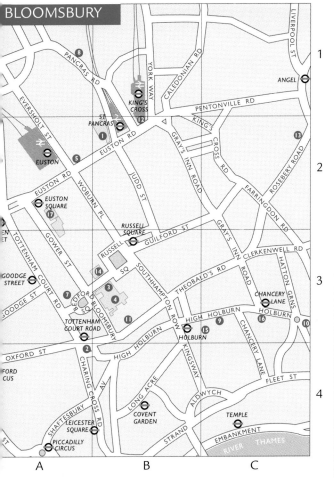

1) British Library B:2
2) Centre Point A:4
3) British Museum,
    Edward VII Galleries B:3
4) British Museum,
    Great Court B:3
5) Euston Fire Station A:2
6) Fitzroy Square A:3
7) Imagination A:3
8) Old St Pancras Church A:1

9) Renaissance London Chancery Court
    Hotel C:3
10) St Andrew's Holborn C:3
11) St George's, Bloomsbury Way B:3
12) St Pancras Station B:2
13) Sadler's Wells C:2
14) Senate House, University of London B:3
15) Sir John Soane's Museum C:3
16) Staple Inn, Holborn C:3
17) University College, Gower Street A:2

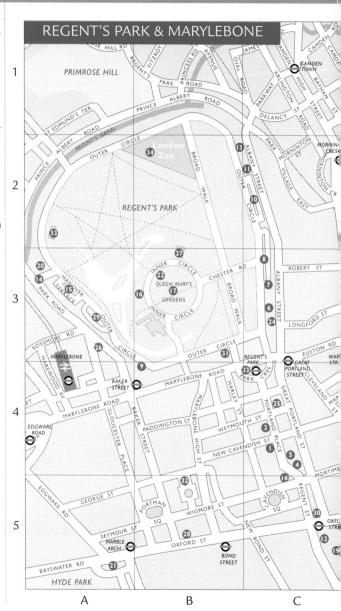

REGENT'S PARK & MARYLEBONE

Regent's Park & Marylebone

1) 17, 21 & 23 Portland Place C:4
2) 27-47 Portland Place C:4
3) All Saints Church, Margaret St C:5
4) All Souls Church C:4
5) BBC Broadcasting House C:4
6) Cambridge Gate C:3
7) Chester Gate C:3
8) Chester Terrace C:3
9) Cornwall Terrace B:4
10) Cumberland Terrace C:2
11) Danish Church (formerly St Katherine's) C:2
12) Dickens & Jones C:5
13) Gloucester Lodge & Gloucester Gate B:2
14) Hanover Gate A:3
15) Hanover Terrace A:3
16) The Holme B:3

17) Inner Circle B:3
18) Langham Hotel C:5
19) Liberty's C:5
20) London Central Mosque A:3
21) Marble Arch A:5
22) Open Air Theatre B:3
23) Park Crescent C:4
24) Royal College of Physicians C:3
25) Royal Instit. of British Architects C:4
26) Rudolf Steiner House A:3
27) St John's Lodge B:3
28) Selfridges B:5
29) Sussex Place A:3
30) Top Shop C:5
31) Ulster Place B:3
32) The Wallace Collection B:5
33) Winfield House A:2
34) Regent's Park Zoo B:2

3.1

Westminster Area Map

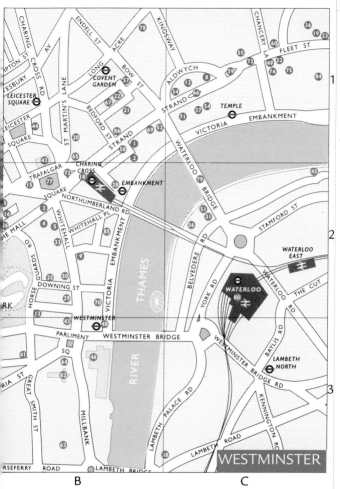

3.1

City Area Map

1) All Hallows Barking C:2
2) All Hallows Church B:1
3) Banco Commerciale Italiana B:2
4) Bank of England Museum B:2
5) Bank of England, Threadneedle St B:2
6) Black Friar, Public House A:2
7) Blueprint Café C:3
8) Britannic House B:1
9) Charterhouse Square A:1
10) Christ Church, Commercial St C:1
11) Christ Church, Newgate A:1
12) The Circle, Queen Elizabeth St C:3
13) City Hall C:3
14) Cloth Fair A:1
15) Daily Express building A:2
16) Dennis Severs House C:1
17) Florin Court A:1
18) Frederick's Place B:2
19) Geffrye Museum (off map)
20) George Inn B:3
21) The Guildhall B:1
22) Haberdashers' Hall A:1
23) Holborn Viaduct A:1
24) Leadenhall Market C:2
25) Lloyds building C:2
26) Mansion House B:2
27) Millennium Bridge A:2
28) Monument B:2
29) Old Bailey A:1
30) Pizza Express, Alban Gate B:1
31) Port of London Authority C:2
32) Reuters building & The Press Association A:2
33) Royal Exchange B:2
34) St Alban B:1
35) St Andrew by the Wardrobe A:2
36) St Anne & St Agnes B:1
37) St Bartholomew the Great A:1
38) St Bartholomew the Less A:1
39) St Bartholomew's Hospital A:1
40) St Benet, Paul's Wharf A:2
41) St Bride, Fleet St A:2
42) St Bride's Printing Library A:2
43) St Clement Eastcheap B:2
44) St Dunstan in the East C:2
45) St Edmund the King & Martyr B:2
46) St Helen's Bishopsgate C:2

A

47) St James Garlickhithe B:2
48) St John's Priory A:1
49) St Lawrence Jewry B:1
50) St Magnus the Martyr B:2
51) St Margaret Pattens C:2
52) St Margaret, Lothbury B:1
53) St Martin within Ludgate A:2
54) St Mary Abchurch B:2

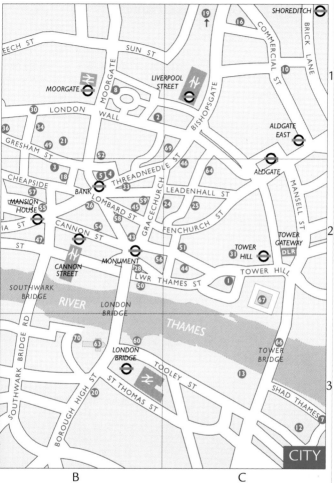

ARCHITECTURE AT A GLANCE

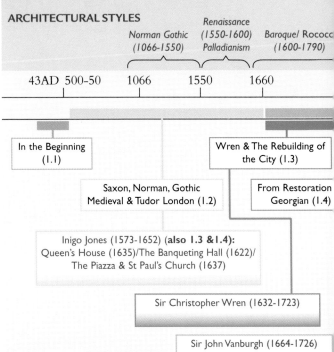

ARCHITECTURAL STYLES

Norman Gothic (1066-1550)

Renaissance (1550-1600) Palladianism

Baroque/ Rococo (1600-1790)

43AD 500-50 1066 1550 1660

In the Beginning (1.1)

Wren & The Rebuilding of the City (1.3)

Saxon, Norman, Gothic Medieval & Tudor London (1.2)

From Restoration Georgian (1.4)

Inigo Jones (1573-1652) (**also 1.3 & 1.4**):
Queen's House (1635)/The Banqueting Hall (1622)/
The Piazza & St Paul's Church (1637)

Sir Christopher Wren (1632-1723)

Sir John Vanburgh (1664-1726)
Nicholas Hawksmoor (1661-1736)
Thomas Archer (1668-1743)
James Gibbs (1682-1754)
William Kent (1685-1748)
Lord Burlington (1694-1753)
Robert Adam (1728-92)
Sir John Soane (1753-1837)
Sir Robert Smirke (1781-1867)

Key Architects & Buildings From The Renaissance to 21st Century

This chart chart gives details of most of London's major architects, examples of their work and where to find them in this book. The prominent modes of architecture for each epoch are given above and will help to understand the historical changes in architecture from Inigo Jones's to the Swiss Re Headquarters.

John Nash (1752-1835):
-Trafalgar Square (1820's)
-Regents Park (1816-30

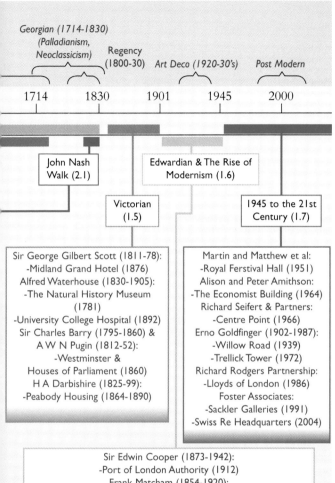

Georgian (1714-1830)
(Palladianism,
Neoclassicism)

Regency
(1800-30)

Art Deco (1920-30's)

Post Modern

1714   1830   1901   1945   2000

John Nash
Walk (2.1)

Edwardian & The Rise of
Modernism (1.6)

Victorian
(1.5)

1945 to the 21st
Century (1.7)

Sir George Gilbert Scott (1811-78):
-Midland Grand Hotel (1876)
Alfred Waterhouse (1830-1905):
-The Natural History Museum
(1781)
-University College Hospital (1892)
Sir Charles Barry (1795-1860) &
A W N Pugin (1812-52):
-Westminster &
Houses of Parliament (1860)
H A Darbishire (1825-99):
-Peabody Housing (1864-1890)

Martin and Matthew et al:
-Royal Ferstival Hall (1951)
Alison and Peter Amithson:
-The Economist Building (1964)
Richard Seifert & Partners:
-Centre Point (1966)
Erno Goldfinger (1902-1987):
-Willow Road (1939)
-Trellick Tower (1972)
Richard Rodgers Partnership:
-Lloyds of London (1986)
Foster Associates:
-Sackler Galleries (1991)
-Swiss Re Headquarters (2004)

Sir Edwin Cooper (1873-1942):
-Port of London Authority (1912)
Frank Matcham (1854-1920):
Coliseum (1904), Hackney Empire (1901), London Paladium (1916)
Sir Edwin Lutyens (1869-1944):
Ex Country Life Offices (1904), Brittanic House (1925)
Modernism
Charles Holden (1875-1960): London Transport Headquarters (1929),
Arnos Grove Station (1930), Senate House (1937)

297

Glossary

Abacus: A flat slab (usually of stone or marble) forming the top of a capital.

Ambulatory: A passage (usually at the eastern end of a church) around the sanctuary.

Amphitheatre: An open-air theatre with tiered seating.

Apse: The semicircular end of a Roman basilica (a building used for administrative purposes). The apse was subsequently incorporated into church architecture.

Arcade: Series of arches supported by columns or piers. Also refers to a covered shopping street.

Ashlar: Stone blocks cut into a regular size.

Atrium: A covered court rising through all storeys of a building (especially Roman or 20th century).

Attached or Engaged Column: One that partly merges into the wall and is thus not freestanding.

Balustrade: A number of vertical supports for a handrail.

Bay: Division of an elevation by regular verticals such as arches or windows.

Boss: An ornamented projection usually at the intersection of vault ribs.

Buttress: A wall built at right angles to the main wall to stabilise it or take the thrust of the arch or vault behind. A 'flying buttress' of the Gothic period transmits the thrust to a heavy abutment by means of an arch.

Capital: The head of a classical column.

Caryatids: Female figures supporting an entablature (as seen on the northern exterior of St Pancras New Church, Euston Road, London NW1)

Chancel: Sited towards the eastern end of a church, separated from the nave. Used by officiating clergy and choir.

Clerestory: The wall above the aisles of a church (especially Norman and Gothic) pierced by windows.

Coade Stone: Artificial stone manufactured in London circa 1769-1840.

Concrete: A mixture of cement (ie calcined lime and clay), aggregate (ie small stones or broken brick), sand and water. First used by the Romans but the knowledge of this material was lost at the end of the Roman Empire and only rediscovered during the 15th century. Reinforced concrete contains steel rods for additional support.

Crypt: Underground vaulted chamber, usually at the eastern end of a church, and which sometimes held specific chambers for relics.

Cupola: A dome, and more usually a small dome placed upon a larger one.

Curtain Wall: Non load-bearing external wall (20th century building); also the wall connecting two towers of a castle or fort.

Dormer: A window projecting from the slope of a roof. 'Dormer' is French for 'to sleep' and often these windows let air and light into roof voids to allow the space to be used as a bedroom.

Eaves: The overhanging edge of a roof.

Entablature: The collective name for the three horizontal members (architrave, frieze and cornice) in classical architecture that is supported by the column.

Fenestration: The arrangement of windows in a building.

Gable: The triangular part of an end wall of a sloping roof.

Hammerbeam: Timber beam projecting from a wall, often elaborately carved.

Hypercaust: Underfloor heating system perfected by the Romans.

Keystone: The top central stone in an arch or vault.

Lancet Window: Long, slim, pointed window.

Lantern: Windowed turret, usually circular, upon a dome.

Lintel: Flat stone or beam above an opening in a wall.

Nave: The central, usually the largest, space in a church.

Pediment: The triangular part above the entablature.

Pilaster: Column, usually square or rectangular, or pillar slightly projecting from a wall.

Rendering: The plastering on the outside wall of a building.

Reredos: Screen, usually painted or carved, behind the altar in a church.

Rood Screen: A partition between the nave and choir of a church - usually carved.

Rotunda: A building or room circular in plan and often with a dome over it.

Rustication: Tooled surface of building stone made to look exaggeratedly rough.

Stucco: A mixture of lime plaster and sand applied to exterior walls - usually to hide inferior brickwork - and often marked to give the impression of stonework.

Vault: Arched stone or brick roof or ceiling.

Resources

Bibliography

A History of London, *Stephen Inwood* (Macmillan. 1998)

Dictionary of British Architects 1600-1840, *Howard Colvin*
(Yale University Press 1995)

English Architecture, *David Watkins* (Thames and Hudson 1979)

In Search of London, *H V Morton* (Methuen 1951)

Liquid History, *Stephen Croad* (Batsford 2003)

London A-Z, The newer editions have the principal buildings marked.

London – Bread and Circuses, *Jonathan Glancey* (Verso 2001).

London: A Social History, *Roy Porter* (Penguin 1994)

London's Riverscape – Lost and Found
(The London's Found Riverscape Partnership 2000)

Museums & Galleries of London, *Abigail Willis* (Metro Publications 2000)

Oxford Dictionary of Architecture, *James Stevens Curl* (Oxford 1999).

Oxford Dictionary of London Place Names, *A D Mills* (Oxford 2001)

Restoration London, *Lisa Picard* (Phoenix 2003)
Lisa Picard has also written **Elizabeth's London** and **Dr Johnson's London**
(Weidenfeld and Nicholson 2003 and 2000 respectively).

Style City London (Thames and Hudson 2003)

The Buildings of England, *Nikolaus Pevsner* (Founding Editor) .
For further information visit www.pevsner.co.uk.

The Great Stink of London, *Stephen Halliday* (Sutton Publishing 1999).
Stephen Halliday has also written **Underground to Everywhere** (Sutton
Publishing 2001).

18 Folgate Street, *Dennis Savers* (Chatto and Windus 2002).

Websites

www.londondiscovery.org.uk A consortium project that has created seven websites about the people, places and buildings of London. There is something to fascinate anyone interested in London and its history.

www.londonopenhouse.org The London Open House is a registered educational charity concerned with London and its architecture. Open House organises an annual weekend event when hundreds of buildings open their doors to the public – private houses, offices, medical schools, theatres, etc, most of which do not usually allow public access. This event usually takes place during the third weekend of September – consult the website for dates and venues.

www.architecturelink.org.uk Provides useful information about architecture, especially buildings in London of the 20th and 21st century.

www.museumoflondon.org.uk Invaluable information about the history and people of the capital.

www.architecture.com The website of RIBA (Royal Institute of British Architects). News and details of exhibitions and projects as well as access to the extensive RIBA library. Also useful information if you are thinking of hiring an architect or becoming one yourself!

www.architectureweek.org.uk An annual event, which usually takes place in June. A collaboration between the Arts Council of Great Britain, RIBA and others – talks, walks, and visits available nationwide.

www.c20society.demon.co.uk Originally called the Thirties Society the society changed its name to the Twentieth Century Society when good post-war buildings became under threat.

www.cityoflondonchurches.com A valuable site packed with information and illustrations of the fifty or so churches within the City of London.

www.artsline.org.uk Information service for people with physical disabilities – gives a comprehensive guide to access to London buildings.

Additional Photography Credits

p.97 © Sir John Soane's Museum / p119 © Leighton House / p143 © Freemason's Hall / p.143 © Bank of England / p.296 View from the Tate Modern © Alexander Hug.